Global Players and the Indian Car Industry

This book is one of the first critical analyses of the automobile industry in India. It studies the sector in general and the passenger car industry in particular, and provides valuable insights into the operation of Foreign Direct Investment (FDI) companies in a technology-intensive industry under changing economic regimes. The volume underlines the influence of the changing nature of foreign investment, the impact of economic reforms, technology regimes and industrial policy on growth, structural changes and development. It offers a detailed account of the trade performance of manufacturers in India's passenger car industry. It also looks at successful cases to draw policy lessons towards encouraging quality FDI and developing India as a base for world production.

A useful addition to industry studies in India, this book with its wide coverage and contemporary analyses will interest scholars and researchers of economics, Indian economy and industrial policy, industrial economics, automobile industry and manufacturing sector, development economics and international economics. It will also appeal to policymakers, practitioners and industrial associations.

Jatinder Singh is Assistant Professor at the Centre for Research in Rural and Industrial Development (CRRID), Chandigarh, India. He obtained his PhD from Jawaharlal Nehru University, New Delhi, and M.Phil. from the Centre for Development Studies, Thiruvananthapuram, Kerala. His research areas include foreign direct investment, technology development and industrialisation in India. He has published nine research papers in refereed national and international journals and five chapters in edited volumes apart from presenting papers at various conferences. Presently, he is coordinating two research studies funded by the Indian Council of Social Science Research, including one on industrial development in Punjab. He has worked in different capacities with various organisations, including the Centre for Development Studies, Thiruvananthapuram; the Centre for WTO Studies, New Delhi; University of Delhi; and National University of Education Planning and Administration, New Delhi.

Critical Political Economy of South Asia
Series editors: C. P. Chandrasekhar and Jayati Ghosh,
both at the Centre for Economic Studies and Planning,
Jawaharlal Nehru University, New Delhi, India

At a time when countries of the South Asian region are in a state of flux, reflected in far-reaching economic, political and social changes, this series aims to showcase critical analyses of some of the central questions relating to the direction and implications of those changes. Volumes in the series focus on economic issues and integrate these with incisive insights into historical, political and social contexts. Drawing on work by established scholars as well as younger researchers, they examine different aspects of political economy that are essential for understanding the present and have an important bearing on the future. The series will provide fresh analytical perspectives and empirical assessments that will be useful for students, researchers, policymakers and concerned citizens.

The first books in the series cover themes such as the economic impact of new regimes of intellectual property rights, the trajectory of financial development in India, changing patterns of consumption expenditure and trends in poverty, health and human development in India and land relations. Future volumes will deal with varying facets of economic processes and their consequences for the countries of South Asia.

Labour Law Reforms in India
All in the Name of Jobs
Anamitra Roychowdhury

Global Players and the Indian Car Industry
Trade, Technology and Structural Change
Jatinder Singh

For more information about this series, please visit: www.routledge.com/Critical-Political-Economy-of-South-Asia/book-series/CRPE

'The major merit of the book is that it analyses both pre- and post-reform periods and questions the view that the passenger car industry in India is an example of success of liberalization.'
—**Sudip Chaudhuri,** Professor, Indian Institute
of Management Calcutta, Kolkata, India

'Jatinder Singh's book is an important study on one dimension of the changing face of Indian capitalism. A follow-up study on the grave environmental implications of increasing supply of and demand for cars should be the logical outcome.'
—**Pritam Singh,** Professor of Economics,
Oxford Brookes Business School, Oxford, UK

'A seminal contribution on India's passenger car industry in a context wherein industry-specific studies are the need of the hour to deepen our understanding on what ails India's manufacturing sector.'
—**K. J. Joseph,** Professor and Ministry of Commerce
Chair, Centre for Development Studies,
Thiruvananthapuram, Kerala, India

Global Players and the Indian Car Industry

Trade, Technology and Structural Change

Jatinder Singh

LONDON AND NEW YORK

First published 2019 by Routledge

2 Park Square, Milton Park, Abingdon, Oxon, OX14 4RN
605 Third Avenue, New York, NY 10017

*Routledge is an imprint of the Taylor & Francis Group,
an informa business*

First issued in paperback 2020

Copyright © 2019 Jatinder Singh

The right of Jatinder Singh to be identified as author of this
work has been asserted by him in accordance with sections
77 and 78 of the Copyright, Designs and Patents Act 1988.

All rights reserved. No part of this book may be reprinted or reproduced or
utilised in any form or by any electronic, mechanical, or other means, now
known or hereafter invented, including photocopying and recording, or in
any information storage or retrieval system, without permission in writing
from the publishers.

Notice:
Product or corporate names may be trademarks or registered trademarks,
and are used only for identification and explanation without intent to
infringe.

British Library Cataloguing-in-Publication Data
A catalogue record for this book is available from the
British Library

Library of Congress Cataloging-in-Publication Data
A catalog record for this book has been requested

ISBN: 978-1-138-55971-4 (hbk)
ISBN: 978-0-367-73353-7 (pbk)

Typeset in Sabon
by Apex CoVantage, LLC

Dedicated to
My Parents and Teachers

Contents

Illustrations

Tables

Figures

Preface and acknowledgements

The development of India's passenger car industry is, in many ways, unique. The industry, owing to passenger cars being considered as a luxury item, was stringently regulated as compared to other industries before the 1980s. Even within the automobile sector, this segment was treated differently for nearly three-and-a-half decades. Two major manufacturers were serving the domestic market with just two models of cars until the early 1980s. The supply of cars remained short of demand so much so that a buyer had to wait for more than two years for delivery of a new car. Such a scenario provided no incentive to car manufacturers to improve quality of products and they kept supplying same models of cars for nearly three decades. The situation changed completely with the onset of policy changes initiated in the 1980s and implemented at a large scale in the early 1990s. The new policy regime marked a paradigm shift in the economy's development strategy in general and the regulations involved around the car industry in particular. It provided a new setting for the industrial sector to grow that also eased the entry and operations of foreign firms. The resultant continuous entry of leading international car manufacturers has not only increased the variety of technologically advanced cars, as manifested in terms of the growing segmentation in the industry, which did not exist until the early 1990s, but also became very stark since the late 1990s. Now cars are available on demand and companies are upgrading and modifying cars on a regular basis to meet the changing choices and preferences of consumers. Besides this transformation, the industry has been recording consistent high growth since the mid-1980s and significantly increased the forward and backward linkages. The impressive growth record of this industry, besides other things, has made it one of the most attractive sectors for foreign investors.

This book contributes towards the understanding of the evolution of the passenger car industry in India, which is presented as one of the successful cases of liberalisation. Broadly, there are two main themes of the present volume. First, it concerns the issues of economic reform policies and the nature of FDI in India and their effect on industrialisation in the country, as also provides a critique of the assertion that the passenger car industry is an example of the success of liberalisation. Second, it analyses the trade performance of firms, especially foreign firms in the industry and their contribution to the Balance of Payment of the country. The study focuses on three main issues, i.e. restructuring, technological development and trade, which are of key relevance to contemporary policy formation and it examines both demand as well as supply side factors which have not been given due attention academically.

The present volume is an outcome of years of research, including the period of my doctoral research. After submitting my PhD thesis at Jawaharlal Nehru University (JNU), New Delhi, I continued to revise, update and sharpen the work. Both for my doctoral thesis and for its culmination in a book, I received support and help from various quarters and I take the pleasure of acknowledging those contributions.

First of all, with sincere gratitude, I thank my PhD supervisor, Professor C. P. Chandrasekhar, who placed confidence in my work and motivated me to come up with this volume. He persuaded and motivated me continuously to improve upon my doctoral research so as to make it a publishable manuscript. My thanks are also due to all the faculty members at the Centre for Economic Studies and Planning, whose constructive criticism and suggestions at various stages of this work were highly useful. I would like to express my special thanks to Prof. Jayati Ghosh, Prof. Praveen Jha; Prof. Biswajit Dhar and Prof. Surajit Mazumder for their help and support.

I take this opportunity to express my gratitude to Dr. Rashpal Malhotra (Executive Vice-Chairman CRRID, Chandigarh), Prof. Sucha Singh Gill and Prof. Ranjit Singh Ghuman, Prof. Satish Verma (Senior Professors, CRRID) for their valuable guidance. I must acknowledge the contributions of Prof. Ghuman in ameliorating my personal and professional outlook. It was Prof. Ghuman who persuaded me to chose to pursue higher studies. My thanks are due to him once again. I am also grateful to my friends and colleagues Dr. Rajeev Sharma and Dr. Vikash Kumar (CRRID), Dr. Kulwinder Singh and Dr. Manjit Sharma (Punjab University Chandigarh) with whom I often engaged in fruitful discussions and received valuable inputs. Dr. Vikash has remained a rescuer in tough times during the work on this volume.

Learning is a cumulative process, and this work too has been benefited from interactions with academicians over a long period of time. I am thankful to Prof. K. J. Joseph and Dr. Vinoj Abraham (CDS, Trivandrum), Prof. Sudip Chaudhuri (IIM, Calcutta), Prof. D. Narayana (GIFT, Trivandrum), Prof. (late) G. S Bhalla (JNU, New Delhi), Prof. Sukhpal Singh (IIM, Ahmedabad), Prof. R. Nagaraj (IGIDR, Mumbai), Prof. Mona Khare (NUEPA, New Delhi), Prof. M. R. Murthy and Dr. Satyaki Roy (ISID, New Delhi) and Dr. Subash S. (IIT, Chennai). My teachers from Panjab University, Chandigarh and Punjabi University, Patiala deserve special thanks for helping me in developing a deep interest in the subject of economics.

The constructive comments and suggestions by anonymous reviewers helped to improve the book in many ways. The publication team of Routledge, especially Ms. Shoma Choudhury, deserves special appreciation for publishing this book. I am thankful to them for their meticulous efforts.

The Indian Council for Social Science Research (ICSSR), New Delhi, has a special contribution in my academic and professional career. I was a recipient of ICSSR's Doctoral Fellowship and presently am working in an ICSSR supported research institute.

I would not have been able to complete this book without the support of my wife, Dr. Maninder Deep Cheema. She made valuable suggestions on the work and was very cooperative and understanding while I was busy in completing this work. My son, Mansukh Singh, whose birth has given birth to a father in me, also provided motivation to complete this work. His cooperation is to be acknowledged as he let me work at a time when he deserved my complete attention. Finally, I thank my parents and parents-in-law for always being encouraging and supportive during all my studies and during the work on this volume.

Abbreviations

ACMA	Automotive Components Manufacturers Association
AIAM	Association of Indian Automobile Manufacturers
AMP	Automotive Mission Plan
BoP	Balance of Payments
CAGR	Compound Annual Growth Rate
CBU	Completely Build Unit
CIF	Cost, Insurance, Freight
CKD	Completely Knocked Down
CMIE	Centre for Monitoring Indian Economy
DGFT	Director-General of Foreign Trade
DIPP	Department of Industrial Policy and Promotion
DSB	Dispute Settlement Body
DST	Department of Science and Technology
FDI	Foreign Direct Investment
FERA	Foreign Exchange Regulation Act
FIB	Foreign Investment Board
FIPB	Foreign Investment Promotion Board
FoB	Free on Board
GATT	General Agreement on Tariffs & Trade
GDP	Gross Domestic Product
GoI	Government of India
HHI	Herfindahl-Hirschman Index
HML	Hindustan Motors Limited
IBRD	International Bank for Reconstruction and Development
IDRA	Industrial Development and Regulation Act
IPR	Industrial Policy Resolution
JV	Joint Venture
M&M	Mahindra and Mahindra

MoU	Memorandum of Understanding
MRTP	Monopolies and Restrictive Trade Practices
MUL	Maruti Udyog Limited
NCAER	National Council of Applied Economic Research
NPC	National Planning Committee
NEP	New Economic Policy
OGL	Open General License
PAL	Premier Automobiles Limited
PMP	Phased Manufacturing Programme
R&D	Research & Development
SIA	Secretariat for Industrial Assistance
SIAM	Society of Indian Automobile Manufacturers
SITP	Science, Technology and Innovation Policy
SKD	Semi Knocked Down
SMC	Suzuki Motor Corporation
SMPIL	Standard Motor Products India Limited
STP	Science and Technology Policy
TELCO	Tata Engineering and Locomotives Company Limited
TPS	Technology Policy Statement
UNCTAD	United Nations Conference on Trade and Development
WIR	World Investment Report
WTO	World Trade Organization

Chapter 1

Introduction

Cross-border flows of direct investment have increased greatly since the early 1980s. The magnitude of worldwide Foreign Direct Investment (FDI) flows swelled from US$ 87.01 billion in 1986 to US$ 958.52 billion in 2005 and further to US$ 1746.00 billion in 2015 (UNCTAD 2017). Several changes at the level of the global economy have reinforced this tendency. The most important ones are: (1) gradual change in the sceptical attitude of the developing world towards FDI; (2) formation of the World Trade Organisation (WTO), which made it essential for all the member countries to follow its various investment and trade-related agreements; (3) increases in the cost of production and slowdown of growth in the developed countries, which worked as a push factor for international firms to shift production to low-cost areas; (4) increase in the flow of Japanese investment as a result of the appreciation of Japanese currency (Yen) in the mid-1980s; and (5) the revolution in information and communication technology, which enabled multinational firms to effectively manage their subsidiaries across geographical boundaries.

One important feature of the rise in FDI flows in recent times is the growing volume of such flows to the developing part of the global economy. These countries are competing intensively among themselves to attract more and more investments in recent years by offering a variety of financial and fiscal benefits along with national treatment to the foreign firms (Naik 2006; Rajan, Rongala and Ghosh 2008; Singh 2010, 2015). The share of developing countries in total world FDI flows has expanded from 18.41 per cent (1986) to 35 per cent (2005) and then to 42.41 per cent (2015) (UNCTAD 2017). This shift is mainly driven, on the one hand, by the desire of foreign investors to deploy their intangible and tangible assets in the developing countries with a view to improve their competitiveness, profitability and to get access to the local market, and, on the other, by the expectations of the developing countries that they would be benefited in multiple ways from the cross border inflows of investment (Subrahmanian, Sastry, Pattanaik and Hajra 1996; Narula and Lall 2006; Jenkins 2006; Dunning and Lundan 2008). From the point of view of the developing countries, in the first instance, the inflow of FDI helps to bridge the savings and investment gap. That, in turn, allows the domestic investment rate to be higher than the domestic savings rate. Secondly, foreign investment inflow is expected to reduce the technology gap between foreign and local firms. It has been argued that transfer of technology from foreign affiliates to local firms takes place through imitation of new knowledge, linkages between domestic and foreign firms, competition effects and hiring of trained workers of foreign firms in the host country (Beugelsdijk, Smeets and Zwinkels 2008; Fu 2008; Singh 2015). It is further argued that transfer of technology and business know-how to local firms boosts the productivity of all firms (not just of FDI-receiving firms) in the economy because of substantial spillovers to the rest of the economy. Third, it is anticipated that the entry of foreign firms would offer relief to the Balance of Payments (BoP) by bringing positive foreign exchange inflows. This expectation is guided by the view that the texture of FDI has changed since the 1980s: (1) It is argued that the motives of foreign investors are no longer limited to exploiting the local market (i.e. market seeking), as international firms are searching to source supplies from appropriate bases, especially in developing countries, given their specific locational advantages; (2) being a part of parent firms' global network, the foreign subsidiaries have access to better technology along with other intangible assets (brand name, managerial skills), which allows them to compete more easily in the international market as compared to their local counterparts in the host country market. Thus, it is hoped that FDI of this kind would not have negative implications for the BoP of developing countries, since FDI would deliver export revenues and develop a positive relationship between trade and FDI.

India joined the bandwagon as the government of India (GoI) intensified the process of liberalisation starting in 1991 and provided a new setting for foreign investors by introducing a series of changes in the economic environment. The 1991 policy changes mark a paradigmatic shift in the economy's development strategy in general and the industrial policy in particular from being a discretion-based and inward looking import-substitution policy to a more de-controlled and market-oriented one based on liberalisation, privatisation and globalisation. The genesis of the current development strategy can be traced back to the early 1980s, when India started relaxing restrictions on the entry of FDI, foreign technology, imports of raw material and capital goods, which were subject to stringent regulations and discriminatory controls between 1950 and the mid-1980s (World Bank 1987; Chandrasekhar 1994, 2010; Kumar 1994; Krueger 2002; Balasubramanyam and Mahambare 2004; Pradhan and Singh 2008; Singh 2014). The primary aim of the economic reform programme in India was and still is to provide an attractive climate to foreign investors. This is not surprising, as the central focus of the neoliberal reform programme always remains to ease regulations on the entry of foreign investors and their operations in the country.

Like other developing countries, the changes in foreign investment policy in India have been guided by the presumption that it would bring capital, modern technology and managerial and marketing skills which are necessary for strengthening the resource-base, ensuring macro-economic stability and improving overall economic performance, and also for enhancing India's participation in the international market. Guided by these anticipations and inspired by the Newly Industrialised Countries and the recent Chinese experience, the successive governments in India, including the current National Democratic Alliance (NDA) government, have been aggressively announcing incentives and progressive relaxations of regulations in order to attract more FDI (Singh 2015; GoI 2016a, 2016b, 2017, 2017–18). According to UNCTAD (2017), India is identified as third most prospective host economy by foreign investors for the period 2017–19.

India's story of attracting FDI remained disappointing relative to the expectations in the initial years of liberalisation, but later, especially after 2000, the inflows of FDI increased significantly. The inflow of FDI increased from US $0.25 billion in 1992 to US $3.59 billion in 2000, and it further increased to US $44.49 billion in 2016 (UNCTAD 2017). Correspondingly, India's share in world FDI flows has moved up from 0.15 per cent to 2.64 per cent and then to 2.48 per cent. The large volume of foreign investment coming into India is unevenly distributed across different industries and states (Singh, Jha and Singh 2011; Singh and Cheema 2015). Some industries have attracted large foreign investment in the post-reform period, whereas others have lagged behind depending upon the influence of the industry-specific characters (demand conditions, growth prospects etc.) as well as the nature of regulations around the industry.

Against this background, the present study is an attempt to understand the impact of foreign investment in the case of India's passenger car industry. The car industry has been selected for this study because of certain distinguishing features attached to this segment both under the regulatory regime as well as in the post-reform period.

First, this industry was stringently regulated within the automobile sector until the early 1980s, as the government classified the passenger car as a luxury good. Accordingly, the government had continuously reduced the foreign exchange allocations to the passenger car manufacturers in order to reduce their imports (HML 1966; Pingle 1999). It adversely affected the growth of the car segment. The passenger car was the only segment to experience negative growth in production during the 1970s, whereas the growth of other segments of the automobile industry remained positive and significantly higher during the 1970s (Table 1.1). Surprisingly, the passenger car industry in India is now seen as one of the most successful cases of the economic liberalisation strategy adopted since the middle of the 1980s (Mani 2011; Kale 2012; Tiwari and Herstatt 2014). The increase in production led to consistently high growth during the reform period. It is worth pointing out that the growth experienced by the car industry after 1980s remains higher than the overall growth of the automobile industry as well as of other sub-segments of the industry (Singh 2014).

Second, this is one of the sectors which attracted huge FDI in the recent period, especially after 2000. On average, per annum

Table 1.1 Category-wise CAGR of production

Time period	Cars	UVs	CVs	2-wheelers	3-wheelers	Automobile industry
1960–69	7	4	3	21	29	10
1971–80	−3	4	7	15	16	14

Source: AIAM (1985), ACMA (1984).

Notes
(1) UVs – utility vehicles, CVs – commercial vehicles.
(2) CAGR – Compound Annual Growth Rate.

FDI equity inflows received by the passenger car industry were US$ 82.63 million from 2000 to 2006, which increased to US$ 515.92 million from 2007 to 2011 and then stood at US$ 794.68 million from 2012 to 2016 (GoI 2007, 2010, 2013, 2016b). The huge volume of FDI reflected the fact that almost all the leading foreign manufacturers have started production of cars in India (Table A.1 in annexure). From 2000 to 2016, the passenger car segment accounted for 43 per cent of total FDI attracted by the automobile industry.

Third, the automobile industry in general and the passenger car industry in particular have received special attention from the government since 2000. The special treatment of the industry is reflected in the government's policy specifically prepared for the automobile industry in 2002, known as 'Auto Policy 2002' wherein a central focus was placed on developing India as a manufacturing hub of small cars and auto ancillary (GoI 2002). Further, in 2006, the GoI released a vision document for the automobile industry known as the Automotive Mission Plan (AMP) (2006–16). The AMP was a ten-year vision document wherein emphasis was placed on developing India

> as the destination of choice in the world for design and manufacture of automobiles and auto components with output reaching a level of US$ 145 billion accounting for more than 10% of the GDP and providing additional employment to 25 million people by 2016.
>
> (GoI 2006: 26)

Following this, GoI and SIAM announced AMP 2016–2026. According to the AMP (2016–26), 'by 2026, the Indian automotive industry will be among the top three of the world in engineering, manufacture and export of vehicles and auto components, . . . growing in value to over 12% of India's GDP, and generating an additional 65 million jobs' (GoI and SIAM 2016: 5). The special attention from the government was warranted, as this is a sector with deep forward and backward linkages with other key sectors (such as iron, steel, rubber, plastics and glass). The contribution of the automotive industry to GDP has increased from 2.77 per cent in 1992–93 to 4.14 per cent in 2008–09 and reached to 7.1 per cent in 2016–17 (GoI 2010–11, 2017–18).

Fourth, the development experienced by the passenger car industry in the recent decade has not only contributed to growth and development within the domestic economy but also improved its international ranking in terms of production. In 2002, India accounted for 1.72 per cent of world production of passenger cars, which increased to 3.22 per cent in 2007 and further rose to 5.21 per cent in 2012 (Chattopadhyay 2013). In the corresponding period, India's ranking in world production also improved from number 15 to 9 and then it stood at 6th place.

Given the series of developments that the passenger car industry in India has witnessed during the last couple of decades, this industry has attracted greater attention from the policy makers as well as from researchers. Existing studies in the area have analysed various aspects of the development of this industry such as technology development, competitiveness, export performance of foreign firms etc. The developments described also influenced the choice of this industry for study by this researcher.

Insights from Literature: considering the scope of the study, this review of literature is restricted to discussing the arguments related to technology development, the competitiveness of firms both in the domestic and international markets as well as development of the industry under the liberal policy regime.

The first set of studies has discussed the development of the passenger car industry in India until the 1980s. For the period before liberalisation, most of the studies are related to the inappropriateness of India's policy environment (Krueger 1975; United Nations 1983; World Bank 1987; Narayana 1989; Kathuria and Vandana 1990). Such studies have found that the regulatory economic environment framed to develop an indigenous car industry in India promoted the indigenisation of manufacturing activities, as the indigenous content in the production of cars reached close to 100 per cent in the 1970s. At the same time, it is argued that the extensive protection adversely affected the development of this industry and placed the car industry far behind in terms of technological development (Agarwal 1987; Narayana 1989; Narayanan 1998). The downside of this group of studies is that, without exploring other factors, it has attributed every failure of this industry to the regulatory economic environment, which might not be the case. It is worth noting that many firms in the automobile industry under the same economic environment have experienced considerable success (Lall 1987; Kathuria 1996; Tyabji 2000). Firms such as Tata Motors, Mahindra and Mahindra, Bajaj, Punjab Tractor entered the automobile industry after India's independence. Operating in a similar regulatory environment, these firms have successfully developed manufacturing and technological capabilities which are comparable to international standards (Desai 1984; Venugopal 2001; Ray and Ray 2011). It suggests that factors other than the policy environment that might also have contributed to the poor performance of manufacturers have not been explored by these studies.

However, the orientation of most of the studies in this set changed with the onset of the economic reforms programme and, subsequently, with the entry of foreign firms. Post-liberalisation studies have highlighted the growth trends in the production of passenger cars under the neoliberal policy regime. It is argued that the industry has witnessed significantly high growth in the post-reform period on a continuous basis for a long time (Gulyani 2001; Singh 2004, 2007; D'Costa 2005; Becker-Ritterspach and Becker-Ritterspach 2009; Chattopadhyay 2013). But the underlying factors behind the rapid growth of the passenger car industry under different phases of new liberal policy regime were not discussed in detail in most of these studies. It is significant to analyse the nature of demand stimulus as the underlying conditions for high growth of passenger car industry might not have remained the same during the 1980s and afterwards. As discussed in the literature, large spending by the state played a critical role in the market expansion of industrial goods until the late 1980s (Patnaik 1979; Chandrasekhar 2010, 2011). As the role of the state was reduced in the era of liberalisation but the passenger car industry continued to grow, the nature of demand stimuli might have been different. Thus, it is critical to understand the changing factors behind the success of the industry. This would facilitate an understanding of the long-term sustainability of growth trends witnessed by the industry during the last couple of decades.

A second set of studies has analysed the implications of policy changes on the structure of the industry as the passenger car industry was dominated by two leading firms until the middle of the 1980s (Mohanty, Sahu and Pati 1994; D'Costa 1995; Narayanan 1998; Singh 2004; Becker-Ritterspach and Becker-Ritterspach 2008, 2009). The major argument of these studies is that the industry has witnessed a structural transformation as new entrants (domestic and foreign firms) started competing for the domestic market. In this process, the consumers have been benefitting, as the variety of cars increased in India in the post-reform period. But these studies did not analyse the long-term costs of these developments for the indigenous industry, on the one hand, and implications for investment and pricing strategies of the manufacturers, on the other.

Third, the researchers have extensively analysed the technology changes experienced by the automobile industry in general and the passenger car industry in particular during the last two decades (Mohanty et al. 1994; Narayanan 1998; Sagar and Chandra 2004; Singh 2004; Mani 2011; Kale 2012; Saripalle 2012; Tiwari and Herstatt 2014). Almost all the studies have claimed that India's passenger car industry has performed remarkably well in terms of technology development. To analyse the development of technology, they have selected indicators like spending on technology, increase in variety of passenger cars, product innovations etc. Based on the growing spending on technology, and the growing variety of passenger vehicles, they have claimed that, during the last decade and a half, technology standards of the passenger car industry in India have not only improved but the technology edge achieved by this industry is comparable with that of advanced countries (Sagar and Chandra 2004; Kale 2012). These studies have claimed that technology development has taken place, but the kind of technology development analysed in this literature is not the same as indigenous technology and technological capability development. Further, the literature related to technology issues is also limited to the main vehicle segment and does not focus on the auto components sector. If components and raw materials are procured by manufacturers from the domestic market to launch the new product as well as upgrade existing products, then it implies that the technological level is improving and India is building manufacturing capabilities. Contrary to this, if these firms are using imported components in the production of vehicles, then India's indigenous manufacturing capabilities are not improving either in main vehicle manufacturing or in the ancillary industry.[1] It would imply that India is emerging as an assembling centre rather than a manufacturing hub. Thus, it is critical to address the issue of the auto components sector while analysing technological development. In a liberal trade and investment regime, the manufacturers can supply the same types of cars in any part of the world by using imported technology along with imports of SKD/CKD kits and other components.

Fourth, the focus of the policy initiatives since 1991 was and remains to develop India as a manufacturing hub of small cars for the world market by attracting large foreign investment. The literature in recent decades has also examined the success that India has achieved in exports of cars and other automobile vehicles (Narayanan 2006;

Singh 2007; Singh 2014). The studies in the case of the passenger car industry have highlighted that exports of passenger cars from India have increased significantly after 2000. It is argued that the increase in exports mainly occurred as car manufacturers, especially foreign firms, have started using India as a manufacturing base for world markets. Given this, they have claimed that the growing exports of cars from India would ease the BoP constraint. The downside of these studies is that they did not examine the exports of manufacturers against their spending on imports of raw materials, components and other technical services. It is of significant importance to examine the import payments and other transactions of manufacturers against their exports. Without analysing the trends of foreign exchange payments of manufacturers it would be misleading to claim that the rising exports would ease the BoP constraints. Another gap in the earlier studies, especially those which have viewed India as an export centre, is that they have failed to pay enough attention to the issue of export sustainability. That is important because the exports of major car manufacturers from India have started declining both in absolute and relative terms in recent years (*The Economic Times* 2014; SIAM 2016a).[2] It is reported that exporters from India have shifted sourcing of exports of some models out of India as other countries offered cost-effective alternatives to start manufacturing in that region. Given this, it is worth examining the sustainability of exports of passenger cars from India in the near future.

Filling the Gaps: In view of the above discussion, it is clear that the development scenario of the passenger car industry in the post-reform period has only been partially discussed in the literature. Almost all the studies carried out in recent times have emphasised the favourable effects of open door policies. The open door policies may have certain unfavourable effects as well; thus, it is necessary to analyse various aspects such as import payments of foreign firms, implications for indigenous manufacturing capabilities and technological development, etc., which are either less studied or completely ignored. It is essential to undertake a study with a balanced view to assess the implications of the neoliberal economic reforms programme, particularly with reference to the impact of foreign entry on the various aspects of development of the passenger car industry.

The present study contributes to the literature by seeking to fill these gaps in the literature relating to the changes witnessed by India's passenger car industry from 1981–82 to 2013–14. To be specific, objectives of the study are: (1) to analyse the structure and growth of the industry and document the underlying factors that led to the changes in structure and were recognised as growth stimuli under different economic regimes; (2) to analyse the impact of changes in structure and foreign entry on the technological development of firms and also document the factors underlying the rapid emergence of technologically advanced cars in India; and (3) to analyse the trade performance of foreign firms and their contribution to the balance of payments and sustainability of export trends in the wake of changing strategies of foreign firms.

Data sources and scope of the study

To analyse the aforesaid objectives, the present study uses secondary data. First, the PROWESS electronic database published by the Centre for Monitoring Indian Economy (CMIE), Mumbai, is the principal source. The PROWESS electronic dataset publishes information from the financial statements on various aspects of the performance of Indian firms. This data is increasingly used for firm-level analysis and is considered as quite comprehensive and reliable. The information published in PROWESS starts from 1989 onwards. This dataset provides almost all the information contained in the balance sheets and annual reports of public limited companies.

The second main sources of data are the annual publications of the Society of Indian Automobile Manufacturers[3] (SIAM) and the annual publications of the Automotive Component Manufacturers Association (ACMA) of India. There are two annual publications of SIAM (namely Statistical Profile of Automobile Industry in India and Profile of the Automobile Industry in India), and one of the ACMA publications (namely Automotive Industry of India: Facts and Figures) which are increasingly used to supplement the information available in the PROWESS electronic dataset. It is worth noting that information provided in these reports is not as comprehensive as available in PROWESS. Third, the information related to country-wise inflows of foreign investment is gathered from the World Investment Report (WIR) published by the United Nations Conference on Trade and Development (UNCTAD), whereas industry-wise trends in inflows of foreign investment are collected from the Secretariat for Industrial Assistance (SIA)

Newsletter published by the Department of Industrial Policy and Promotion (DIPP), GoI. Other than these sources, we have also collected data from published research, which is reported as a source wherever it is used.

Data Limitations: The main dataset used in the current study, CMIE PROWESS, has some limitations; it is not a census data and the coverage of firms also varied over the years. These limitations are to be kept in mind while drawing inferences from the analysis.

For empirical investigation, we have used various statistical measures. The discussion on methods used and selection of firms is provided in the respective chapters. The time span of this study is 1981–82 to 2013–14. In this period, there has been a major change in the regulatory environment affecting the development of the passenger car industry in many ways.

Organisation of the book

The book is organised into nine chapters, including the introduction. The introductory chapter describes the broader context in which the objectives of the present study have been developed. Further, it discusses the importance and likely contribution of the present study to the literature.

Chapter 2 develops an understanding of the policy framework which has evolved around the passenger car industry in India since 1947. Based on the varying nature of regulations, we have divided the whole period into four sub-periods. The first phase covers the period from 1947 to the mid-1960s. In this phase, the state granted protection to the domestic industry by imposing quantitative restrictions, increasing tariffs and regulating the nature and form of foreign presence with a view to promote indigenisation of production activities. The second phase stretches from 1966 to 1980. In this phase, the regulations around the industry tightened as the Indian economy experienced a foreign exchange shortage in the late 1960s. The third phase starts in 1981 and ends in 1990. In this phase, the regulatory framework installed in the 1950s and afterward was relaxed in order to promote competition between domestic manufacturers as well as to modernise the industry. And the fourth phase starts from 1991 onwards, wherein the government introduced a series of changes in the economic environment and the policies dealing with entry of foreign firms and their operations in the country.

Chapter 3 analyses the changes in the structure of the industry on account of the entry of foreign players as well as the growth episodes of the industry from 1981 onwards. To understand the relationship between foreign entry and structure, we develop an understanding based on existing theoretical as well as empirical studies. Following this, we have separately analysed the changes in structure and growth trends for two sub-periods (i.e. 1981–90 and 1991 onwards). Further, the implications of changes in structure and the varying nature of the growth stimulus for the investment strategies and pricing behaviour of manufacturers are discussed.

In Chapters 4 and 5, we extend the previous analysis by investigating the impact of changes in structure and large foreign entry on the technology development and technology acquisition strategies of firms. After developing an analytical understanding, we estimate the change in expenditure on technology in the case of the individual selected firms as well as of the industry as a whole. Further, we have estimated the changes in the composition of raw materials and components procured by manufacturers from domestic as well as from the international market to manufacture final vehicles.

Chapters 6 and 7 investigate the contribution of the passenger car manufacturers, especially foreign firms, to the BoP of the country. After discussing the possible linkages between foreign entry and exports of the host country, we have analysed the trends in the firms' export earnings from, as well as import spending on, goods in order to understand the net contribution of manufacturers. This analysis is further extended as the earnings and spending of manufacturers are not only limited to imports and exports of goods as firms earn from and spend on various other services. Thus, the actual contribution of firms can be known only after analysing the total transactions of firms. The analysis in Chapter 7 also discusses the sustainability of export earnings of manufacturers and export potential of various sub-segments in the car industry.

Chapter 8 provides case studies of MUL and Hyundai. The performance of these two firms has remained unique since their entry in the industry. The chapter tries to understand the factors and their strategies which would have contributed to their performance. The case studies also facilitated in drawing some policy lessons for other firms.

The final chapter summarises the findings of the study and draws some policy implications.

Notes

1 The segment producing components holds the key to the development of the entire industry, especially because it determines the cost, quality and technological parameters of finished vehicles (World Bank 1987; Karmokolias 1990).

2 The exports of major passenger vehicle manufacturers (Maruti, Hyundai, Honda, Mahindra and Mahindra, Toyota, Tata Motors and Nissan) have declined during 2013–14, 2014–15 and 2015–16.

3 Until 2000, the SIAM was known as the Association of Indian Automobile Manufacturers (AIAM).

Chapter 2

Exploring the basics

Development of the passenger car industry in the changing regulatory framework

This chapter aims to understand the economic environment provided by the state in the form of policies and regulations for industrial sector development in general and the passenger car industry in particular in the period following the attainment of India's independence in 1947. It is well recognised that state intervention plays a significant role in the development of a nation's industrial sector (Patnaik 1979; Chakraborty 1987; Ghosh 1992; Evans 1995; Cimoli, Dosi and Stiglitz 2009; A. Singh 2009; Chandrasekhar 2010, 2011). Government intervention influences industrial development both directly and indirectly. We define direct intervention of the state as its participation in the production of goods and services. Indirect intervention occurs through policy that affects size, location and form of private investment and the operations of private firms. Therefore, any analysis of the development of the industrial sector remains incomplete without a discussion of the policy framework that governs it.

The Indian industrial sector, including the passenger car industry, was subjected to strict regulations until the early 1980s, the significant ones being protection, capacity licensing, restrictions on foreign collaborations, price control etc. However, a shift in the development strategy has been noticed since the 1980s. The shift essentially involved a gradual reduction in the role of state, both in direct and indirect forms, and a corresponding increase in the role of the market and private agents in shaping a long-term development path. To observe the changes along the development path of this industry, the whole period after 1947 is divided into different sub-periods. The periodisation of this industry can be based either on episodes of growth and deceleration or in terms of changing policy regimes since the attainment of independence in 1947.[1] In this study, periodisation is done on the basis of changes recorded in the policy regimes. The objective of this research is to understand the role of regulatory regimes, particularly the nature of foreign entry in the development of passenger car industry. The policy regime plays a critical role in influencing the magnitude, nature, pattern and form of foreign presence.

To understand the policy framework governing the evolution of the passenger car industry, the period after 1947 is divided into four phases. The first phase covers the period from 1947 to the mid-1960s. In this phase, the state granted protection to the domestic industry by imposing quantitative restrictions on imports, increasing tariffs and regulating the nature and form of foreign presence in a view to promote indigenisation of production activities. The second phase stretches from 1966 to 1980. This phase started with worsening macro-economic conditions and the transfer of power to Ms. Indira Gandhi. These developments led to the tightening of regulations in the form of a selective and restrictive foreign investment policy. The third phase starts in 1981 and ends in 1990. This was a phase of partial liberalisation because the regulatory framework installed in the 1950s and thereafter still existed, but the extent of regulation was not as effective as it was when originally implemented. And the fourth phase started with the onset of a severe BoP crisis in 1991. It led to comprehensive changes in the policy environment dealing with firm size, capacity expansion, time-bound Phased Manufacturing Programme (PMP) etc. and in the policies dealing with foreign firms' entry and their operations in India.

Against this background, the present chapter examines the main features of the relevant policies relating to the industrial sector in general and the passenger car industry in particular since 1947. The main focus of discussion here is on: (1) operating environment; (2) foreign investment policy and (3) nature of technology development. Before providing a detailed discussion on the different phases of policy regimes regulating the industry, a brief discussion on the origin of the passenger car industry before 1947 is provided.

2.1 Origin of India's passenger car industry

The origin of India's car industry lies way back in 1898 with the import of the first motor car (Narayana 1989; Pingle 1999; Nayak 2008). For almost three decades, the demand for cars and other vehicles in India was continuously met through imports, as no attempt was made to establish an assembling plant in India until 1928. During this period, the demand for automobiles increased substantially. According to the New York Times (1922: 106) 'there were already 45,983 cars and trucks plying on India's roads by the end of June 1921, making it the ninth largest automobile market ahead of countries such as Spain, Russia and even Japan.' Responding to growing demand, subsidiaries of foreign firms established assembling plants in India in the late 1920s. In 1928, General Motors India Limited started assembling cars and trucks in India based on the imports of components and parts from the USA in the form of CKD kits. The General Motors plant was located in Bombay. Following this, Ford Motors entered and started assembly of vehicles in Madras in 1930 and in Bombay and Calcutta in 1931 (Venkataramani 1990; Kathuria 1996; Nayak 2008).

During World War II, the demand for vehicles increased rapidly and kept the General Motors and Ford Motors plants in India very busy. The annual combined demand for commercial vehicles and passenger cars crossed 20,000 units, with passenger cars accounting for the major share of the total demand(Narayana 1989).

In response to the growing demand, various committees which were set up at different points of time since the late 1930s argued for the creation of an indigenous motor vehicle industry. First, the National Planning Committee (NPC) appointed by the Indian National Congress (INC) in 1938 analysed various aspects of India's industrialisation and emphasised the need for developing an indigenous automobile industry. Second, after World War II, the government of British India established a Panel on Automobiles and Tractors in 1945 to explore the feasibility of setting up manufacturing activities in the country. According to the panel's report submitted in 1947, development of a motor vehicle industry was in the national interest and the industry could be identified as of basic importance to the country's economic development (GoI 1947). Besides these committees, a group of leading Indian industrialists developed a separate document in 1944–45 wherein they not only recognised the importance of state support for industrial development but also emphasised its direct role in the development of capital goods sector.

These developments paved the way for the entry of two Indian business houses (namely Birla group and Walchand Hirachand group) into the automobile industry in the early 1940s. Birla group established Hindustan Motors Limited (HML) in 1942 and Walchand

Table 2.1 Automobile industry in India up to 1947

S. no	Automobile firms	Nature of production
1	Hindustan Motors Ltd., Calcutta	Firms initiated manufacturing activities
2	Premier Automobiles Ltd., Bombay	
3	General Motors India Ltd., Bombay	Assemblers
4	Ford Motor Company of India Ltd., Bombay	
5	Addison and Co. Ltd., Madras	Automobile import dealers
6	Dewar's Garage and Engg. Works, Calcutta	
7	Peninsular Motor Corporation Ltd., Calcutta	
8	French Motor Car Co. Ltd., Bombay	

Source: Prepared based on GoI (1953), Narayana (1989), Pingle (1999), Tyabji (2000).

Hirachand group established Premier Automobiles Limited (PAL) in 1944. Initially, these companies also offered import-intensive products but, nonetheless, they had a programme of progressively indigenising manufacturing of complete vehicles. Initial progress by HML and PAL towards indigenisation of manufacturing activities was very slow mainly on account of tough competition from already established foreign subsidiaries and dealers of foreign firms supplying a wide variety of imported complete vehicles as well as assembled vehicles (Agarwal 1987; Pingle 1999). Table 2.1 indicates that the industry comprised of eight firms and, out of eight, four firms were the dealers of imported vehicles whereas two firms were offering completely assembled products. The subsidiaries of foreign firms did not have any long-term programme to start manufacturing activities in India. Thus, the process of development of an indigenous automobile industry started only after the attainment of India's independence.

2.2   Evolution of the automobile industry after 1947

At the time of India's independence, around 180 models of automobiles (61 of cars and 119 of commercial vehicles) were available in the domestic market, the size of which was only 20,000 to 25,000

units per annum (HML 1966; Agarwal 1987). The resource constraints at the time of independence made it impossible to continue
with imports of a large variety of automobiles and components; the
government showed interest in developing an indigenous automobile industry, as was suggested in the recommendations of a number
of committees set up prior to independence. Accordingly, the state
intervened with a series of supportive policies as well as administrative measures with the sole aim of developing an indigenous
automobile industry. The regulations covered the whole range of
manufacturing decisions including entry, size, expansion of firm,
diversification of product line, final prices, import of technology
and raw materials and the role for and nature of foreign participation etc. These regulatory measures were modified periodically
after 1947, and these modifications swung between regulation and
liberalisation.

2.2.1   Phase I: 1947 to 1965

With a view to speed up the industrialisation process, the GoI
announced its first Industrial Policy Resolution (IPR) in 1948. Under
this policy, government specified the role of the state in the process
of development of industrial sector by dividing the whole industrial sector into four groups. The automobile industry was grouped
under the category of industries of basic importance. Industries of
basic importance were planned, regulated and controlled by the
central government. In 1956, the government announced its second
IPR. Under IPR-1956, the industrial sector was classified into three
categories. The automobile industry was classified under the third
group and was left to the initiatives of the private sector for its
development.

Operating Environment: Besides the two industrial policies, the
government also adopted a number of administrative regulations
and policies which played a critical role in shaping the operating
environment surrounding this industry.

Protection and Indigenisation: As a first step, the Ministry of Industry, GoI, announced its first automobile policy in 1949, wherein the
government banned the import of fully built vehicles (Singh 2004).
The ban was aimed at preventing unfair competition from imports
of complete vehicles and providing space to indigenous manufacturers. The automobile policy of 1949 permitted firms to continue
assembling activities through the imports of CKD kits, but their

imports were regulated through the foreign exchange allocation policy. While allocating foreign exchange to the manufacturing firms, priorities were given to those firms which had already initiated the process of indigenisation of components and other parts (Agarwal 1987; Narayana 1989; Venkataramani 1990).

To ensure long-term development, the government sought advice from the Tariff Commission set up in 1952. The commission submitted its report in 1953. After considering all aspects of protection and state support, the commission advised the government to reserve the automobile industry for firms which had already started indigenous manufacturing or showed willingness to indigenise production activities in a phased manner. In line with the commission's recommendations, the government directed the assemblers to either implement the PMP or terminate the activities of their assembling units within a period of three years. This was done with a view to restrict the domestic market only for firms which were willing to act according to the state's economic policy. Two foreign firms (General Motors and Ford) which were serving the Indian market since late 1920s with assembled vehicles wound up their business in the stipulated time (up to 1956). According to them, it was not viable for them to continue production in line with the government's guidelines regarding the PMP. With the exit of foreign firms, three firms were left in the passenger car segment to serve the whole domestic market. Initially two firms (HML and PAL) were recognised by the commission for manufacturing automobiles, as these firms had already embarked upon the process of indigenisation of components. In 1954, Standard Motor Products India Ltd. (SMPIL) also got approval from the government to produce passenger cars in India.[2]

What to produce and how much to produce was not left to the firms. It was subject to the type of license and the production capacity of licenses issued by the government. Licensed capacity issued to the manufacturers was decided in line with the requirement of vehicles, as per the estimates of the five-year plan document.

The process of indigenisation was further intensified after the foreign exchange shortage of 1957. To deal with the foreign exchange constraint, as a first step, government directed the manufacturers to increase local content in the production of vehicles from 50 per cent to 80 per cent by the end of 1960–61 (Singh 2004; Ranawat and Tiwari 2009). As a second step, the allocation of foreign exchange to the manufacturing firms was reduced significantly in

Table 2.2 Firms in the automobile industry, 1950s

S. no.	Automobile firms	Passenger vehicles	Production of commercial vehicles
1.	Hindustan Motors Ltd.	Hindustan 14, Studebaker Champion	Studebaker
2.	Premier Automobiles Ltd.	Dodge, De Soto, Plymouth Fiat	Dodge, De Soto, Fargo
3.	Standard Motor Products India Ltd.	Standard Vanguard	–
4.	Ashok Motors*	Austin	Austin, Leyland
5.	TELCO	–	3 to 5 tonne diesel truck
6.	Mahindra and Mahindra	Willy's jeep	–

Source: Prepared based on GoI (1953, 1957), Narayana (1989), Pingle (1999), Tyabji (2000).

Note: *Ashok Motors was renamed as Ashok Leyland after equity collaboration with British Leyland. After collaboration, the firm discontinued production of cars.

the following years. This led to a reduction in the import of motor vehicle components, and the production of passenger cars fell in the following years. For instance, the production of cars declined from 13339 units in 1956 to 8114 in 1958 (AIAM 1985). It happened because it was not possible for manufacturers to increase indigenisation of imported components quickly as it required time as well as resources. It was argued that the promotion of indigenisation through the PMP led to a high degree of vertical integration (World Bank 1987; Gumaste 1988; Narayana 1989; Pingle 1999). According to D'Costa (1995: 493),

> older Indian firms relied heavily on components made in-house. Indian firms were motivated to "make" rather than "buy" components from external vendors because of the underdeveloped ancillary industry . . . and the need to enhance market control through vertical integration.

According to Kujal (1996), the tax structure before the economic reforms was cascading as intermediate goods were being taxed at each stage of production. To avoid being taxed at each stage of production, the passenger car manufacturers were producing most of the components and parts within the assembling plant, as no sales tax was levied on within firm transfers. The decline in the production of cars created the backlog of unsatisfied car demand, which increased to up to two years in the following period (Kujal 1996; Okada 1998; Bhargava and Seetha 2010). These developments led to a sharp increase in the prices of passenger cars on account of the mismatch between demand and supply.

To deal with the rising prices and declining production of cars, government intervened at two levels. First, to control rising prices, government came up with an informal price control mechanism,[3] which was accepted by the manufacturers. Under the informal price control mechanism, a potential buyer of a car was required to place the order with a dealer and deposit partial payment with the Indian Postal Savings. The car was delivered to the buyer in a sequence in which the order was registered with Indian Postal Savings[4] (Kathuria 1996; Ranawat and Tiwari 2009). Second, to increase production of auto parts and components, the government came up with an elaborate policy on auto components and parts in the early 1960s[5] (Krueger 1975; Narayana 1989; Pingle 1999). It led to division of auto components into two categories, list A and list B. Under list A, government included those parts and components which could be manufactured by either vehicle producers or the ancillary sector. All the components and parts under list B were strictly reserved for manufacturing by the ancillary sector. Within the ancillary sector, policy initiatives were directed to encourage small-sized manufacturers.[6] The elaborate classification of auto components widened the structural base of India's automobile industry, and led to its three-tier structure: the first tier consisting of manufacturers of final auto products; the second tier manufacturers producing relatively sophisticated components namely filters, oil seals, radiators etc. and known as original equipment manufacturers, and the third tier (consisting of small-scale units)[7] producing for original equipment manufacturers and the replacement market.

In response to the state's new ancillary policy to develop separate ancillary units, indigenous ancillary production increased dramatically during the 1960s (Tables 2.3 and 2.4). According to Krueger (1975), the production of auto ancillaries increased by around four times between 1961 and 1968 and product variety also expanded significantly. It is further evident from Table 2.3 that the import content in all passenger cars produced by HML, PAL and SMPIL declined. The decline in import content was largely the result of

Table 2.3 Distribution of value of components (percentages)

Car model	Sources of components	1961–62	1962–63	1963–64	1964–65	1965–66
HML (Ambassador)	I	29.9	25.4	15.5	15.5	9.9
	BO	16.7	21.7	29.7	30.2	31.5
	SM	53.4	52.9	54.8	54.3	58.6
PAL (Fiat)	I	51.1	43.1	35.2	30.4	19.3
	BO	21.1	26.1	27.9	32.2	41.7
	SM	27.0	30.8	36.9	37.4	39.0
SMPIL (Herald)	I	56.6	54.9	43.0	40.4	27.8
	BO	17.4	16.5	20.8	23.0	29.3
	SM	26.0	28.6	36.2	36.6	42.9

Source: GoI (1968).

Note: I = Directly Imported; BO = Bought Out from ancillary manufacturers in the country; SM = Self-Manufactured.

Table 2.4 Composition of indigenous and import content (percentages)

Year	HML (Ambassador)		PAL (Fiat)		SMPIL (Herald)	
	IC	I	IC	I	IC	I
1956	–	–	30	70	20	80
1960	70.5	29.5	47	53	32.5	67.5
1959–60	70.5	29.5	47.3	52.7	32.5	67.5
1961–62	70.1	29.9	48.1	51.9	43.4	56.6
1962–63	74.6	25.4	56.9	43.1	45.1	54.9
1963–64	84.5	15.5	64.8	35.2	57.0	43
1964–65	84.5	15.5	69.6	30.4	59.6	40.4
1965–66	90.1	9.9	80.7	19.3	72.2	27.8
1968–69	99.36	0.64	99.06	0.94	95.0	5
1971–72	99.82	0.18	99.64	0.36	99.3	0.7

Source: GoI, (1968), Agarwal (1987).

Note: IC = Indigenous Content; I = Imported.

purchases from the ancillary manufacturers (Table 2.3). The value of bought-out components from local ancillary units to total value of components used in the manufacture of Ambassador, Fiat and Herald cars increased (Table 2.3). This means that increased indigenisation of manufacturing over time was not only an outcome of the PMP and other regulatory measures applied on vehicle manufacturers, but also an outcome of systematic state intervention in the process of development of ancillary units.

Industrial Licensing Policy: The enactment of the Industries Development and Regulation Act (IDRA) in 1951 marked the beginning of licensing policy. The IDRA provided enough space to the government to regulate industrial activities and to make effective use of resources in accordance with national priorities. According to IDRA (1951), manufacturers with 50 or more workers (100 or more workers without power) were bound to get a license from the licensing authority for the establishment of a new unit, expansion of output by more than 5 per cent, manufacture of new product, change in location and for all other purposes. The act also aimed at limiting the entry of manufacturers in the industry in order to encourage scale economies. It was expected that a large number of firms in a small-sized market may hinder the process of indigenisation as well as add to the cost of production. The costs of indigenisation decrease with increase in volume of production and vice versa. According to Baranson (1968) an increase in indigenous content from 28 to 97 per cent increased the index of production costs from 152 to 300 for a volume of 3000 cars per annum. But (for the same increase in indigenous content) the index of cost of production rose from 143 to 204 for a volume of 12000 cars per annum.

Licensing policy sought to allocate vehicle production among segments and producers according to the nation's requirement as well as the availability of scarce resources, particularly foreign exchange. It is evident from the fact that, after the BoP problem of 1957, the government replaced general licensing with product-specific licensing[8] with an aim to restrict the outflow of foreign exchange.

Foreign Investment Policy: The presence of leading foreign firms (General Motors and Ford) in the passenger car industry was noted well before 1947. However, the nature and pattern of foreign presence in the industrial sector changed with the attainment of political independence in 1947.

Until the middle of the 1960s,[9] India's attitude towards FDI was marked by gradual liberalisation. The IPR presented in April 1948 recognised the importance of foreign capital as an important supplement to domestic savings for facilitating national economic development. To ensure national interest and use of foreign capital according to national priorities, it was proposed that majority control would remain, as a rule, in Indian hands. To ensure increased foreign collaborations, the Prime Minister's Foreign Investment Policy Statement of April 6, 1949 declared that the government would not impose any kind of regulations that implied discriminatory treatment of foreign vis-à-vis indigenous firms. Instead, government intended to frame a policy which would encourage foreign investment on mutually beneficial terms. There would also be no restrictions imposed on remittances of profits and dividends (Kidron 1965; Kumar 1994, 2005). The business lobby in India was not completely against the Prime Minister's statement on foreign investment. The main demand of the indigenous business lobby was that the government specify the sphere of activities of foreign capital. Further, the government should not allow foreign capital in those areas where it could adversely affect the interests of indigenous firms (Kidron 1965).

The push for foreign collaboration was further intensified in the late 1950s in view of India's BoP problem as it led to a shortage of foreign exchange for importing necessary capital goods and raw materials. Thus, the government extended various fiscal incentives to foreign firms in the late 1950s and the early 1960s. The fiscal incentives included the concessional rates of dividend tax and reduced taxes on technical service fees and income from royalties. Given the liberal attitude of the government towards foreign investment,[10] automobile firms also signed a number of technical and financial collaborations with foreign firms during the 1950s. The most important ones included TELCO with Mercedes-Benz; HML with Morris Motors (UK); PAL with Fiat (Italy); Ashok Motors with Leyland; SMPIL with Standard-Triumph (UK) etc.

Technology Policy: In line with the overall objectives of the import-substitution industrialisation strategy, the GoI also pursued the objective of self-reliance on the technology front. Towards that end, the government took a number of concrete steps. It established a number of state-funded research centres[11] to undertake R&D and also set up a separate Ministry of Scientific Research and Cultural Affairs under the direct control of the Prime Minister in 1949.

To provide a broad perspective and guidelines for future efforts towards technology development, the government released a Scientific Policy Resolution in 1958. The Scientific Policy Resolution (1958) stated that 'the key to national prosperity, apart from the spirit of the people, lies, in the modern age, in the effective combination of three factors, technology, raw materials and capital, of which the first is perhaps the most important' (GoI 1958: 4).

Along with internal efforts towards technological capability development, India recognised the role of foreign skills in developing local science and technology in the early years of independence. To get access to external technology, government provided incentives and also clearly defined the role of foreign firms and forms of participation in different industries. At the same time, emphasis was given to rapid indigenisation or absorption of technical skills by local technical personnel and the quickest possible replacement of expatriates by Indians (Kumar 1987). In line with the government's attitude toward technology imports, a number of technological agreements were signed between domestic automobile manufacturers and foreign firms. For instance, in 1954, HML entered into a technical collaboration with UK-based Morris Motors Ltd. and launched its Ambassador car, which was an upgraded model of Morris-3. PAL entered into technological collaboration with Fiat, Italy, to produce cars in India and manufactured Fiat 1100 Delight for the Indian market. Similarly, the SMPIL entered into technological collaboration with Standard-Triumph of the United Kingdom and started production of the Herald Model of car for Indian consumers. Although these firms started production based on imported designs, they systematically absorbed the technology and also replaced imported components and parts by developing them domestically. The extent of technology learning is evident in terms of success achieved in indigenisation of production activities which promoted systematic learning and added to the technological capability of the firms (Tables 2.3 and 2.4).

To summarise, it can be argued that the policy measures implemented in this phase worked successfully to develop the passenger car industry. The development of the industry is manifested in terms of the systematic reduction of import content in the production of passenger cars and increased use of indigenous components. According to the AIAM (1965), the inception of the Indian automobile sector was largely dependent on protection given to the industry during the 1950s. Corresponding to the main vehicle segment, the component segment also observed growth during the early 1960s in response to wide-ranging policy measures.

2.2.2 Phase II: 1966 to 1980

The beginning of the second phase was marked by major changes in the economic situation as well as changes in the political scenario of the country. On the economic front, India was experiencing a fiscal crunch on account of the huge expenditure on wars with China (1962) and Pakistan (1965), on the one hand, and an agrarian crisis due to successive droughts in the middle of the 1960s (1965–66 and 1966–67), on the other. On the political front, the appointment of Ms. Indira Gandhi as India's Prime Minister in 1966 and her success in the general election in 1967 changed the political situation in the country.[12] These developments led to a shift in the operating environment, foreign investment and technology policies.

Operating Environment: The regulations initiated and implemented during the previous one and a half decade remained in place, but Indira Gandhi's government also introduced additional regulations which led to the tightening of the operating environment. *First*, the government set up the Third Tariff Commission in 1966 to examine the issues of protection granted to the automobile industry and the informal price control mechanism. Tariff Commission recommended that: (a) the number of models in each segment of the automobile industry be reduced to an absolute minimum in order to ensure minimum economic scales of production; (b) the informal price control mechanism be continued for passenger cars.

In the case of the car segment, the number of models had already been reduced to a minimum as the product-specific licensing policy permitted each manufacturer to produce only a single model. Thus, the first recommendation of the Tariff Commission did not bring any change in the case of the passenger car segment. With regard to the price control mechanism, the government replaced the informal price control mechanism with a rigid system of 'statutory price control' in 1969 in the case of the car segment, whereas it was abolished in the case of commercial vehicles and jeeps. It adversely affected the profits of manufacturers operating in the car industry. PAL challenged the statutory price control policy of the state in the Supreme Court. The Supreme Court set up a committee to examine the validity of PAL's claim. Based on the committee's report, in 1975, the court's decision favoured PAL and accordingly statutory price control was eliminated and manufacturers were allowed to determine the prices of their own products.

Second, based on the suggestions of the Monopolies Inquiry Commission (MIC) report, the government passed the Monopolies and Restrictive Trade Practices (MRTP) Act in 1969. The Act was enacted with a view to empowering the government to effectively control concentration in the industrial sector as the large industrial houses managed to get a disproportionate share of industrial licenses issued under the IDRA 1951, which led to a high concentration (Hazari 1966; Narayana 1989). Under MRTP Act 1969, the companies or undertakings with assets amounting to Rs. 200 million or which held a dominant position in the market with one-third (or more) market share were identified as MRTP firms. Firms identified as MRTP companies were asked to get an additional clearance under the MRTP Act, as well as under the IDRA 1951, to enter an industry, expand, relocate or merge. A number of firms operating in the automobile industry were subjected to MRTP scrutiny for future expansion and capacity licensing.

Third, another set of changes was observed with the onset of global oil shocks witnessed in 1973. Following the oil shocks, India's import bill for crude oil increased sharply which badly affected the BoP of the country.[13] To reduce oil imports, it was decided to modernise the automobile industry in order to increase fuel efficiency. For this purpose, the government appointed a committee for evaluating and making recommendations on the issue. Based on the recommendations of the committee, the industry was sub-divided into luxury (passenger car) and non-luxury (rest of the industry) segments and the government decided to develop the non-luxury segment as opposed to the luxury segment. Following this, foreign exchange allocation to the luxury segment (passenger car firms) was reduced, which affected the imports of critical components that were not manufactured in India at that time (GoI 1973). Consequently, the production of the passenger car industry declined in the following years (Table 1.1 in Chapter 1).

To develop the non-luxury segment, particularly the commercial vehicle segment, a series of relaxations were announced after 1973, which were solely aimed at boosting growth and technology development in the non-luxury segment. (1) The government brought the non-luxury segment under the Appendix I list in 1973. With this, the applications of units in the non-luxury segment for capacity expansion, modernisation requiring foreign exchange and foreign collaboration got more favourable treatment than earlier. (2) The government also amended the IDR Act-1951 in 1975 and permitted automatic capacity expansion of up to 25 per cent during a period of five years. This expansion was over and above that already sanctioned under the IDR Act (Kathuria 1996; Singh 2004). This policy did not, however, apply to the passenger car segment. In 1975, the government facilitated expansion without limit to non-MRTP/Foreign Exchange Regulation Act (FERA) firms operating in the commercial vehicle, ancillaries and scooter sectors (Pingle 1999; Ranawat and Tiwari 2009). In line with changing priorities of the government across segments of the automobile industry, no additional capacity was allocated to the passenger car segment under the fifth five-year plan, whereas the production capacity of the commercial vehicle and two-wheeler segments was increased substantially.

Initially, the discriminatory attitude of the government towards the car segment was attributed to the shortage of foreign exchange on account of the 1973 oil crisis. But this attitude continued even in the following years when the BoP situation improved after the mid-1970s.[14] These policy measures suggest that the state policies did not favour the development of the passenger car segment.

Foreign Investment Policy: The attitude of the government towards foreign investment changed in this phase. Broadly, three types of changes were noticed at the policy level to streamline the procedure for foreign approvals.[15]

As a first step, the government formed a committee on foreign collaboration known as the Mudaliar Committee (1966). On the advice of committee, the government established a Foreign Investment Board (FIB) in 1968. The sole aim of the FIB was to regulate the equity participation in joint ventures (JVs) between domestic and overseas firms and to approve foreign collaborations (Singh and Kaur 1999; Sinha 2004). FIB was empowered to deal with all those cases of foreign investment where total foreign investment amounted to less than Rs. 20 million or the proportion of foreign equity did not exceed 40 per cent (Singh and Kaur 1999). All the other cases[16] were referred to the Cabinet Committee on Economic Affairs for approval because these were considered to be special cases. It pressured foreign investors to restrict equity up to 40 per cent as equity participation beyond 40 per cent was to be granted in rare cases. Within the FIB, a sub-committee was also formed to deal with the cases involving foreign collaborations where foreign firms held equity up to 25 per cent or foreign equity investment was not more than Rs. 10 million.

A second move to regulate foreign presence was observed in January 1969 when the nature and presence of foreign firms was made selective (Natarajan 1988; Subrahmanian et al. 1996). The government divided the whole industrial sector into three groups: (a) where foreign collaborations were deemed to be necessary; (b) where foreign presence was limited to technical collaborations; and (c) a third in which no collaboration was considered necessary. In the subsequent year, the government announced an industrial policy (1970) which further specified regulations regarding the presence of foreign firms in the core industries (or industries listed in Appendix I).

Finally, to influence the operations of foreign investors in the country, the Indira Gandhi government passed the FERA in 1973. FERA aimed at conserving the foreign exchange resources of the country. The Act made it mandatory for the foreign firms and subsidiaries to reduce their equity share to 40 per cent or less. Section 29 of FERA covered all the foreign firms and subsidiaries which were operating in India in 1974 with more than 40 per cent foreign equity. These firms were directed to convert themselves into Indian firms with minimum 60 per cent of local equity participation. Once the firms reduced foreign equity participation up to 40 per cent, they were treated like local firms. All the firms exceeding the 40 per cent limit of foreign equity were required to get permission from the Reserve Bank of India (RBI) to continue operations. Due to this, many firms wound up their businesses in India during this period. Among them, IBM and Coca-Cola were the major ones (J. Singh 2009).

Thus, it can be argued that the regulations on FDI became very strict in this phase. The changes in the regulatory environment not only influenced the inflow of foreign investment but also regulated its nature. The same holds true for the passenger car industry, which was tightly regulated and its products treated as luxuries. Thus, in this phase, this segment of the automobile industry failed to get even a single approval for foreign collaboration.

Technology Policy after 1966: Changes in technology policy were observed both in relation to the imports of technology and the efforts towards indigenous technology development. The government took several steps to accelerate the pace of indigenous technology development. First, the GoI initiated a scheme for recognising the in-house R&D units of industrial firms in 1974. The recognised

units received benefits in terms of easier access to imports of equipment, raw materials etc. used for their R&D work under OGL
(Kumar 1987). In addition, the expenditure incurred on scientific
research was also deducted (100 per cent) from profits of the firm for
the purpose of income tax calculation. As a result, per firm expenditure on technology increased from Rs. 1.16 lakh in 1967–68 to Rs.
5.32 lakh in 1977–78 and further reached above 8 lakh in 1980–81
(Subrahmanian 1987). Second, the Patent Act was amended in the
1970s as foreign firms were using vague provisions of the Act to
impede local innovation activities in the 1960s (Parthasarthi 2007).
The new Patent Act abolished product patents and also reduced the
life of process patents. Life of patent was reduced from 14 to 7 years
from the date of the filing of the patent and 5 years from the date of
the sealing of the patent, whichever was earlier (Joseph and Abrol
2009). Following this, a significant upsurge was observed in adaptive research and copying of technologies. For instance, the share of
Indian firms in total patents sealed in India was 13.02 per cent in
1969, which increased to 26.13 per cent in 1977–78 (Kumar 1987).

Correspondingly, the government tightened the regulations dealing with the import of technology in the middle of the 1960s. As
a first step, the government discouraged purely financial collaborations and preferred to purchase technology through licensing.[17]
Technology import through licensing encourages importing firms to
do local R&D to absorb, adapt and upgrade imported technology
according to the domestic resource endowment. This process adds
to the technology capability of firms through learning and doing
as well as enables firms to make more efficient and effective use of
imported technology. In addition, the government also regulated
the various aspects of technical collaboration agreements, which
included a ceiling on royalties and lump-sum payments, the duration of technology contracts, the right to sub-license and the right
to export technology. In the case of royalty payments, the ceiling
was set at 5 per cent of the value of sales, which was lower than
international standards (Lall 1984). Further, the life of contracts
was reduced from 10 to 5 years and renewal of a contract was
also restricted.[18] The state did not permit collaborations involving
restrictive clauses related to sub-licensing of technology within the
domestic economy and its export. A Technical Evaluation Committee was set up in 1976 that aimed at assisting the government
on deciding on the desirability of technology imports after analysing all aspects of proposed collaborations as well as analysing the

possibility of extension of existing collaborations in order to avoid the repetitive imports of technology and to promote the use of locally available technology.

The restrictive measures initiated during the second half of the 1960s also influenced the import of technology in the car industry. This industry was not classified in any of the two groups of industries where foreign collaborations were allowed in any form. As a consequence, the passenger car firms were neither allowed to form any new collaboration nor permitted to renew their existing contracts. For instance, the technical collaboration between Fiat and PAL expired in 1972. As this firm was denied renewal of the contract, PAL replicated the old model (Fiat 1100), which was manufactured in collaboration with Fiat until 1972. Further, firms in the passenger car industry applied for the approval of foreign collaborations in order to improve the quality of cars produced in India, but the government rejected their proposals on the grounds of huge foreign exchange outflow (D'Costa 1995).

To sum up, it can be argued that the operating environment around the industrial sector in general and the passenger car industry in particular witnessed a tightening of regulations from 1966 to 1980. This was aimed at saving foreign exchange, encouraging the development of indigenous manufacturing capability and providing protection to local technology. On account of increased regulations, scholars' views differed significantly on the implications for technology. One set of studies has argued that the rigid policies of the government did not permit firms to purchase the latest technology available in the international market (Lall 1980, 1984; Desai 1985; Kumar 1987). It was so because foreign firms were not willing to transfer their best technology to Indian firms under the conditions laid down in this phase. Contrary to this, Subrahmanian (1986) argued that tightening of the regulations on imports of technology strengthened the bargaining position of the Indian buyers. The strengthening of bargaining power was inversely related to the costs of transfer of technology.

2.2.3   Phase III: partial liberalisation (1981 to 1990)

Phase III began with the success of the Congress party in the general elections, which led to the reappointment of Ms. Indira Gandhi as Prime Minister of India. Her return to power brought a number of changes in the regulatory environment around the industrial sector in the country. The changes in the policy environment occurred on account of various economic and non-economic factors (Manor 1988; Marathe 1989; D'Costa 1995; Pingle 1999).

Non-economic factors included the personal interest of Ms. Indira Gandhi to re-establish Maruti, which was started by Sanjay Gandhi in the early 1970s, as well as political obligations incurred during her years in the opposition (Pingle 1999). Another factor was the macro-economic setback experienced by the world economy on account of the second oil shock in 1979, which led to the deterioration of external balance (Ahluwalia 1986; Ghosh 1990; Jalan 1991). Unlike the first oil crisis, the government could not curtail the volume of imports, including oil imports, as is evident from the continuously mounting trade deficit after the second oil crisis.[19] This led to a change in the attitude of the state, which now viewed export promotion as a way to earn foreign exchange. The Industrial Policy Statement of 1980 placed emphasis on the modernisation and development of export-oriented units. To realise this, the GoI announced a number of export promotional measures (Kathuria 1996). The important ones include: (a) reimbursement of tariffs on imports of raw materials and components through a duty draw-back scheme; and (b) permitting import of inputs at international prices through the import replenishment scheme. Along with export promotional measures, the government also loosened its control and provided a more flexible internal environment to the manufacturing firms.

Operating Environment: The operating environment around the automobile industry was significantly liberalised in order to provide flexibility to the firms in their operations and to encourage firms to achieve greater international competitiveness. First, the capacity re-endorsement scheme was announced by the government on April, 1982. This scheme was applicable to firms that had achieved 95 per cent capacity utilisation during any one of the previous five years. Firms fulfilling that condition were to automatically get approval for additional capacity up to one-third of the highest production level achieved in any year during the previous five years. This scheme was modified in 1986, wherein the capacity utilisation requirement was reduced to 80 per cent. This scheme was applicable to Appendix I MRTP/FERA companies as well. Second, the government replaced its product-specific licensing policy with the broad-banding policy in January 1985. The new licensing policy allowed manufacturers to diversify their production activities into similar product lines without any prior approval from the licensing authority. Once the license was issued for a broad category, the manufacturers did not require any additional clearances for diversifying within their product group, provided the diversification did not require new investment in machinery. Third, the government increased the floor limit for identifying MRTP companies from Rs 200 million worth of assets to Rs. 1000 million in the middle of the 1980s and also exempted 25 broad categories of industries from the licensing provision (Kathuria 1996; Singh and Kaur 1999). Fourth, in May 1985, all automobile and auto-component manufacturers were exempted from the provisions of section 21 and 22 of the MRTP Act. As a result of this, large business firms were no longer required to seek approval under the MRTP Act for substantial expansion or for starting a new business, but approval from IDRA 1951 was still required for further expansion of capacity (Mohanty et al. 1994). Fifth, the passenger car industry was added to the list of core industries (Appendix I) in 1982. Sixth, in 1986, the government announced its minimum economic scale scheme, wherein it encouraged firms to realise economies of scale in their operations. The minimum economic scale varied across segments within the automobile industry. For instance, these scales were 50,000 units for cars with engine capacity up to 2000 cc and 30,000 for those with engine capacity beyond 2000 cc[20] (Kathuria and Vandana 1990; Kathuria 1996). All these changes suggest that the operating environment was substantially liberalised during the 1980s, which provided the manufacturing firms with more decision-making space.

Foreign Investment Policy: The attitude of the government towards foreign participation also changed significantly in this phase. This is reflected in terms of reduced restrictions and increasing incentives to attract FDI into the country. To start with, the restrictions on remittances, royalties, dividends and technology fees were relaxed (Subrahmanian et al. 1996). Second, foreign investors were allowed to apply for permission to enter even before choosing an Indian partner in a JV (Sinha 2004). But the government also directed all JV firms to increase the usage of indigenous content up to 95 per cent of overall cost of vehicle within a period of five years from the date of commencement of production. Third, a 'fast channel' for speedy clearance of Japanese private investment and technology agreements was set up in May 1988. This was to exploit the opportunity created by the appreciation of the Japanese currency, which pressured Japanese manufacturers to search for new manufacturing locations to remain competitive. The 'fast channel' scheme was later extended to other developed countries such as USA, UK, West Germany and France (Kumar 1994). Given the changes in the foreign investment regime, the rejection rate relative to approvals recorded a sharp fall from 30 per cent during the 1970s to 5 to 8 per cent towards the end of the 1980s. It also resulted in an increase in the number of foreign collaborations approved during the 1980s as compared with the previous phase. For instance, the total number of approvals increased from 239 during 1966–79 to 724 during 1980–90 (Subrahmanian et al. 1996).

Thus, following the relaxation of the investment regime, foreign presence in the industrial sector in general and the automobile industry in particular increased considerably during the 1980s (Table A.1 in annexure). According to Narayana and Joseph (1993), 182 foreign collaborations were approved in the automobile industry from 1982 to 1991. Of the total, 70 per cent were purely technical and 20 per cent in the form of both financial and technical collaborations, and the remaining 10 per cent consisted of agreements to transfer design and drawings. In the case of the passenger car industry, with one exception (namely MUL), foreign presence was mainly in the form of technical agreements, as the existing firms in the industry were permitted to sign technical JVs only.

Technology Policy: The policy dealing with technology development also changed during the 1980s. The changes were noticed with regard to both imports of technology and internal efforts towards technology development. First, the government issued a Technology Policy Statement (TPS) in 1983. It called for developing indigenous technology, on the one hand, and ensuring the efficient use and adaptation of imported technology in accordance with national priorities, on the other. It was stated that the import of technology would not be allowed at the expense of national interest. It was decided that a list of technologies that had been developed adequately within the country be prepared and upgraded periodically, so that the import of these technologies could be restricted. Secondly, the government enacted the Cess Act in 1986. Under the Act, a 5 per cent cess was imposed on royalty payments for imported technology. The Technology Development Board of the

Department of Science and Technology (DST) was to use this fund to promote indigenous technology development and to promote absorption and adoption of imported technology. The indigenous technology development efforts were accompanied by the imports of technology as well. In January 1987, the policy of delegating the right to approve foreign collaborations to the administrative ministry, in the case of projects not involving foreign equity participation and with an outflow of foreign exchange not exceeding Rs. 5 million, was revised, with the foreign exchange outflow limit now set at Rs. 10 million (Natarajan 1988; Kumar 1994; Singh and Kaur 1999). In addition, a Technical Development Fund was launched in 1976 in order to facilitate existing manufacturers to import technology/capital goods/consultants with the sole aim of upgrading technology, so as to modernise capacity and enhance exports (Kathuria 1996). Under this scheme, existing manufacturers were allowed to import technology and capital goods of a value equal to Rs. 12.5 million in foreign exchange, which was raised to Rs. 30 million in March 1989. Further, the imports of capital goods were gradually liberalised in the mid-1980s and the tariff rates were slashed (Joseph and Veeramani 2001). For instance, capital goods under the OGL category were increased from 150 in 1984 to 200 in 1985 (Kumar 1994). The gradual liberalisation of imports of capital goods occurred into the aftermath of the Industrial Policy Statements of 1980 and 1982, wherein the role of capital goods was recognised as critical to the process of modernisation of the industrial sector.

All these changes indicated that efforts towards technology development either through in-house R&D or imports of technology had intensified during the 1980s. How these changes have influenced the path of technology development is an empirical issue. It is addressed in Chapters 4 and 5 of this study.

In sum, it can be argued that the policy environment around the passenger car industry was considerably relaxed during the 1980s as compared to earlier periods. The changing policy environment not only changed the operating environment, but also relaxed restrictions on technical collaborations and imports of raw material and capital goods, as well as provided various incentives to promote exports. These changes were aimed at inducing competition in the domestic market, modernising industry by developing its technology base (through in-house R&D and imports of technology) and promoting exports.

2.2.4 Phase IV: external liberalisation

The beginning of the fourth phase was marked by the severe BoP crisis of the early 1990s. The gross fiscal deficit as a percentage of GDP increased from 6.1 per cent to 8.4 per cent from 1980–81 to 1990–91 (Nayyar 1996). This led to an increase in internal debt as a percentage of GDP from 35.6 per cent to 53.5 per cent. Accordingly, interest payments increased from 2 per cent to 4 per cent of GDP in the same period. Further, the increase in debt-finance government spending was accompanied by a liberalisation of import policy aimed at modernising the industrial sector. The result was a significant increase in foreign exchange payments and the trade deficit during the1980s (Jalan 1991; Joshi and Little 1994).

The prevailing economic atmosphere at that time provided a basis for arguing that the ongoing development strategy had failed and any persistence with it would deepen the crisis further. The Economic Survey 1991–92 explained this situation as follows:

> By June 1991, the balance of payments crisis had become overwhelmingly a crisis of confidence – of confidence in the Government's ability to manage the balance of payments. . . . A default on payments, for the first time in our history, had become a serious possibility in June 1991.
>
> (GoI 1991–92: 10)

To deal with this crisis, India approached the International Monetary Fund (IMF) and the International Bank for Reconstruction and Development (IBRD) and received a US$7 billion loan to manage the crisis. To access this loan, the international institutions directed India to adopt a stabilisation-cum-structural adjustment programme. As part of the structural adjustment programme, international agencies advised the country to remove restrictions related mainly to the supply side of the economy and also cut fiscal and BoP deficits. Accordingly, the GoI proclaimed a 'New Economic Policy' (NEP) in July 1991. The central focus of the NEP was to open up the economy by removing restrictions on the private sector, reducing the role of government in many areas and removing restrictions on trade and foreign investment.

Operating Environment: In line with changes in the economic environment of the country, the industrial policy of the country also changed significantly. The industrial policy statement of 1991 eliminated or considerably relaxed the regulations introduced during the 1950s, 1960s and 1970s (A. Singh 2009). The policy changes initiated in the early 1990s removed the requirement of industrial licensing, abolished the MRTP clearance requirement, suspended the PMP, removed the ban on imports of raw material and capital goods by bringing them under OGL etc. As a result, firms were free to expand business, diversify according to market demand, enter new markets, acquire or merge with a view to gaining market strength. In other words, the changing regulatory environment enabled the industrial sector, including passenger car firms, to expand and diversify their business in accordance with the changing global conditions without any approval from different authorities.

Foreign Investment Policy: The foreign investment policy in this phase has been progressively liberalised (Sahoo, Nataraj and Dash 2014). For the first time in the history of independent India, foreign firms in the car industry were allowed to participate as holders of majority equity (up to 51 per cent via automatic route) in JVs. Following the changes in FDI policy, a large number of foreign firms entered the industry in the middle of the 1990s through JVs with local firms (Table A.1 in annexure).

Fearing that large foreign firms may resort to and, therefore, prevent mere assembly of cars based on imports of raw material, components and CKD/SKD kits, the government adopted some measures towards the end of the 1990s. The imports of CKD/SKD kits were restricted for passenger car manufacturers. The imports of restricted items were permitted against a specific import license issued by the Director-General of Foreign Trade (DGFT). For this, manufacturers were required to sign a Memorandum of Understanding (MoU) with the DGFT, which required manufacturers to accept the conditions set out in advance in a Public Notice No. 60 issued in December 1997. A car manufacturer that did not sign the MoU or did not fulfil the obligations defined under it could be denied a license for the import of SKD/CKD kits (GoI 1997, 2002).

Under the Public Notice, the government announced a certain uniform set of conditions that all the foreign car manufacturers had to comply with if they wanted to invest in India's car industry. This was an attempt to encourage manufacturers to establish actual production activities instead of selling assembled products. These conditions were as follows:

1   The signatory of the MoU must establish actual production facilities for the manufacture of cars, and not for mere assembly of imported kits/components.

2   A minimum foreign equity of US$50 million to be brought in by the foreign partner within the first three years of the start of operations. The condition was applicable only to those JV firms which hold majority foreign equity ownership;

3   The signatory must achieve a minimum level of indigenisation of 50 per cent in the third year and 70 per cent in the fifth year from the date of clearance of the first lot of imports. Once the MoU signing firm had reached an indigenisation level of 70 per cent, there will be no need for further import licenses from DGFT.

4   The firm must ensure trade balancing of foreign exchange flows over the entire period of the MoU, in terms of balancing the actual cost, insurance, freight (CIF) of imports of CKD/SKD kits/components with the free on board (FoB) value of exports of cars and auto components over that period. The period of export obligation will commence from the third year of commencement of production. But the value of imports made during the first two years must be balanced in subsequent years.

These conditions were to apply to all existing and future entrants into the car industry. However, companies intending to set up units to manufacture light or heavy commercial vehicles, tractors, earthmoving equipment etc., with foreign collaboration, were not required to sign any MoU. Their request for CKD/SKD kit imports were to be considered by the Special Licensing Committee on merit on an annual basis (GoI 1997).

Opposing the conditions set out by India for JVs in the car industry, the EU approached the Dispute Settlement Body (DSB) of the WTO. The US and Japan also supported the case filed against India. In view of the US and EU complaints, the Director-General of WTO established a panel to analyse the basis used by India to impose various conditions on the entry and operations of foreign firms in the car industry, which announced its decision in December 2001. The Panel concluded that: (a) India had acted inconsistently with its obligations under Article III: 4 of the GATT 1994 by imposing a restriction to use a certain proportion of local parts and components in the manufacture of cars and automotive vehicles, and (b) India had acted inconsistently with its obligations under Article XI of the GATT 1994 by imposing a restriction to balance imports with exports of equivalent value (WTO 2002). Given the decision, the GoI was not in a position to continue with the conditions imposed on the ground of BoP in December 1997. However, it is worth noting that the Indian government had already scrapped many of these restrictions in April 2001. In the words of Chandrasekhar (2002: 1):

> Many of the conditions that the DSB has deemed violative had been withdrawn by India in April 2001, when as part of an agreement reached with the US regarding all import-licensing conditions imposed on BoP grounds, India abolished the import licensing scheme for cars imported in the form of CKD/ SKD (completely knocked-down/ semi-knocked-down) kits. The 'agreement' with the US essentially involved succumbing to pressures to advance (from April 1, 2003 to April 1, 2001) the date on which import restrictions imposed for balance of payments reasons needed to be withdrawn.

To make policy accord with the WTO's recommendations, the Ministry of Industry announced a separate policy for the automobile industry in 2002 known as *Auto Policy 2002*. The stated aim of this policy was to promote modernisation and to develop indigenous designs through in-house R&D by developing a conducive economic environment; and to develop India as an international hub for manufacturing small, affordable passenger cars as well as a global source for auto components with the assistance of foreign firms. Further, GoI increased foreign participation up to 100 per cent through the automatic route both in the vehicle segment and auto components. As a result of this, the passenger car industry attracted a large entry of leading international firms in the industry in the following years. At the same time, the policy proposed to fix import tariffs in such a way that actual production was facilitated within the country as against mere assembly, without providing undue protection at the same time (GoI 2002; Ranawat and Tiwari 2009).[21] Along with the reductions in overall tariffs in order to open up India for international trade, the government has also progressively rationalised its domestic tax structure to provide a level playing ground for the domestic manufacturers against the international competition. For instance, the excise duty on passenger cars was brought down from 66 per cent in 1991–92 to 24 per cent in 2003–04 and reduced further in the following years. In line with the objective of Auto Policy 2002 to develop India as a hub of small car production, the government reduced the excise duty on small cars from 17 per cent in 2006–07 to 13.5 per cent in 2015–16 (SIAM 2016a). At the same time, excise duty for non-small cars has been kept significantly higher than small cars. Favourable treatment toward small cars indicates that the government wanted to see India as a global hub for small cars.

Technology Policy: The policy dealing with technology development also changed substantially on account of the economic reform measures initiated in the early 1990s and continued after that.[22] The changing economic environment has eased the restrictions on various aspects of imports of technology, including nature of technology imports, amount spent on technology imports and duration of technology agreement. In addition, India also pronounced specific policies to speed up indigenous technology development.

To secure indigenous development of technology particularly in the automobile industry, the government offered a series of fiscal and financial incentives to the corporate sector for boosting R&D, and developing technological know-how. First, in 2002, a Weighted Tax Deduction (under I.T. Act 1961) of more than 125 per cent was provided for sponsored research and in-house R&D expenditure on vehicle and component manufacturers. This limit has been increased up to 150 per cent in the AMP 2006–2016 (GoI 2006). Second, vehicle manufacturers were also considered for a rebate on the applicable excise duty for every 1 per cent of the gross turnover of the company spent during the year on R&D. This would include R&D leading to adoption of low emission technologies and energy saving devices. Third, the government decided to increase allocation to the automotive cess fund created for R&D in the automotive industry and expand the scope of activities covered under it. Fourth, tax breaks and concessional duties on imported equipment were also announced for those manufacturers who set up an independent auto design unit.

Above all, the government formulated a new Science and Technology Policy (STP) in 2003. Among various objectives, the major thrust of this policy was to promote public-private partnership in science and technology. Further, Science, Technology and Innovation Policy (STIP) 2013 placed an emphasis on developing world-class infrastructure for R&D and also on increasing gross spending in R&D to 2 per cent of GDP in the next five years, provided private-sector spending on R&D also matches public-sector investment. In line with STP 2003and STIP 2013, the government prepared ten-year vision documents for the automotive industry, popularly known as AMP 2006–2016 and AMP 2016–26. The underlying objective of these programmes remains to develop India as an emerging destination of choice for design and manufacturing. Accordingly, the government has adopted measures to set up world-class automotive testing facilities and R&D infrastructure in the country in the form of the National Automotive Testing and R&D Infrastructure Project (NATRIP) (GoI 2006). To what extent the Indian automotive industry in general and the passenger car segment in particular has succeeded in this direction is yet unclear.

2.3   Main observations and issues for research

The broader objective of this chapter is to develop an understanding of the policy framework which has evolved around the passenger car industry in India since 1947. It gives an understanding about the development trajectory of the industry from a completely closed and highly restrictive environment to an open regime with hardly any restrictions on import of components and parts, technology and FDI. It is observed that the industrial sector was regulated by a series of policy measures, the significant ones being protection, capacity licensing, restrictions on foreign collaborations, price controls, reservation of certain products and components for small-scale units for production etc. These regulatory measures continued to apply to Indian industries until the early 1980s, but the nature and extent of regulations did not remain the same throughout the reference period. The extent of regulations followed the changing priorities of the government over time as well as the changing foreign exchange constraints of the country.

The significant changes in the economic environment and the policies were noticed in July 1991 and thereafter. Besides providing investors with a free hand in their operations, free imports of technology and other components were also encouraged by lowering tariffs and removing quantitative restrictions. These developments might have various implications for the chosen industry, including strategies of technology development and indigenisation of manufacturing activities. It is expected because the government did not put in place any safeguard to avoid the adverse impact of unregulated entry of foreign operators and continuous import of technology and other spare parts and components. Given this, there is a high risk associated with the new policy regime in relation to the development of local manufacturing and technology capabilities. As manufacturers are permitted to import components and technology without any commitment towards the development of the local technology base, they, especially foreign firms, have no incentive to develop local technology. It is easy for these manufacturers to use tangible and intangible knowledge available with parent firms. If that holds true, the current strategy may prove damaging for the country.

Therefore, it is worth understanding the implications of new investment, technology and trade policies on the structure of the industry, technological development and technology strategies as well as BoP.

Notes

1 The first two phases (1947 to mid-1960s and 1966 to late 1970s) are almost the same whether we consider growth episodes or the policy regimes as the basis for periodisation. But after the 1980s, it makes a difference if the base of periodisation is changed. This is because, in terms of growth episodes, the whole period after the 1980s can be considered as one since there was a continuous growth in the passenger car industry but in terms of policy regimes, this period has observed significant changes in the early 1980s and 1990s and therefore needs separation.

2 Besides HML, PAL and SMPIL, four more firms, namely Automobile Products of India Ltd. (APIL), Ashok Motors Ltd. (AML); Mahindra and Mahindra (M&M) and Tata Engineering and Locomotives Co. Ltd. (TELCO), were allowed entry by the government in the mid-1950s as these firms came up with a PMP but none of them actually entered the car industry (Table 2.2).

3 Under the informal price control mechanism, the manufacturers were not permitted to charge excessive prices. In order to change prices, manufacturers were required to give advance notice to the concerned authority of any such intention.

4 The imposition of the informal price control mechanism led to the emergence of an illegal market. This was evident in terms of growing bogus allotees. 'The situation developed because premiums were offered to allotees by persons who wanted to avoid the lengthy period of waiting to get a new car. Thus while in any developed country a newly purchased automobile would begin to depreciate in value from the moment it was driven away from the dealer's showroom, in India it could actually be sold at a premium of several thousand rupees!' (Venkataramani 1990: 11).

5 Ancillary production was divided into three groups: (1) components produced in India in requisite quantities (or in which India was self-sufficient). In 1960, these components included spark plugs, brake parts,

mufflers, car and truck bodies, and non-mechanical components such as paints, upholstery and rubber components; (2) components whose production was partially done in India but demand was not completely met (or partially being imported due to lack of production capabilities or non-availability of requisite designs). These included mechanical items such as shock absorbers, brake linings, piston and clutch parts, fuel injection equipment and various filters. (3) Components whose production was not started in India but production licenses were already given; these included electrical equipment and key mechanical parts (wheels, steering, machinery) (Narayana 1989; Pingle 1999).

6 To realise this objective, the government further sub-divided the list B into two sub-parts, that is, large-scale and small-scale manufacturers. Accordingly, 60 to 80 components were exclusively reserved for small-scale units. The reservation for the small-scale sector led to the entry of a large number of such units.

7 Besides protection from foreign and domestic large/medium enterprises, small-scale units were granted easier credit facilities and infrastructural support and considerably less degree of licensing requirements (Krueger 1975; Tyabji 2000).

8 According to the product-specific licensing policy, an automobile manufacturer was eligible to produce only one model against a license and for producing an additional model, the manufacturer was required to get an additional license from the licensing authority.

9 The discussion in this part is based on GoI (1948), GoI (1961), Kidron (1965), Narayana (1989), Kumar (1990, 1994), Subrahmanian et al. (1996).

10 Due to this, the number of approvals for foreign collaborations increased suddenly during the early 1960s. For instance, in 1956, the number of foreign collaborations approved was just 82 which jumped to 380 in 1960 and further to 403 in 1964 (Kumar 1994).

11 For example, Council of Scientific and Industrial Research (CSIR), Indian Council of Medical Research (ICMR), Indian Council of Agricultural Research (ICAR) and some government departments.

12 During her rule (1966 to 1977), the focus was more on populist policies such as Garibi Hatao and nationalisation of banks. Due to this, the leading industrialists continuously criticised her.

13 The Organisation of the Petroleum Exporting Countries (OPEC) hiked prices of petroleum products in 1973. It resulted in a five-fold increase in the value of Indian imports of petroleum products in the following fiscal year (Ghosh 1990); foreign exchange reserves reached its lowest level (Jalan 1991).

14 From 1976–77 to 1979–80, the Indian economy witnessed a small surplus in the current account (0.6 per cent of GDP) and the available foreign exchange reserves were sufficient to finance imports for next seven months (Jalan 1991). It is worth mentioning that the improvement in the BOP situation was an outcome of two things – a slowdown in the imports and a sharp increase in the remittances of Indian workers, which in turn led to a sharp increase in net invisibles (excluding official transfers) (Jalan 1991; Ahluwalia 1986). The earnings in the

net invisibles account increased from Rs. 193 crores in 1974–75 to Rs. 1388 crores in 1977–78 and further to Rs. 2486 crores in 1979–80 (Jalan 1991).

15 Discussion in this part is primarily based on Goyal (1979), Malik and Vajpeyi (1988), Kumar (1990, 1994, 2005), Subrahmanian et al. (1996), Singh and Kaur (1999), Forbes (2002), Sinha (2004).

16 It involved all those cases where foreign equity investment crossed Rs. 20 million or 40 per cent of equity share.

17 The number of technology collaborations increased from 199 in 1971–72 to 231 in 1975–76 and further to 240 in 1977–78, whereas the share of financial collaborations declined from 46 to 40 and then to 27 in the corresponding years (Kumar 1987).

18 Renewal of contract was subject to the content of new technology, export orientation etc.

19 The trade deficit of the government increased from Rs. 34400 million in 1979–80 to Rs. 64940 million in 1981–82 and further to Rs. 95860 million in 1985–86. These trends continued throughout the 1980s (Jalan 1991; Joshi and Little 1994).

20 In commercial vehicles and two-wheelers, the scale capacity was 25,000 units and 200,000 units, respectively.

21 In view of this, the GoI announced differentiated tariff rates for components, CBU/CKD kits, and vehicles. In order to encourage the development of an indigenous automobile industry, the government followed a discretionary tariff rate policy wherein tariffs imposed on vehicles and CBU/CKD were kept much higher than the tariff imposed on components' imports. High tariffs on vehicles/CBU/CKD kits would discourage imports in these forms.

22 This section is mainly based on the published information in various government documents such as Auto policy 2002, Automotive Mission Plan 2006–2016 and 2016–26, Annual Reports of Ministry of Heavy Industries and Public Enterprises.

Chapter 3

Restructuring of the passenger car industry

This chapter focuses on understanding the impact of the changing nature of foreign presence on the restructuring of the passenger car industry. India initiated the process of liberalisation in the early 1980s. But a more paradigmatic shift in its industrial policy from a highly controlled regime to a more de-controlled and market-oriented policy regime became noticeable in 1991. Consequently, a large number of foreign firms entered and started production of passenger cars in India. This change was likely to influence the structure and development of the passenger car industry.

However, the nature of foreign entry did not remain the same during the three decades starting from the early 1980s. There was a major overhaul of the policy regime during the early 1990s, which also changed the nature of foreign presence in the car industry. To capture this, the period since 1981 is divided into two phases: the phase first covering the period from 1981 to 1990, and the second phase being the period from 1991 onwards. The major focus of this discussion is to understand: (a) the nature of foreign entry into the car industry; and (b) how the changing nature of foreign presence influenced the structure of the car industry.

Further, there may be factors other than foreign entry that are expected to influence the pattern of growth of this industry. These factors are credit policies of financial institutions, distribution of income, etc. So, while analysing the impact of foreign presence, we have introduced a discussion on other factors wherever necessary for understanding the structural changes. Any change in these factors has implications for the industry. For instance, the expansion of credit for automobile purchases would obviously add to the growth of this industry by bringing new buyers into the market, whereas changes in the distribution of income would influence the nature of the demand for cars.

3.1   Foreign firms and industrial structure: an analytical background

The relationship between foreign presence and industrial structure is a widely studied issue (Lall 1979; UNCTAD 1997; Driffield 2001; Wang and Wong 2004; Dunning and Lundan 2008; J. Singh 2009; Singh, Joseph and Abraham 2011). As discussed in the literature, this relationship is not uniform across countries or across industries within the same country. Amongst various factors, the nature of the relationship has been found to be largely determined by the institutional set-up of the host country, local production and technological capabilities, mode of entry of foreign firms (greenfield investment or merger and acquisition) and the nature of the industry where foreign firms are entering.

The most important factor that determines the nature of the above-mentioned relationship is the pre-existing structure of the domestic industry into which foreign firms are entering (UNCTAD 1997, 2006; J. Singh 2009). The entry of foreign manufacturers through greenfield investments in a concentrated industry will directly add to the number of manufacturers in the market. The newly established foreign firms will be able to compete with existing market leaders because of their financial strength, managerial and marketing skills and access to modern technology (Pillai 1978; Peria and Mody 2004; Singh et al. 2011). Consequently, the intensity of competition in the market is likely to increase at least in the initial years. The long-run effect of foreign presence on market structure is uncertain because it is conditioned by the competitive strength and technological capabilities of host country firms and the institutional set-up within which foreign firms operate in the host country (Fu 2008; J. Singh 2009).

Consequently, in the long run, competition is likely to increase if the host country firms have a minimum threshold level of technological capabilities, as then they are more likely to upgrade in the wake of rising competition from foreign firms. Firms can advance basic capabilities through various types of investment linkages, vertical transformation of technology and technology spillovers from foreign firms and also through investment in R&D activities (Geroski 1990; Sutton 2007; Beugelsdijk et al. 2008). The process of learning from foreign firms facilitates local firms in improving their technology base, which subsequently enables them to reduce the technology gap between the two sets of firms. This narrowing technological gap permits existing domestic suppliers to compete successfully with new entrants, resulting in an increase in the intensity of competition in the host country.

However, the entry of foreign firms may also increase concentration in the host country in the long run. This is specifically true under two conditions: First, in those cases where local firms are not equipped with adequate absorption capabilities (Fu 2008; Lundin, Sjoholm, He and Qian 2007). Instead of capitalising upon their technological capabilities, local firms may get discouraged due to unregulated competition from foreign firms which will reduce investment in R&D activities over time. The reduction of investment in technology will reduce the degree of learning and new innovations of such firms. Consequently, the technology gap between local and foreign firms will widen. The widening technological gap may lead to displacement (crowding out) of local firms from the market. The displacement of local firms will increase the degree of market concentration in the host country (Joseph 1997; Haller 2004).

Secondly, increased concentration is also possible when foreign firms are entering into industries where technology is changing rapidly (or the life span of technology is very short). If domestic firms are not able to keep pace with rapidly changing technology, the technological gap between foreign firms and domestic firms widens substantially over the years. The widening gap becomes difficult to bridge for local firms. With the passage of time, modern technology becomes inaccessible to local firms (Kaplinsky 1984). Consequently, foreign firms take over the control of the market and an oligopolistic structure may emerge (J. Singh 2009). Oligopolistic market structures have their own implications for investment in technology-related activities. Earlier research opined that an oligopolistic market structure does not provide any incentive for market leaders (or big size firms) to put serious efforts into long-run technological improvement (Kathuria 1996; Narayanan 1998).

The above discussion clearly states that the influence of foreign presence on the industrial structure of the host country is ambiguous. It may intensify competition or it may increase concentration in the host country. Given this understanding, we conduct an empirical analysis in this chapter to understand the influence of an increase in foreign presence as well as the changing nature of the industrial structure in the Indian passenger car industry.

3.2   Data sources and methodology

The information relating to sales and production is gathered from the 'Statistical Profile of Indian Automobile Industry' published annually by the SIAM. That information is supplemented with data provided by the ACMA in its annual publication titled 'Automotive Industry of India: Facts and Figures.'

The empirical analysis is conducted at two levels to measure changes in industrial structure and emerging pattern of the industry. First, structural changes at the level of the car industry as a whole are analysed by measuring the percentage share of the respective passenger car firm in total production of the industry. This provides information on the changing relative position of manufacturers over a period of time. In addition, concentration in the industry is also measured by using the Herfindahl-Hirschman Index (HHI).[1]

Second, the change in the structure of different sub-segments of the passenger car industry has been analysed using the same measures. It will facilitate an understanding of the changes in a particular sub-segment of the car market, as cars produced in India vary widely in terms of size, price and other features. Given the strong heterogeneity in the nature of cars available in the market, it may be the case that foreign firms have entered in larger numbers in one sub-segment as compared to others. Given this possibility, changes at the sub-segment level in the passenger car industry are analysed by adopting the classification developed by SIAM. Given the heterogeneity within the passenger car industry in terms of length and prices of cars, the SIAM divides the industry into six sub-segments as follows: Mini size car (length up to 3400 mm); Compact (3401–4000 mm); Mid-size (4001–4500 mm); Executive (4501–4700mm); Premium (4701–5000 mm); and Luxury (above 5000 mm).

3.3   Empirical analysis

The empirical analysis in this section intends to address the following issues: The *first* part discusses the restructuring of the passenger car industry during the 1980s and its implications for investment and pricing behaviour. The *second* part analyses the nature of restructuring, after 1990, of the industry as a whole as well as within sub-segments of the industry on account of heterogeneity within the car industry. Implications of these developments for investment and pricing behaviour are also discussed.

3.3.1   First phase of restructuring: 1981 to 1990

The liberalisation process of the 1980s brought changes in the regulatory environment and eased the entry of foreign firms. This coincided with the time when the automobile industry in Japan was experiencing saturation in production and manufacturers were searching for new markets (Venkataramani 1990; D'Costa 1995). Due to this, the Japanese firms aggressively exploited the opportunities provided by the changing regulatory environment around the industrial sector in India. Accordingly, the presence of Japanese firms in the automobile industry increased as local firms signed a number of financial and technical JVs with Japanese firms during the 1980s (Table A.1 in annexure).

Nature of Foreign Presence: Foreign presence can be of different types. First, it can be in the form of technical collaboration, wherein foreign firms are supplying technology to host country firms against technical fee and lump-sum payments but they are not directly involved in manufacturing activities in the host country. Second, foreign presence can be in the form of a JV, in which foreign firms take part in manufacturing activities in collaboration with the host country partner and also supply technology. Third, entry can be in the form of fully owned subsidiaries wherein foreign firms fully control the unit's activities.

The nature of foreign presence is influenced by the regulatory policies of the state. In India, foreign presence in the car industry during the first phase (1980s) was mainly of the first kind (technical collaborations). State policies also allowed for the formation of JVs (both financial and technical) during this phase, but they were subject to approval from the government.

The passenger car segment of the automobile industry witnessed the entry of a number of foreign firms during this phase (D'Costa 1995; Singh 2015). Collaboration with foreign firms in any form was restricted during the 1960s and 1970s[2] (D'Costa 1995). Once the government allowed technical collaborations with overseas automobile manufacturers, existing indigenous manufacturers (HML, PAL and SMPIL) in the passenger car industry exploited this opportunity and signed a number of technical agreements with foreign firms. In 1984, HML entered into a technical collaboration with Vauxhall Motors, a subsidiary of General Motors, to manufacture Contessa, which was touted as one of the first technologically advanced cars in India. Subsequently, HML signed a technical collaboration agreement with Isuzu (Japan) to manufacture petrol and diesel engines for the Contessa Classic. In 1987, HML also entered into technical collaboration with Ricardo Consulting Engineers of the United Kingdom with a view to modernising the petrol and diesel engines of the Ambassador. Similarly, PAL signed a technical agreement with Nissan Motors Company (Japan) to improve the fuel efficiency of petrol engines used in its Fiat 124 model. The company also introduced an economy version of its Padmini model and a new car 'Premier 118 NE' in 1986. In 1986, PAL also entered into technical collaboration with Technolicence Limited (UK) to make diesel engines for Padmini. Further in 1987, PAL entered into an agreement with AVL of Austria to upgrade Padmini's engine for fuel efficiency and improve horsepower, emission control, etc. In the same year, PAL signed a technical collaboration agreement with Power Design Intranet to improve aerodynamic features, reduce body weight, increase safety and comfort, and generally restyle interiors and exteriors of its car models. In the changing policy environment, Standard Motors re-entered[3] the market and imported technology from Austin Rover (UK) to produce its 'Standard 2000' car.

Most significantly, however, MUL was chosen as the only firm in the car industry to be allowed access to both foreign equity and technology through the formation of a JV with a foreign firm. In 1982, a JV was signed between the GoI (MUL) and Suzuki Motor Corporation (SMC). Initially, SMC was given 26 per cent equity holding and the rest was in the hands of the GoI. The first product of this JV was introduced in 1983 under the name of Maruti 800 and in 1984 the Maruti Van was launched with the same three-cylinder engine as used in the Maruti 800. The government did not allow any other car manufacturer to form a JV involving financial collaboration with foreign players during this phase.

Thus, India's passenger car industry was characterised by the increased presence through technical collaborations of many foreign firms in response to the liberalisation measures initiated in the 1980s. Increased foreign presence in this industry had obvious implications for the pattern of development of this industry as well as the economy. Firstly, foreign presence would encourage imports of components from firms related to the foreign technology supplier. This is seen as discouraging indigenisation of manufacturing activities (an issue that is empirically analysed in the following chapter). Such a development would run contrary to the core objectives of the import-substitution industrialisation strategy initiated in the mid-1950s. Evidence suggests that the volume of imports by the car industry grew without any significant change in its export earnings (Mohanty et al. 1994; D'Costa 1995). Secondly, a growing volume of technical collaborations would obviously lead to large outflows of foreign exchange in terms of royalty and technical fee payments to foreign partners. Therefore, the sudden increase in technology collaborations was expected to contribute negatively to the BoP of the country. This tendency was compounded by the sharp appreciation of the Japanese Yen during the late 1980s.[4] That appreciation added significantly to the outflow of foreign exchange from India, as the 1980s were the years when major technical and financial collaborations were signed with Japanese firms in the automobile industry.

Structure of the Car Industry: Structural changes in the car industry are defined for our purposes in terms of: (1) changing market share (changing ranking) of manufacturing firms in the industry, (2) increase or decrease in concentration based on the HHI. Table 3.1 presents the change in market shares of firms as well as the change in intensity of competition in terms of the HHI during the 1980s.

During the 1960s and 1970s, the passenger car industry was under the control of two manufacturers (HML and PAL) (Figure A.1 in annexure). The dominant position of HML and PAL and absence of changes in their relative market positions over time rendered the market in this industry oligopolistic. Moreover, the oligopolistic structure of the industry was stable in character in the sense that the ranking of firms remained more or less the same until the late 1970s. Stability in the market position was an outcome not only of the economic strength of business firms but also of the policy environment. Among other things, these manufacturers were being provided protection to insulate them from external competition. On the other hand competition within the domestic industry was also muted because the manufacturers were provided product-specific licenses, which restricted diversification. Thus, it can be argued that the policy measures proved to be very significant in the evolution of the structure of this industry.

As discussed above, the policy amendments of the 1980s regarding entry of foreign firms enabled existing firms to sign technical agreements with foreign firms and also allowed one new entry in the form of a JV (Maruti-Suzuki). The changes induced by these developments influenced the structure of the passenger car industry (Table 3.1). The old market leaders, which were manufacturing cars for Indian consumers since the 1950s, experienced a sharp decline in their market shares. The market shares of HML and PAL declined from 55 per cent and 45 per cent respectively in 1981 to 13.9 per cent and 23.7 per cent respectively in 1990–91. Other old manufacturers, namely SMPIL and SAL, could not hold their ground even after entering into technical collaborations with overseas firms and disappeared from the industry in the second half of the 1980s (Table 3.1).

These were unanticipated changes and the principal factor behind these changes was the entry of the new JV formed between Japanese private capital and Indian state capital. This entry under the name of MUL weakened the position of established firms. The loss in market shares of the established firms constituted gains for MUL, as evident from the fact that the market share of MUL rose significantly within a short span of time; within a period of eight years

Table 3.1 Structure of car industry, 1980s

Year	Share of manufacturers (percentages)					HHI
	HML	PAL	MUL	SAL	SMPIL	
1981	55.09	44.82	0.00	0.07	0.01	0.50
1982	51.17	48.53	0.00	0.30	0.00	0.50
1983	52.47	46.47	0.39	0.67	0.00	0.49
1984	35.95	43.25	19.29	1.51	0.00	0.35
1985	25.61	33.66	40.11	0.60	0.01	0.34
1985–86	22.61	28.48	48.38	0.51	0.01	0.37
1986–87	18.22	21.29	58.04	1.23	1.23	0.42
1987–88	17.48	22.09	59.80	0.32	0.32	0.44
1988–89	17.09	23.40	59.50	0.00	0.00	0.44
1989–90	16.04	23.63	60.33	0.00	0.00	0.45
1990–91	13.91	23.73	62.36	0.00	0.00	0.46

Source: AIAM (1985), ACMA (1991).

(1983 to 1989–90), MUL's market share increased from 0 per cent to 60.3 per cent (see Table 3.1).

The nature of the restructuring of the industry during this phase, as revealed by the changing value of the HHI, is also interesting (Table 3.1). The value of HHI initially declined with the entry of MUL into the car industry and then started rising after 1985. The value of HHI declined from 0.50 in 1981 to 0.34 in 1985 and then started increasing to touch 0.46 in 1990–91. The increase in the HHI value from 1985 to 1990–91 was mainly on account of a sharp decline in the market share of PAL, which added to the market strength of MUL (Table 3.1). These trends illustrate how, in the initial years, the entry of MUL intensified competition, while later MUL gained a leadership position in the market. This trend tallies with that predicted in the earlier conceptual discussion.

In actual fact, MUL worked under a systematic strategy to gain leadership. It initially dumped low-priced passenger cars on the market. MUL kept the prices of its passenger cars below those of other cars available in the market, but, after the middle of the 1980s, MUL price increases were higher than those of other firms (Table 3.3). It points to the systematic strategy adopted by MUL to capture a leadership position in the market. This aspiration of MUL was supported by various other factors. For the purposes of this discussion, we have classified these factors into (1) political factors, (2) economic factors and (3) social factors.

Political Factors: MUL's performance was the outcome of a strategy adopted by the state to support MUL's drive to become the market leader. It was given special treatment, with a set of policy measures that were specifically crafted to favour the company (Venkataramani 1990; Pingle 1999; D'Costa 1995, 2005; Becker-Ritterspach 2007). The measures were many. *First,* except for the Maruti Suzuki JV, no new firm was permitted to enter the car industry with foreign equity participation, whereas in the commercial vehicle segment four new firms entered in the early 1980s in collaboration, both technical and financial, with foreign firms. The most significant proposal that the government rejected was the one involving collaboration between Tata and Honda (Japan), despite the fact that it fulfilled the basic conditions set for forming a JV. Prime among those conditions was agreement to ensure 50 per cent local content in the first year of production and to increase that figure to 90 per cent by the fifth year of production. The government suddenly raised the local content requirement to 70 per cent in the first year of production. The promoter companies were not in a position to meet the enhanced requirement and their proposal was rejected on the ground of excessive foreign exchange outflow (Agarwal 1987; D'Costa 1995). This suggests that the government created a protected environment for MUL by blocking entry of any other Indian or international firm. *Second*, on February 25, 1983, Ministry of Industry persuaded the Finance Ministry to reduce rates of excise and customs duties imposed on automobile vehicles with engine capacity up to 1000 cc. Accordingly, the central excise duty was reduced from 25 per cent to 15 per cent ad valorem and the special excise duty from 5 per cent of the basic excise duty to 0.75 per cent (Venkataramani 1990). This duty structure was designed to benefit only MUL since no other firm was manufacturing cars below 1000 cc capacity. Not only this, excise and customs duties on small and fuel efficient components used by MUL and Sipani were also reduced significantly in the same period.[5] It is worth pointing out that Sipani's total production of cars was only 302 in 1983 (AIAM 1985). This suggests that MUL was the main beneficiary of the duty concessions given on auto components. *Third*, MUL was directly controlled by the Ministry of Industry, and senior bureaucrats were generally selected to monitor its development. The nexus between bureaucrats and MUL's management benefited this firm, as reflected in the production capacity allocated to it from the very beginning. Production capacity allotted to this firm crossed the figure of 1 lakh units during the second half of the 1980s, which allowed it to realise economies of scale, whereas the annual production capacity of HML and PAL was only 60,000 and 54,000 units, respectively, until 1991. Within a period of five years, the number of passenger vehicles produced by MUL reached 115048 units, whereas all the other manufacturers together produced only 71364 cars. And, *fourth*, to raise resources for investment, the government allowed MUL to enter the Euro currency market for a US$ 75 million loan. This decision of the government was contrary to earlier policy decisions, wherein it aimed to curb international commercial market borrowing, especially by public sector enterprises (Venkataramani 1990; Pingle 1999). All the evidence suggests that these political factors played a critical role in the success of MUL.[6]

Economic Factors: There were also many economic factors underlying the rapid growth of MUL. Important among them were the following. (1) The prices of MUL cars in the initial years were significantly lower than those of passenger cars offered by other existing firms, which added to the demand for its products in the market. For instance, the products manufactured by MUL in the initial years were 21 per cent cheaper than the lowest-priced model available in India in the mid-1980s (Humphrey, Mukherjee, Zilbovicius and Arbix 1998; Pingle 1999). (2) MUL was able to produce technologically advanced cars because of its collaboration with Suzuki, which had expertise in the production of small-sized cars7 (Ishigami 2004; Okada 2004; Nayak 2008; Motohashi 2015). Production of advanced cars by MUL helped it to out-compete its competitors, who were selling relatively low technology products. (3) Passenger cars launched by MUL were fuel efficient as compared to passenger cars offered by rival firms. The fuel consumption rate in the case of the Ambassador in city driving varied from 8 to 9.5 km per litre, whereas in the case of PAL Padmini it varied between 9.5 and 11 km per litre. On the other hand, Suzuki claimed a fuel consumption rate of 19.9 km per litre (Venkataramani 1990).

Social Factors: MUL's decision to enter into the production of small-sized cars with an engine capacity of less than 1000 cc in collaboration with Suzuki, a specialist in manufacturing small cars, can be understood in the light of the socio-economic conditions of the country. According to a survey of potential purchasers conducted by the Indian Market Research Bureau (IMRB) in 1981 on MUL's request, only 20–30 per cent of the respondents were willing to buy a car at the then existing prices, but for a price range little less than that (below HML and PAL), this proportion went up to 43–45 per cent. Further, 37 per cent of the respondents preferred a small car, as against 18 per cent who preferred a medium-sized car. The survey also revealed that fuel efficiency and initial capital cost were the two important factors in buying a car (Shirali 1984; World Bank 1987). It suggested that there was a huge untapped market for small-sized, fuel efficient and low-price cars. The cars manufactured by HML and PAL were larger than MUL products,[8] which excluded a large number of consumers (D'Costa 2005). MUL tried to tap this market by launching new models with an engine capacity of 800cc that were not available previously on the Indian market. MUL also initially kept prices of its models low. These features brought new buyers into the market who were previously not able to buy a car. Increase in total car production[9] on account of MUL's entry fulfilled a huge demand backlog existing from the period prior to the 1980s, since the combined annual production of the two main manufacturers of passenger cars (HML and PAL) was

Table 3.2 Expansion of passenger car industry, 1980s

Year	Growth rate
1981–82	35.70
1982–83	2.55
1983–84	7.67
1984–85	62.24
1985–86	35.11
1986–87	22.43
1987–88	20.66
1988–89	9.17
1989–90	8.13
1990–91	1.42
	CAGR
1981–82 to 1985–86	24.73
1986–87 to 1990–91	9.63

Source: Same as Table 3.1.

less than half of the total demand for cars in the 1970s (Narayana 1989; Okada 1998; Bhargava and Seetha 2010).

Given the nature of the market and MUL strategy, MUL proved successful in acquiring a large market share in a short time.

The discussion in this section suggests that India's passenger car industry went through a major restructuring process during this phase. Initially, there was an oligopolistic structure led by HML and PAL. But with the entry of the Maruti-Suzuki JV, the hitherto stable oligopolistic power enjoyed by HML and PAL could not be protected by them, as is clear from the falling market share of these firms. But one common feature of the two policy regimes was that, in the new environment as well, an oligopoly market structure existed though the power shifted into the hands of MUL, the giant, because of the various policy benefits given to it and other factors that led to its success. The preferential treatment given to MUL is also suggestive of a change in the relationship between the government and the old private business houses.[10] The changed relationship reduced the ability of domestic private capital to influence policy decisions. This reduced influence is reflected in the fact that market leaders like HML and PAL (owned by big business groups) were denied permission to enter into financial collaboration with foreign firms and that Tata (belonging to the most influential business family) was also not allowed to form a JV with Honda to manufacture cars in India.

Implications for investment strategies and price/non-price competition

The investment behaviour and pricing behaviour of firms was likely to change in response to the policy changes and restructuring observed in the 1980s as it brought new challenges and opportunities.

Investment Behaviour: In the 1980s, some major policy changes with their likely impact on the investment behaviour of firms were observed. (1) As noticed in the previous chapter, until the early 1980s, firms were not free to form collaborations with foreign firms in any form, and the imports of capital goods were severely restricted. As the government permitted the domestic firms to form technical collaborations with foreign firms, old manufacturers facing stiff competition from MUL signed a number of technical agreements with foreign firms in order to launch new technologically advanced products to compete with the new entrant. (2) The number of capital goods under OGL was expanded (Kumar 1994; Panagariya 2004). With a view to improving their competitiveness in the changing economic environment, manufacturers took this opportunity to modernise and expand their production facilities by heavily importing capital goods (Table 4.4 in Chapter 4). Using imported goods, HML and PAL expanded production capacity from 20,000 and 18,000 units per annum, respectively, to 60,000 and 54,500 units from 1982 to 1992. Correspondingly, the production capacity of the industry rose to 2,70,000 units per annum in 1991 from just 74,400 units per annum in 1982.

Despite the aggressive investment and modernisation strategy followed by the old private firms (HML and PAL) in the industry, their market position worsened. Capacity expansion added to the excess capacity of HML and PAL, as that was much higher than the increase in actual production. For instance, the capacity utilisation[11] of HML and PAL fell from 72.79 and 115 per cent, respectively, to 41.94 and 78.76 per cent from 1982 to 1991 (AIAM 1985, 1995). Contrary to this, MUL registered high levels of capacity utilisation (80.59 per cent in 1991). The high rate of capacity utilisation of

MUL alone pulled up the capacity utilisation of industry as a whole from 57 per cent in 1982 to 67 per cent in 1991.

Pricing Behaviour: Until the early 1980s, any kind of price and non-price competition was almost absent because: (1) due to the product-specific licensing policy, cars manufactured by old indigenous firms until the early 1980s were not close substitutes for each other as the Ambassador car manufactured by HML was big in size as compared to PAL Padmini. Absence of direct substitution muted the direct price/non-price competition as the targeted customers of HML and PAL were completely different. Adding to this, the check on new entry through licensing policy granted captive domestic market for their products and facilitated them to retain their oligopoly; and (2) given the policy of administered prices, producers were not allowed to determine the prices of their products. After the mid-1970s, the administered price policy had been dismantled, which enabled firms to determine their product prices according to market conditions, and the changing market conditions of the 1980s were likely to affect the price policy of firms.

As compared to this, during the 1980s, non-price competition emerged as a result of replacement of product-specific licensing policy with the policy of broad-banding. Now, the firms could produce differentiated products and compete on non-price basis. The rise of non-price competition is reflected in the fact that the available variety of passenger cars increased considerably during this phase. Not only this, the price deregulation allowed manufacturers to determine the prices of their products themselves. Along with this, internal competition among firms increased due to change in market positions with the entry of MUL. These factors were likely to increase price competition.

But, contrary to expectations, the information presented in Table 3.3 indicates that, in general, prices of all the products have increased. This happened because MUL, the market leader in the new structure, increased its prices. Initially, MUL kept the prices of its products lower than those of the others, but later MUL increased its prices and set them above those of the others. The higher price increase resorted to by MUL was mainly because of its market strength, and its differentiated higher-quality products. In a free market, the prices of products are determined by market forces, with the combination of product quality, demand and manufacturer's control of the market playing an important role. Therefore,

Table 3.3 Trends in car prices (in Rs.)*

Year	HML (Ambassador)		PAL (Premier Padmini)		MUL (Maruti 800)	
	Net Dealer Price	Index	Net Dealer Price	Index	Net Dealer Price	Index
1984	48587	100	46080	100	39594	100
1987	59547	122	54300	118	55570	140
1990	78692	161	62090	135	65875	166
1992	95992	198	77510	168	90789	229

Source: AIAM (1985, 1995).

Note: *1984 considered as the base year because MUL's production started in this year.

the other two manufacturers could only follow but could not match the increase in prices quoted by MUL.

From the above discussion it can be concluded that the car industry witnessed significant restructuring during the 1980s. The impact this had on pricing strategies, investment behaviour and production growth reflected increased competition in the industry. For the first time in the history of independent India, internal competition was vibrant.

3.3.2 Second phase of restructuring

The policy changes announced in July 1991 and thereafter covered almost the whole industrial sector. With the announcement of the liberalisation policy relating to the passenger car industry, new foreign entry was allowed into the industry, imports of critical components and capital goods were allowed at reduced customs duties, and the excise duty was rationalised. These policy initiatives considerably transformed the environment in which automobile firms were operating. They not only granted greater space to manufacturing firms in their operations and decision-making but also attracted large entry of foreign and domestic firms into the car industry (Table A.1 in annexure).

Nature of Foreign Presence: In this phase, the nature of foreign presence in the car industry changed completely from one of being a technology supplier to that of equity participation. As discussed earlier, until the early 1990s, except for the JV between Maruti and Suzuki, foreign presence in the passenger car industry was limited to the supply of technology and designs to local firms. But following the policy changes in the early 1990s, the car industry witnessed the entry of several global players in the form of JVs and wholly owned subsidiaries.

During the 1990s, foreign firms mainly entered in the form of JVs with domestic firms (except Hyundai, which managed to enter as a subsidiary of the parent company in 1997). The principal reason behind the entry only through formation of JVs in the early phase of liberalisation was that the government allowed foreign participation in equity of up to 51 per cent through the automatic route and if any foreign firm wanted to increase the stake beyond 51 per cent it was required to get approval from the Foreign Investment Promotion Board (FIPB). Therefore, it was easier to establish a JV than wait to get approval. Major JVs signed between domestic and foreign firms during the 1990s included: HML and General Motors (USA); PAL and Peugeot (France); PAL and Fiat (Italy); DCM and Daewoo Corporation (Korea); M&M and Ford Motors (USA); Usha International of Siddharth Shriram Group and Honda (Japan); Tata Motors and Mercedes-Benz (Germany); Kirloskar Group and Toyota Motors Corporation (Japan).

However, the nature of foreign presence further changed after the year 2000 when almost all foreign players started entering as subsidiaries of the parent firm as foreign investors were permitted to increase their stake to up to 100 per cent through the automatic route after 2000 (GoI 2002). Accordingly, a large number of foreign players set up wholly owned subsidiaries. As a result of these developments, it is to be expected that the behaviour of the foreign firms would determine the structure and development of the domestic car industry. Further, it is to be expected that, ultimately, foreign firms would have major control over the market either by acquiring shares of indigenous firms or by displacing them from the market through various strategies including dumping and predatory pricing.

Structure of Passenger Car Industry: Table 3.4 presents the market share of different firms in the industry and HHI for the industry. It is observed that the market structure of the car industry has altered in this phase and the emerging structure increasingly approximates a competitive market. The growing competition is evident from the fact the value of HHI has fallen over the reference period. For instance, the value declined from 0.59 in 1992–93 to 0.39

Table 3.4 Structure of car industry, 1990 onwards

Year	Share of passenger car firms (in %)																		HHI
	BMW India	Fiat India	Ford India	General Motors	HML	Honda Cars	Hyundai Motor	M&M	MUL	Mercedes-Benz In	Nissan Motor	Skoda Auto	Tata Motors	Toyota India	Volkswagen India	PAL	DM	PP	
1992–93	–	–	–	–	13.4	–	–	–	74.8	–	–	–	2.4	–	–	9.4	–	–	0.59
1993–94	–	–	–	–	12.5	–	–	–	72.1	–	–	–	3.5	–	–	11.9	–	–	0.55
1994–95	–	–	–	–	9.9	–	–	–	75.1	–	–	–	4.7	–	–	10.3	–	–	0.59
1995–96	–	–	–	–	8.0	–	–	–	77.3	0.3	–	–	3.0	–	–	5.8	2.6	3.0	0.61
1996–97	–	–	–	1.8	6.2	–	–	–	80.7	0.4	–	–	1.8	–	–	2.5	4.3	2.2	0.66
1997–98	–	–	–	1.9	5.7	–	–	–	86.4	0.6	–	–	1.3	–	–	2.9	0.3	0.9	0.75
1998–99	–	2.5	–	0.8	5.2	–	4.6	–	84.6	0.3	–	–	1.2	–	–	0.7	–	0.1	0.72
1999–2000	–	2.8	–	0.5	4.6	–	12.6	–	69.4	0.1	–	–	9.9	–	–	0.01	–	–	0.51
2000–01	–	–	1.0	1.6	5.0	0.5	16.8	–	66.1	0.2	–	–	8.8	–	–	–	–	–	0.48
2001–02	–	–	2.9	1.6	3.9	2.1	18.8	–	57.7	0.3	–	–	12.9	–	–	–	–	–	0.39
2001–02	–	–	2.9	1.6	3.9	2.1	18.8	–	57.7	0.3	–	–	12.9	–	–	–	–	–	0.39
2002–03	–	–	2.8	1.4	3.3	2.5	20.2	–	54.8	0.2	–	–	14.7	0.2	–	–	–	–	0.36
2003–04	–	–	2.6	1.9	1.8	2.6	21.8	–	52.3	0.2	–	0.4	15.1	1.2	–	–	–	–	0.35
2004–05	–	–	2.7	1.7	1.5	3.8	23.6	–	48.7	0.2	–	0.8	16.1	1.1	–	–	–	–	0.32
2005–06	–	0.1	2.4	1.2	1.4	4.0	24.9	–	47.9	0.2	–	0.9	16.2	0.8	–	–	–	–	0.32
2006–07	0.01	0.1	3.2	1.2	1.0	4.8	25.4	0.1	46.7	0.2	–	1.0	15.8	0.5	–	–	–	–	0.31

(Continued)

Table 3.4 (Continued)

Year	Share of passenger car firms (in %)																		HHI
	BMW India	Fiat India	Ford India	General Motors	HML	Honda Cars	Hyundai Motor	M&M	MUL	Mercedes-Benz In	Nissan Motor	Skoda Auto	Tata Motors	Toyota India	Volkswagen India	PAL	DM	PP	
2007–08	0.2	0.2	2.5	3.2	0.8	4.4	25.7	1.9	46.9	0.2	–	1.0	12.6	0.5	–	–	–	–	0.31
2008–09	0.2	0.6	1.6	3.0	0.5	3.1	33.1	0.9	45.6	0.2	–	1.0	9.8	0.6	–	–	–	–	0.33
2009–10	0.1	1.4	1.9	3.6	0.5	3.4	30.5	0.3	47.6	0.2	–	0.8	9.2	0.5	0.02	–	–	–	0.33
2010–11	0.2	0.9	4.5	3.7	0.3	2.5	24.2	0.5	45.0	0.2	3.1	0.9	11.1	0.8	2.2	–	–	–	0.28
2011–12	0.4	0.7	4.6	3.4	0.1	1.9	24.8	0.7	38.7	0.3	5.1	1.4	11.0	3.6	3.1	–	–	–	0.23
2012–13	0.3	0.3	4.5	2.8	0.1	3.0	26.3	0.6	40.3	0.2	5.6	1.2	7.6	3.9	2.7	–	–	–	0.25
2013–14	–	0.5	2.9	2.1	0.1	5.8	26.7	0.4	42.5	–	5.9	0.6	4.6	3.6	3.8	–	–	–	0.27

Source: AIAM (1995), ACMA (2003), SIAM (2006a, 2010a, 2012a, 2014a, 2016a).

Notes
(1) – indicates non-existence of firm in those years or non-availability of data.
(2) DM- Daewoo Motors; PAL- Premier Automobiles Ltd; HM- Hindustan Motors Limited; PP- Pal Peugeot; MUL-Maruti Udyog Limited; M&M- Mahindra and Mahindra; HHI- Herfindahl-Hirschman Index.

in 2001–02 and further to 0.27 in 2013–14 (Table 3.4). Second, the market share of all the firms including MUL has declined and new entrants in the industry succeeded in getting a foothold in the market.

In the changing market structure, indigenous firms (HML and PAL) experienced a sharp decline in their market share (Table 3.4). To protect themselves from the onslaught of severe competition with the entry of foreign firms, both the firms formed JVs with leading foreign firms in the mid-1990s in order to use international brand names to compete in the domestic market as well as to launch technologically advanced passenger cars at competitive prices. HML launched Opel Astra cars in the middle of the 1990s in collaboration with General Motors and also manufactured Mitsubishi models (namely Pajero during the late 1990s and early 2000s). Similarly, PAL launched the Peugeot 309 model and the Uno model of Fiat. But these efforts did not help these firms protect their market position and the situation worsened so much for PAL that it completely disappeared from the car market in the late 1990s (Table 3.4).

Not only this, the growing intensity of the competition affected the market leader, MUL, which recorded rapid expansion during the 1980s and most of the 1990s. Though MUL is still the largest manufacturer in India's car market, its market share has consistently declined from 86.4 per cent in 1997–98 to 42.5 per cent in 2013–14. The fall in the market share of MUL is mainly because of the entry of a foreign firm (Hyundai) and an indigenous firm (Tata) in the industry, which was deliberately restricted by the government during the 1980s in order to benefit MUL. These firms started manufacturing close substitutes of MUL models. For instance, these firms launched models such as Santro (Hyundai Motor) and Indica (Tata Motors). They achieved considerable success, as is manifested in changes in their market position during the last decade (Table 3.4). Hyundai emerged as the second-largest car manufacturer in India with a 26.7 per cent market share in 2013–14.

These developments suggest that India's automobile industry is moving towards a scenario of intense competition in which foreign firms are better placed as compared to domestic firms. The passenger car market, which used to be characterised as a seller's market up to the early 1990s has been transformed into a buyer's market since then. This characteristic of being a buyer's market is evident in the growing variety of products available on the market, on the one hand, and the intensity of competition, on the other. Growth in variety of products is a reflection of the competitive strategies which manufacturers adopt in order to differentiate their products from available substitutes on the market.

Segmentation of Car Industry: A major development witnessed by the passenger car industry in this phase of high growth is the increasing degree of segmentation within it, which was not so stark until the mid-1990s. This is an important development as it has significant implications for the intensity of competition, and for the production and pricing strategies of firms. Segmentation of the car market is associated with growth in the variety of passenger cars that has made competition intense during the last one and a half decades. In the wake of intense competition, rather than focusing on a whole range of passenger cars, manufacturers started targeting those sub-segments where they were either competitive enough or the market potential would allow them to manufacture considerable volumes in future. So, instead of manufacturing a variety of cars, each one is interested in specialising in a particular segment. These changes reflect the competitive strategy of manufacturers. Targeting a specific segment limits direct competition to only those manufacturers who produce similar vehicles and also enables producers to target a particular section of consumers.

Figure 3.1 presents segment-wise distribution of cars produced in India. It is interesting to note that the composition of production has changed during the last one and a half decades. It is biased towards the 'compact segment,' which accounted for almost 80 per cent of total car production in India in 2010–11, having risen from 50 per cent in 2001–02 (Figure 3.1). At the same time, the production share of the mid-size car segment, with some fluctuations, stayed intact but that of the mini car segment recorded a sharp decline from 29.87 per cent in 2001–02 to 8.03 per cent in 2006–07 and further to 4.37 per cent in 2010–11. Another interesting feature is that the premier and luxury segments have observed an increase in production from 2001–02 to 2012–13. The combined production of the premier and luxury segment increased from 3999 units in 2001–02 to 13610 units in 2010–11 and further to 14661 units in 2012–13 (SIAM 2006a, 2012a). Irrespective of an increase of more than 3.67 times during 2001–02 and 2012–13, the combined production share of these two segments continuously fluctuated around 0.55 per cent of total car production in India until recently.

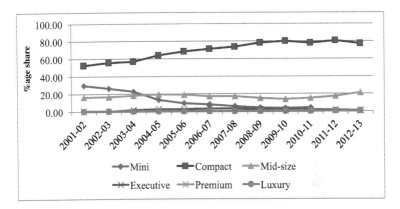

Figure 3.1 Sub-segment-wise composition of car production

Source SIAM (2006a, 2010a, 2012a, 2014a, 2016a)

Note: Since 2011–12, compact segment includes mini segment.

It is clear that the emerging pattern of production in India's car industry is skewed in nature, in the sense that only one segment has observed rapid expansion, namely the compact segment. Given this, it can be expected that the large entry into the car industry may not be uniformly distributed across sub-segments because business firms always try to enter in those areas where growth prospects are higher. Given this, it is very likely that the changes witnessed by a particular segment would not have been the same as by other sub-segments in the industry. Restructuring would be greater in that segment where new entry and entry of a new variety of products happened to be larger as compared to others.

Table 3.5 presents the changes experienced by different sub-segments after 2000. It is worth pointing out that rapid expansion of the compact segment attracted new as well as existing manufacturers. A number of firms that initially entered the mid-size, executive and premium segments have recently changed their product line to incorporate compact size and mid-size cars. This is reflected in an increase in the number of manufacturers in the compact segment from three in 2001–02 to five in 2005–06 and 12 in 2013–14 (SIAM 2016a). Major firms which initially entered in the executive or premium segments but recently shifted to the compact segment

Table 3.5 Share of dominant firms (% of respective segment)

	Mini*				Compact				Mid-size			
	2001–02	2005–06	2010–11	2013–14	2001–02	2005–06	2010–11	2013–14	2001–02	2005–06	2010–11	2013–14
Ford India	–	–	–	–	–	–	4.74	3.06	17.32	12.65	5.09	2.21
General Motors	–	–	–	–	–	0.11	3.88	1.77	9.64	2.10	1.09	4.21
HML	–	–	–	–	–	–	–	–	23.42	7.45	1.94	0.74
Honda Cars	–	–	–	–	–	–	0.18	4.95	11.15	18.96	13.47	11.33
Hyundai Motor	–	–	–	–	27.69	30.18	28.13	27.07	22.64	21.14	15.37	24.06
M&M	–	–	–	–	–	–	–	–	–	–	3.16	1.38
MUL	100	100	36.66	–	47.86	52.06	48.84	48.89	15.84	15.53	35.82	4.34
Nissan Motor	–	–	–	–	–	–	3.93	4.63	–	–	–	14.24
Skoda Auto	–	–	–	–	–	–	0.59	0.06	–	–	–	3.44
Tata Motors	–	–	63.34	–	24.45	17.57	7.5	5.25	–	22.12	16.28	1.05
Toyota India	–	–	–	–	–	–	–	1.82	–	–	2.32	14.01
Volkswagen India	–	–	–	–	–	–	1.52	1.65	–	–	5.41	17.33

(Continued)

Table 3.5 (Continued)

Firm	Executive			Premier				Luxury		
BMW India	—	4.79	—	—	—	20.88	—	—	—	—
Fiat India	—	17.42	21.17	—	—	—	—	—	—	—
General Motors	26.48	22.91	8.47	—	—	—	—	—	—	—
HML	3.91	—	—	—	—	—	—	—	—	—
Honda Cars	—	9.13	—	34.5	64.64	18.41	3.59	—	—	—
Hyundai Motor	5.8	0.04	27.35	58.7	10.61	1.55	9.88	—	—	—
Mercedes-Benz India	96.1	2.94	4.55	6.78	16.48	21.13	—	100	100	100
Nissan Motor	—	—	—	—	—	—	—	—	—	—
Skoda Auto	33.72	13.35	10.18	—	8.27	31.69	61.08	—	—	—
Toyota India	31.06	20.83	18.47	—	—	—	25.45	—	—	—
Volkswagen India	—	6.99	12.49	—	—	6.33	—	—	—	—

Source: Same as Figure 3.1.

Notes
(1) — indicates non-existence of firm in those years or non-availability of data.
(2) * Since 2011–12, compact segment includes mini segment.

include Ford, General, Honda, Volkswagen, Nissan, Renault, Toyota and Fiat. For instance, Ford India introduced Figo, Nissan launched Micra, Toyota launched Liva, Renault introduced Pulse, General Motors introduced Spark, Volkswagen introduced Polo and there are many more firms that are still entering into this segment. The large entry of firms in the compact segment has deepened the competition in this as well as the mid-size segment. Irrespective of entry of new firms in the compact segment, MUL and Hyundai have maintained their market position in the compact segment from 2001–02 to 2013–14. Interestingly, the share of MUL increased from 47.86 per cent in 2001–02 to 48.89 per cent in 2013–14. In the case of the mid-sized segment, MUL recorded a downturn, whereas Hyundai increased its market share during the reference period. It emerged that MUL and Hyundai are the dominant firms in the compact and mid-size segment, which accounted for around 70 per cent of total car production in India in 2013–14.

It is worth pointing out that the structural changes in the car industry (high growth and skewed nature of growth) are not exclusively the result of the changed policies that led to foreign entry and, hence, increased competition. There are some other factors which provided the backdrop for the observed structural changes and influenced these changes. These factors are independent of the increasing foreign presence in the passenger car industry and were the result of changes taking place in the overall economy during this phase.

Other Factors: India's market has undergone drastic changes starting in the early 1990s. These changes can be discussed in terms of: (1) expansion of demand and changes in its pattern in the phase of high economic growth and (2) the role of credit in boosting demand.

Until the early 1990s, structural changes in the car industry were mainly influenced by state policy and that also influenced the growth pattern of this industry. For instance, by facilitating the entry of a public sector firm (MUL) in collaboration with a leading multinational firm (Suzuki) and promoting its growth by modifying various policies, the state played a significant role in shaping the structure and growth trajectory of the car industry during the 1980s. But under globalisation (1990s and afterwards), consumer sovereignty also plays an important role in generating demand, and private consumption behaviour directly influences the growth and pattern of demand. Private consumption behaviour is generally driven by the disposable income of households, on the one hand,

and access to finance from various sources including institutional credit, on the other. Therefore, to analyse structural changes in the car industry during this phase, it is important to understand the pattern of domestic demand expansion in relation to the car industry. The changes in income and access to finance of households over time are analysed to delve deeper into the issue.

The data collected by the National Council of Applied Economic Research (NCAER) relating to the period of 1985–86 to 2009–10 on income of households is used for this discussion[12] (Table 3.6). In the first instance, it is important to note that the proportion of households belonging to the low-income group recorded a sharp decline, especially from 1998–99 to 2006–07 and, correspondingly, the size of other income groups has expanded, including both middle and high income groups. This implies that low income households have observed upward income mobility. As compared to the early 1990s, the size of the middle, upper middle and high income households expanded substantially in the late 1990s and early 2000s (Table 3.6). In 2009–10, around 67 per cent of India's population belonged to the broad middle class (lower middle + middle + upper middle).

The middle income section of society is such that its basic necessities of life are fulfilled and it can afford some luxury products as

Table 3.6 Changing dynamics of India's population: income-group wise (percentages)

Annual income (Rs.At 1998–99 prices)	1985–86	1989–90	1992–93	1998–99	2006–07	2009–10 (est.)
Low (L) (<=35,000)	65.24	58.84	58.16	39.66	17.7	15.83
Lower middle (LM) (35001–70000)	25.22	26.95	25.42	34.53	39.4	36.17
Middle (M) (70001–105000)	6.95	10.11	10.35	13.89	20.4	22.12
Upper middle (UM) (105001–140000)	1.53	2.66	3.74	6.22	10.8	9.44
High (H) (>140000)	1.07	1.44	2.33	5.7	11.7	16.44

Source: NCAER (2002), Bijapurkar (2007), Shukla (2010).

well, specifically, the middle and upper middle sections. So, any increase in their income would directly show up in demand for durables and luxuries, including passenger cars. It has been argued that middle income households have a high demand for consumer durables (Shukla 2010). According to NCAER, based on 2001–02 prices, the income of middle class households varied between 2 and 10 lakhs per annum. Given that income size, most of the households can afford only compact-sized cars because prices of compact cars varied roughly between 3 lakhs and 8 lakhs (Table A.3 in annexure) and the maintenance cost of these cars is minimal.

All these changes were taking place at a time when the Indian economy was experiencing its highest ever growth rate (around 9 per cent) (Nagaraj 2013). The high growth raised the incomes of households, which appears to be clear in terms of falling share of low income households. Further, during the second half of the 2000s, salaries of central government employees increased substantially with the implementation of the sixth pay commission's recommendations. A majority of central government employees can be classified under lower middle, middle and upper middle income class. These developments in general raised the disposable income of households, especially middle income households, which has direct positive implications for the demand for durable goods in general and automobiles products in particular. Therefore, the expanding size of the middle class can be argued as one of the most significant factors behind the rapid expansion of the car industry in general and the shaping of the unique pattern of demand for cars in India in particular.

Another important influence on the high growth and specific pattern of growth of the automobile industry is credit expansion during the period of liberalisation. Economic growth and the changing international financial scenario since 1991 policy changes attracted large volumes of foreign private capital into India in the form of equity and debt, which contributed to an increase in liquidity in the system (Chandrasekhar 2011). The easy availability of credit that the expansion of liquidity led to influenced the growth of the Indian economy in general and the automobile industry in particular through its impact on private consumption and investment. Credit expansion by commercial banks during the last couple of decades remained significant, especially for housing and consumer durables including automobiles. As compared to the late 1990s, growth in credit became explosive during the early 2000s. From 2000–01 to 2006–07, growth of personal loans ranged between 23 per cent and 57 per cent (Table 3.7). It increased the share of personal loans in total credit of commercial banks from 9.28 per cent in 1995–96 to 12.25 per cent in 2000–01 and reached the highest ever level (23.33 per cent) in 2005–06. The explosive growth of personal loans coincided with the phase of rapid growth of the Indian economy. Even after excluding the share of housing loans from personal loans, the remaining share of personal loans fluctuated around 10 per cent of total commercial bank credit. This suggests that the share received by durables, including automobiles, is significant (Table 3.7).[13] Therefore, it can be argued that

Table 3.7 Share and growth of personal loans in total bank credit (percentages)

Year	Share in total bank credit	Share in bank credit (excluding housing loans)	Growth rate	Growth rate (excluding housing loans)
1995–96	9.28	6.48	–	–
1996–97	9.92	7.12	19.35	22.65
1997–98	10.53	7.61	23.23	24.02
1998–99	10.35	7.12	13.92	8.33
1999–2000	11.22	7.20	30.44	21.68
2000–01	12.25	7.53	27.70	22.39
2001–02	12.58	7.58	25.14	22.61
2002–03	15.07	8.58	38.08	30.55
2003–04	20.34	10.65	57.17	44.49
2004–05	22.21	11.21	42.94	37.81
2005–06	23.33	11.30	37.99	32.41
2006–07	22.27	10.51	22.74	19.63
2007–08	20.08	9.80	11.96	15.80
2008–09	19.44	9.44	14.04	13.42
2009–10	16.71	7.55	0.97	−6.03
2010–11	16.44	7.95	19.90	28.35
2011–12	15.62	7.73	11.94	14.56
2012–13	17.92	8.36	16.15	9.5
2013–14	16.19	7.74	16.73	19.7
2014–15	16.63	7.33	12.48	3.6

Source: Reserve Bank of India, *Basic Statistical Returns of Scheduled Commercial Banks in India*, various issues.

credit expansion remained an important aspect of the high growth of the passenger car industry.

Not only this, the distribution pattern of personal loans (including and excluding share of housing loans) is very specific in nature in the sense that it remained biased towards the urban sector (Table 3.8). On an average, more than 87 per cent of total personal loans are accounted for by urban areas,[14] whereas around 70 per cent of the population in the rural areas received only 10 to 12 per cent of personal loans in recent years. Further, the growth rate of credit in urban India remained more than that in rural India.

Table 3.8 Region-wise growth and distribution of personal loans (percentages)

Year	Rural				Urban			
	Share	Growth	Share (excluding housing)	Growth (excluding housing)	Share	Growth	Share (excluding housing)	Growth (excluding housing)
1995–96	14.93	–	16.45	–	85.07	–	83.55	–
1996–97	15.31	22.34	16.59	23.69	84.69	18.83	83.41	22.44
1997–98	15.18	22.21	16.28	21.73	84.82	23.41	83.72	24.48
1998–99	14.43	8.29	16.00	6.42	85.57	14.92	84.00	8.70
1999–2000	14.37	29.91	16.66	26.70	85.63	30.52	83.34	20.73
2000–01	14.08	25.12	16.66	22.44	85.92	28.13	83.34	22.38
2001–02	13.86	23.13	16.65	22.54	86.14	25.47	83.35	22.63
2002–03	13.65	36.06	15.68	22.92	86.35	38.41	84.32	32.08
2003–04	12.23	40.79	15.14	39.53	87.77	59.77	84.86	45.42
2004–05	12.26	43.22	14.20	29.28	87.74	42.90	85.80	39.33
2005–06	11.64	31.06	13.39	24.83	88.36	38.96	86.61	33.67
2006–07	10.52	10.91	12.50	11.68	89.48	24.30	87.50	20.86
2007–08	11.92	26.86	12.81	18.64	88.08	10.21	87.19	15.40
2008–09	9.11	−12.85	11.21	−0.73	90.89	17.67	88.79	15.50
2009–10	11.50	27.50	15.51	30.05	88.50	−1.69	84.49	−10.58
2010–11	11.00	14.72	14.79	22.41	89.00	20.58	85.21	29.44
2011–12	9.32	−5.14	12.01	−7.02	90.68	14.05	87.99	18.31
2012–13	9.23	15.01	12.63	15.17	90.77	16.27	87.37	8.69
2013–14	8.76	10.75	11.29	7.02	91.24	17.34	88.70	21.48
2014–15	9.12	17.05	12.13	11.23	90.88	12.04	87.87	2.65

Source: Same as Table 3.7.

This pattern of credit distribution suggests that the rapid growth of credit in urban areas would have certainly contributed to expanding luxury goods demand as the households in urban areas, especially middle and upper middle income households, generally avail themselves of credit facilities to purchase luxury products, including passenger vehicles and other durables. This argument also finds support from the circumstances prevailing in the economy at that time.[15]

From the analysis of credit expansion it can be argued that personal credit expansion has boosted demand during the last one and a half decade under liberalisation. It is evident from the fact that an individual having income well below the level at which he can afford an automobile could rely on dis-saving and increase his consumption. For instance, more than 70 per cent of the value of passenger vehicles gets financed through credit, as almost all the automobile firms have tie-ups with banks and other financial institutes to finance their cars (IBEF 2012; Singh 2015). Such credit policies have brought new buyers into the market who are buying goods which their income may not allow.

Based on this understanding, it can be argued that the credit-financed demand of automobiles in general and passenger vehicles in particular played an important role, along with other factors, in sustaining the car industry's growth and shaping its patterns under the liberal policy regime.

Asymmetric market distribution: what attracts new entrants?

Tables 3.4 and 3.5 indicate that, in spite of new entry into the industry and the compact segment, two dominant firms, MUL and Hyundai accounted for 76 per cent of market share in the compact segment and 70 per cent of market share in the overall passenger car industry in 2013–14. Their ranking in terms of market share has stayed intact, and these firms have emerged as market leaders in India's car industry. It implies that all other 15 firms in the industry are serving only 30 per cent of the total market. Therefore, it remains to be understood what attracts new entrants into this industry.

There are various factors behind the continuous entry of new firms. Evidence suggests that the size of the car industry has increased quite significantly during the last couple of decades. In terms of volume of production, the size increased from 0.19 million in 1991–92 to 0.58 million in 1999–2000 and finally to 2.42 million in 2013–14. The rapid expansion of the car industry in India also is reflected in terms of consistent high growth for over more than two decades (Table 3.9). Given the expansion and liberal investment regime, a large number of foreign firms made their way into the industry and are continuously entering to exploit India's growing market.

The other important underlying factor is that car penetration in India is still very low in comparison to even BRICS (Brazil, Russia, India, China and South Africa) countries and far lower in comparison to developed countries. Data suggests that the car penetration ratio in 2010 stood at 13 per thousand in India, as compared to 249 in Brazil; 200 in Russia; 44 in China and 565 in Germany (World Bank 2011). This is suggestive of the large potential for market expansion in India as the economy grows and the size of the middle class expands, whereas markets in the advanced countries are getting saturated. The potential market expansion is further revealed by figures from the NCAER's Centre for Macro Consumer

Table 3.9 Expansion of passenger car industry, 1990 onwards

Years	Growth rate
1992–93	12.81
1995–96	31.64
1999–2000	47.90
2005–06	8.91
2006–07	18.34
2007–08	15.20
2008–09	6.36
2009–10	27.40
2010–11	26.93
2011–12	3.43
2012–13	−4.26
2013–14	−4.39
	CAGR
1991–92 to 2000–01	13.42
2001–02 to 2010–11	19.32

Source: Same as Table 3.4.

Research. According to NCAER estimates, middle class households are expected to grow from 31.4 million households (160 million individuals) to 53.3 million households (267 million individuals) from 2009–10 to 2015–16 (*The Economic Times* 2011). Further ahead, by 2025–26, this number is likely to reach 113.8 million households (547 million individuals). The study also projected that the middle class will form 20.3 per cent of the total population of the country by 2015–16 and 37.2 per cent by 2025–26. The growth of middle class households will create a huge market for white goods and automobiles since such families have a strong demand for consumer durables, including cars (Shukla 2010).

But there is a downside associated with the structure of the industry. As mentioned, two dominant firms are controlling a large share of the market (70 per cent approx.), whereas the remaining large number of firms are competing for just 30 per cent of the total car market. So, it can well be expected that the limited market share of the follower firms would not permit them to realise economies of scale. As a result, these firms may restrict themselves to assembly and serve the market by offering highly import-intensive products. Evidence suggests that the liberal trade regime allowed significant inroads of import-intensive products into the domestic market. A strategy of this kind has obvious implications for indigenous manufacturing capability and the BoP of the country. India's indigenous manufacturing capacity is already adversely affected, as reflected in the displacement of indigenous firms from the car market. To fully analyse the implications for the BoP, we need to understand the changes made in the import policy during the last couple of decades, especially with respect to automobile imports (a detailed analysis on this issue is available in the chapter dealing with trade issues).

Implications for investment and pricing

Implications for Investment Strategy: Unlike the previous phase, the industrial licensing policy no longer exists in this phase. The abolition of licensing in the early 1990s has had two consequences: (1) manufacturing firms are now free to expand production capacity, and (2) potential entrants are now free to exploit emerging opportunities. The same scenario holds in the passenger car industry as well. These factors, combined with the growth potential of the industry and the increasing intensity of competition, have set off a race towards creation of capacity among passenger car firms. Existing manufacturers and new entrants are continuously creating capacity, especially in the compact and mid-size segments. These two segments are likely to grow further in the near future because a large chunk of the country's population can afford such cars (Table 3.6). The production capacity of the car industry as a whole has increased from 1.88 million to 4.2 million between 2005–06 and 2011–12 and then stood at 4.96 million units in 2014–15. As per SIAM's estimates, installed capacity of the industry would expand to 6.96 million units by the end of 2017. Given the pattern of domestic demand, the increase in production capacity was mainly recorded in firms operating in the compact and mid-size segments. For instance, installed capacity of MUL and Hyundai Motor increased from 0.35 million and 0.12 million respectively in 2002–03 to 1.5 million and 0.7 million respectively in 2014–15. These two firms are the market leaders in the car industry and these firms are mainly producing compact and mid-size cars (Tables 3.3 and 3.4).

This jump in production capacity is an outcome of unregulated entry and the growing variety of passenger vehicles in the wake of a rapidly growing market. The downside of this development is that the industry is showing signs of overcrowding. Overcrowding is reflected in the fact that a large number of new firms, especially those entering after the middle of the 2000s, failed to achieve expected market share (Tables 3.4 and 3.5). But they have continuously added to production capacity with a view to exploiting the growth potential of the car industry. This has led to an increase in excess capacity in this industry (Table A.2 in annexure). The average capacity utilisation in the industry reached its maximum in 2006–07, after which it has been declining (Table A.2 in annexure). The average capacity utilisation of the industry declined to 65 per cent in 2014–15, as against 79 per cent in 2011–12. It will further decline if we take out MUL and Hyundai, which have made use of more than 90 per cent of total installed capacity in 2014–15.

Though average capacity utilisation has fallen, the fall has not been uniform across manufacturers. It is important to note that the decline is more visible among firms shifting their product line (Ford, Fiat, Toyota, General Motors; Renault and Volkswagen) and firms operating in high-end car segments (Mercedes-Benz India and BMW). For instance, data on capacity utilisation in 2012–13 suggests that MUL and Hyundai remained on top in terms of capacity utilisation, whereas firms such as HML, Fiat and International Cars and Motors Ltd. were placed at the bottom with 9.79 per cent, 3.97 per cent and 1.08 per cent capacity utilisation respectively (Table A.2 in annexure). The large excess capacity has adverse implications as it implies inefficient use of resources. Further, in the process of capacity expansion, firms are heavily dependent upon imported plant and machinery, which is associated with high outflow of foreign exchange resources.

Implications for Pricing Strategies: With structural changes in the car industry and increasing competition, pricing strategies have become more complex. As mentioned earlier, the pattern of demand for cars in India is biased towards small-sized cars, which are demanded by middle-income households, whose demand is very sensitive to prices. On the other hand, the market for high-end cars has also expanded during this phase, and that demand is not very sensitive to prices because these products are demanded by high-income households. For them, features other than prices, which make the product unique, are more important. Moreover, the demand of the high-income class in a developing country is generally influenced by the international demonstration effect.

Another uniqueness of this phase with regard to price competition is that, unlike under the previous phase, the one-to-one relationship between prices and models of cars has blurred. In response to growing competition and increasing availability of substitutes under globalisation, the one-to-one relationship has been replaced with price-bands (Table A.3 in annexure). Within a price band, variation in prices does exist because of product differentiation, but the variation is not too high because products offered in a particular segment remain close substitutes.

As a result, *non-price competition* has become more aggressive in recent years in the passenger car industry. It is visible in terms of a growing variety of products offered by each manufacturer and the continuous replacement of existing models of cars with advanced ones. The fundamental aim behind product differentiation is to strengthen competitive advantages. The extent of product differentiation directly adds to the inelasticity of demand which to some extent (by giving market power to producers in determining product price) enables manufacturers to decide prices of products. Further, after-sales services, which were almost absent until the late 1980s, have become an essential feature of product profile in a competitive market. In the case of closely substitutable products, consumer choice gets influenced by such factors. Finally, the tie-up between financial institutions and manufacturing firms has become critical in order to promote sales of passenger vehicles. Under this tie-up, financial institutions provide loans to the consumers for purchasing cars. These strategies fundamentally aim to promote sales that ultimately affect market share.

To conclude, the main observations of this section are as follows: (1) The growing foreign presence in the form of equity holding has transformed the structure of this industry from being a seller's market to a buyer's market. (2) The growth of the car market was initially driven by the pent-up demand that was released when new, hitherto unavailable, products became available after the import liberalisation of the early 1990s. But since the late 1990s demand is mainly driven by credit offered for purchases of passenger vehicles and partly contributed by the growing disposable income in the phase of high economic growth. And (iii) the rapid growth observed in this industry is biased towards the compact segment. This pattern of demand was mainly driven by the growing size of middle-class households that aspire to a life of luxury. As their incomes increase, they prefer to spend on non-essential goods.

3.4   Observations and implications

Empirical analysis undertaken in this chapter suggests the structure of passenger car industry has significantly changed since the 1980s. But the restructuring observed from 1980 to 1990 was unique in certain senses, as compared to the restructuring observed after 1990. From 1980 to 1990, most of the regulatory measures initiated in the 1950s and afterwards were in place with a limited degree of relaxation. Using these measures, the government drafted policy in such a manner that old established firms were placed in a disadvantageous position because the government policy aimed at providing space to the new JV. This strategy of the government led to significant restructuring of the passenger car industry, which is reflected in the changing relative positions of manufacturing firms. Contrary to the experience of the 1980s, the structural changes observed after 1990 were mainly shaped by the entry of foreign firms, though the importance of other factors cannot be ignored. Since 1991, the government allowed foreign firms to establish manufacturing units, which led to an increase in the number of manufacturers in the passenger car industry. As a result of this, the industry witnessed a significant increase in competition that led to a downturn in the market share of MUL and other established firms, on the one hand, and to an increase in the variety of technologically advanced passenger cars on offer, on the other. The increase in the variety of cars since the late 1990s resulted in segmentation within the car industry.

At the same time, external factors also played an important role in determining the growth and structure of this industry since the 1990s. As suggested by the empirical analysis, the pattern of growth of this industry under the liberal policy regime is unique in the sense that mainly one segment, namely the compact segment, accounted for around 80 per cent of total cars manufactured in India during the second half of the 2000s. Detailed analysis suggests that this pattern of development was mainly driven by the growing size of middle-class households that aspire for a luxury lifestyle. The growing demand of the middle class is sustained (or supported) by the easy availability of credit.

These developments may have certain implications for indigenisation of manufacturing activities and local technology development. These issues are addressed in detail in the following chapters.

Notes

1 This index is defined as the sum of squares of sales share of all firms in an industry, symbolically $\sum S_i^2$ where i = 1, 2,. . . . ., n and S_i is the sales share of ith firm in the particular industry or market. This index is widely used in the literature to measure market power. The value of the HHI varies between zero and one. If all firms are equal in size, then the value of HHI is zero (or negligible). If firms are unequal in size, then the value of index is greater than zero and is close to one if size inequality is very high.

2 Until the early 1980s, the nature, duration, extent and pattern of foreign presence in the passenger car industry were subject to strict regulation. Though collaborations between domestic and foreign firms existed before the 1980s, these collaborations were established during the 1950s. No foreign alliance in the car industry was permitted during the 1960s and 1970s because policy changes in the mid-1960s classified the passenger car industry among those where foreign entry in any form was restricted. Requests for foreign technical collaborations by HML and PAL were denied by the government in the late 1960s and 1970s. The rationale behind stronger forms of regulation on foreign presence in the mid-1960s was (1) the need to minimise the outflow of foreign exchange, and (2) the view that passenger cars were a luxury good.

3 Standard Motors stopped manufacturing cars in the early 1970s.

4 Available evidence indicates that the value of the Japanese currency (Yen) appreciated approximately 90 per cent against the US dollar from 1985 to 1988. For instance, Yen-to-dollar exchange rate moved up from 260 to 123 during February, 1985 to November, 1988 (Chandrasekhar 1997).

5 'Customs duty on components imported by Maruti's competitors would range from 60 to 150 per cent ad valorem, depending on the engine capacity of the vehicle. For fuel-efficient cars of 1000cc or less like Maruti (and the 'Dolphin' produced by the small Sipani Automobiles), basic customs duty was 25 per cent plus an auxiliary duty of 15 per cent, making a total of 40 per cent' (Venkataramani 1990: 220–221).

6 What explains the government's decision to do all this? Maruti Udyog Limited was established by Sanjay Gandhi in 1970. Initially, the company was established under the name of Maruti Technical Services Private Limited and later renamed as Maruti Limited. Sanjay Gandhi became the first Managing Director and Maruti Limited was incorporated under the Companies Act in June 1971. Sanjay Gandhi established this firm with the sole aim of manufacturing a completely indigenous small car for the Indian middle class. The firm got approval from the government, but it failed to produce any car until the late 1970s and was finally liquidated in 1977 on account of various controversies which evolved around this firm (Becker-Ritterspach and Becker-Ritterspach 2009; Kale 2012). To fulfil Sanjay Gandhi's dream, Indira Gandhi's government in 1980 acquired Maruti Limited as a public sector firm and started searching for a foreign collaborator. Given the personal interest of the most powerful political family of that time, the government modified a number of policy measures regulating the passenger car industry.

7 The Suzuki Motor Corporation was well known for her specialisation in the production of small-sized cars not only within Japan but also in other developed countries. Suzuki had achieved success in USA in collaboration with General Motors in manufacturing compact cars. According to Japan Automotive Manufacturers Association (1991), Suzuki Motor doubled her production of small cars in every five years during the 1980s. Before entering in India, this firm had successfully formed joint ventures with many leading international firms to manufacture small cars (Venkataramani 1990; Motohashi 2015).

8 Two existing manufacturers (HML and PAL) were only offering passenger cars with engine capacity of more than 1000 cc.

9 Annual growth of car production was quite high in most of the period during the 1980s. CAGR of production from 1981–82 to 1985–86 was 24.73, which declined to 9.63 per cent from 1986–87 to 1990–91 (Table 3.2). Though the growth has declined in the second half, absolute volume of production of the passenger car industry increased from 42480 units in 1981–82 to 125870 units in 1986–87 and further to 181820 units in 1990–91.

10 The protectionist measures announced following India's independence were not only an end result of state ideology to promote industrialisation,

but also shaped by the nexus between political leaders and leading industrialists (Frankel 1978; Chenoy 2015; Tyabji 2015). It was argued that the relations established between Indian industrialists and political leaders played a crucial role in shaping the post-colonial industrial policy environment (Chenoy 2015; Tyabji 2015).

11 Capacity utilisation is defined in terms of percentage of actual production to total installed capacity of the manufacturers.

12 The sample size of the NCAER dataset is small. Given the absence of any alternative data, we have used this data. Thus the results may be taken to be indicative only.

13 Until 2009, share of personal loans in total credit of commercial banks is not separately available. Due to the non-availability of data on vehicle loans before 2009, we have clubbed the share of consumer durables and others.

14 It can be justified as mainly salaried class and other assured income households reside in the urban areas. Due to their assured monthly income, they are in a position to get loans very easily as compared to rural households, whose income is mainly coming from agriculture and other activities. Income from these sources is not as assured as salary. Hence banks prefer to extend loans to salaried households.

15 A specific feature related to economic growth during this phase is that it was the service sector which was contributing significantly to GDP. Share of service sector in GDP has risen from 39.2 per cent in 1980–81 to around 53.5 per cent of GVA from 2014–15. It is well known that growth of services sector leads to increase in share of a class of people having high demand for consumer durables including cars. It can be seen in relation to large growth of middle and upper middle income population during this phase as discussed above. Further, it has already been explained that the middle income section in India can mainly afford small-sized cars.

Chapter 4

Technological development of the passenger car industry (1981–2000)

The empirical analysis presented in the previous chapter suggests that the shift to a liberal economic environment with easier entry conditions for foreign firms since the early 1980s had intensified competition in the passenger car industry in India. Further, the nature of competition and underlying factors behind market restructuring were different during the 1980s and the 1990s and afterwards. During the 1980s, competition was among local firms and MUL, which was a JV, whereas, during the 1990s and afterwards, competition was largely among foreign firms. This resulted in a significant restructuring of the industry, converting it from a seller's market to a buyer's market.

This chapter aims at extending the empirical analysis to analyse the technology strategies of the passenger car firms towards technology development and technology acquisition in the context of the changing structure and the new policy regime. It is to be expected that, in response to the changes in the nature of the competition and the policy regulations, technology strategies of firms would be affected.[1] This is because the policy set-up influences the pace of technology development by affecting the incentive system and regulating the mode of technology acquisition of firms (Dahlman 1984; Lall 1987; Gumaste 1988; Narayanan 1998; Tyabji 2000).

The importance of technological development for the survival and success of firms has been well recognised in the literature (Fransman and King 1984; Lall 1992, 1996; Kathuria 1996; Tyabji 2000). First, evidence suggests that the technology base that firms develop over the years in the course of production is assumed to be a key input to compete successfully in a globalised world (Reddy 1997; Okada 2004). It allows manufacturers to offer technologically advanced products at competitive prices. Second, the firms with some level of technological capability are better able to identify the value of advanced technology and internalise that technology according to local resource conditions and market demand.[2] Scholars have observed variation across local firms in terms of diffusion of technology from foreign firms and inferred that this difference was mainly due to varying degrees of technological capabilities of local firms (Fu 2008; Blalock and Gertler 2009).

This chapter argues that India has succeeded in dealing with the stagnant-technology problem as the supply of technologically advanced cars increased considerably since the 1990s; this has happened at the expense of the development of indigenous technology and manufacturing capabilities along with the adverse BoP implications.

4.1 Analytical background

In this era of globalisation, building and maintaining technological capabilities has become a key input for firms to remain competitive in both domestic and international markets (Kim and Nelson 2000; Okada 2004). Technology is the application of scientific knowledge and skills (Lall 1987). In this study, *technological capability* is the absorption capacity or the ability to make effective use of technology. In other words, technological capability refers to the internal ability of a firm, an industry or an economy to assimilate or adapt new technologies and disseminate new technical knowledge. *Technological change* involves change, however minor, in the way in which inputs are transformed into outputs, including changes in the quality of the output (Rosenberg 1982).

It is a known fact that firms in developing countries can acquire technology through different channels.[3] Broadly, these channels are classified into three categories. First, the internal efforts through in-house R&D activities are an important source of technological development. Spending in in-house R&D activities does not only mean the production of new technology (i.e. innovation), as a large chunk of R&D spending in developing countries aims at modifying existing technology, and upgrading products and processes according to changing market needs (Gumaste 1988; Cohen and Levinthal 1989; Bell and Pavitt 1992; Ernst, Ganiatsos and Mytelke 1998; Mani 2011). Second, the imports of technology can also supplement the internal efforts of firms towards technological development. It is argued that the adaptation of imported technology in accordance with the local raw material conditions would require the same kind of technical efforts as developing new technology on their own; therefore, the importance of technological imitation in the process of technological development cannot be ignored.[4] Third, learning by doing is another way through which firms can strengthen their technological capabilities. Learning by doing is a long-run process through which firms get to know about better usage of available technology and thereby can produce more output with the same amount of resources (Bell 1984). Evidence from developing countries has strongly supported views emphasising the contribution of learning by doing in developing technological capabilities (Fransman and King 1984; Bell 1984; Lall 1984, 1987; Tyabji 2000).

The importance of building and maintaining technological capabilities through the use of imported technology in developing countries has received a lot of attention (Stewart and James 1982; Fransman and King 1984; Lall 1985; Bell and Pavitt 1993; Romijn 1997; Ernst et al., 1998; Narayanan 1998). Neoclassical theory perceives that the access to technology of a firm is a cost-less and automatic process. Technology is available at zero cost to all countries and all firms within a country. The use of technology neither requires firm-specific learning nor any kind of adaptation to internalise it in the local production process (Lall 1992). This view is not of much relevance in the real world even in relation to developing countries that have the benefit of using technological innovations already present in the developed countries. In this context, earlier studies in the context of developing countries, including India, mainly focused on (a) the transfer of technology from developed to developing countries (Pillai and Subrahmanian 1977; Pillai 1979; Ito 1985; Mohanty et al. 1994) and (b) the costs and benefits of technology transfer to the host country (Balasubramanyam 1971; Desai 1972; Subrahmanian 1972; Balasubramanyam 1973; Pillai 1979; Kumar 1985). These studies highlighted some important issues related to the use of imported technology. The imported technology is usually not completely suitable to local conditions and to the resource endowments of the recipient country, as it is originally developed under different circumstances, for different resource endowments and for different markets. As a result of this, the recipient country is unable to utilise it in efficient ways and at rated efficiency levels. This inefficiency can be reduced only through a process of adaptation of the technology to local requirements and through processes of learning by doing.

Given this, it is clear that technology is not a product that can be imported and put to use in its given form. Effort is involved in selecting the correct technology, copying, assimilation, adaptation, etc. To put it precisely, use of imported technology benefits from some firm-level technological capability and promotes that capability as a result of a continuous learning process through the activities undertaken to absorb, adapt and create new technology (Nelson and Winter 1982). Absorption requires conscious learning effort; adaptation is required to make imported technology suitable to local production scales, resource endowments, climate, skills and market needs. It may also be explained as a firm's knowledge, skill and experience required to improve upon the original performance standards of the technology in use and modify its inputs, outputs and processes in response to a changing input and product market (Bell and Pavitt 1993). Efforts at the end of firms are required in unpackaging/re-engineering, reverse engineering, analytical designing and system engineering of imported technology (Stewart and James 1982; Bell 1984; Dore 1984; Stewart 1984; Tyabji 2000). It indicates that the process of indigenisation requires long-term commitment and investment in R&D in order to bring imported technology into use in an effective way. This process ultimately strengthens the technological capabilities of firms, as minor changes could lead to a paradigmatic shift. Accordingly, the technology trajectory of the recipient firm shifts, which creates potential for further improvement in the technological capabilities. Every step towards technology absorption adds to the existing technological base of the firm.

It is worth noting that, irrespective of all the efforts of firms towards technology development, the importing firms cannot fully realise benefits of the imported technology as sellers of technology would not provide all relevant information for the full usage of technology. The technology market is far from being a competitive market (Lall 1985). Firms with a technology edge in the international market try to retain their monopoly by using this differential advantage. Thus, when the technology is licensed for use for a fee, these firms provide limited knowledge on the usage of the technology and also incorporate certain kinds of restrictions into technical collaboration agreements which constrain absorption of imported technology. In addition, it has been argued that technology has certain implicit characteristics, complete information about which is usually limited to the seller of that technology (Nelson and

Winter 1974; Stewart and James 1982). The seller has better information about the use and potential of technology than the buyer,
and this information cannot be passed on with certainty through
training, blueprints etc. As a result, the importers of technology
face various issues before putting the imported technology to use
(Lall 1996; Ernst et al. 1998). The situation can be worse when the
gap between imported technology and the technology base of host
country firms is substantially high (Kathuria 1996). This often leads
to even poorer applicability of imported technology.

With this understanding, it is clear that the process of technological development in developing countries is different from that
in developed countries. As argued in the literature, in developed
countries, technological development is often linked to product and
process innovations (Lall 1987, 1992). In developing countries,
incremental innovations are an important source of technological
development in terms of use of local materials, processes, equipment and designs (Stewart and James 1982; Bell and Pavitt 1997).
According to Rosenberg (1982), major R&D activities in developing countries are incremental in nature. These innovations are invis-
ible or low-visible[5] because incremental innovations are an addition
to existing technology in terms of downgrading technology according to local scale requirements and/or improvement of products and
processes. But these innovations could add to the competitiveness
of the manufacturing firm by reducing the cost of production. Thus,
understanding technological development only in terms of product
and process innovations may be narrow and misleading, especially
in the context of developing countries. It is argued that knowledge
may be embodied in the hardware and software, in people and
in institutionalised practices and procedures (Fransman and King
1984; Ernst et al. 1998).

Inter-Firm Variation: Technology development is influenced by
the social and economic environment that surrounds a firm (Stewart
1984). But differences in technology learning or acquisition can also
be observed among firms operating in the same industry and under
the same economic or institutional set-up. According to the neoclassical understanding, differences existing between firms were
attributable to the differences in the markets in which they operate
(Lall 1992; Narayanan 1998). Contrary to this, the evolutionary
approach of Nelson and Winter emphasises the inherent heterogeneity of firms. Irrespective of the economic and social environment,
certain differences can exist between firms in the same industry

which are associated with variation in technological capabilities that firms have developed over a period of time. The institutional set-up can influence the mode of technology import and strategies of firms or can create incentives to acquire technology, but the acquisition of technology is conditioned by the technological capabilities (or absorption capacity) of firms. The accumulation of knowledge is a highly specific process (Najmabadi and Lall 1995) and the role of firm-specific factors such as area of operation, investment on R&D, internal knowledge etc. is critical to building technological capabilities at the firm level, ceteris paribus (Ernst et al. 1998). Thus, even in the same industry, all firms do not operate on the same production frontier (Lall 1992; Kim and Nelson 2000).

The above discussion suggests that firm-specific factors and the policy environment in which firms operate contribute significantly towards technological development. Firm-specific factors (R&D and learning) add to the incremental innovations, whereas the external environment influences the incentive structure and subsequently influences the strategies of technology development. It would be useful to analyse the experience of India's passenger car industry, which was subject to varying technology regimes, based on this understanding (Narayanan 1998). As discussed in Chapter 2, the industrial sector in general and the passenger car industry in particular happened to be largely regulated by a complex web of licensing and trade policies until the 1980s. But policy changes initiated since the mid-1980s relaxed a number of restrictions on technology imports, which would have influenced the technology strategy of firms and the strategy to develop the technology capability of firms in the car industry.

4.2   Data sources and methodology

Data Sources: Empirical analysis is conducted using firm-level data mainly collected from the CMIE PROWESS electronic dataset. The information that we have collected from all data sources is related to various technology indicators, which have either direct or indirect influence on the technology acquisition and technology development strategies of firms. In the PROWESS electronic database, the data on expenditure for technology development or technology acquisition through imports are available under the following heads: (1) expenditure in in-house R&D activities and (2) expenditure on import of technology (embodied and disembodied form). In addition to this, we have also collected information related to the usage of imported raw materials. It needs to be noted that use of imported raw material may facilitate a firm's successful competition in the market by offering assembled products based on imported components and parts which are equipped with advance technology, but may not add to the local manufacturing capability as well as learning capabilities which enhance technological capabilities. The data on indigenous content and import content is available in PROWESS from 1999–2000 onwards. We have collected information for some earlier years from published research.

Selection of the Firms: This study being a comparative assessment of two policy regimes, the intention here is to select those passenger car firms for which data are available for a longer period i.e. under both the policy regimes. Until the early 1980s, only two leading manufacturers (HML and PAL) were manufacturing cars in India. In 1981, MUL entered in the industry, but production activity started in 1983. These three firms are selected for empirical analysis for the period of 1980–81 to 1990–91. As mentioned earlier, for the period since 1990 the PROWESS dataset has been used. Information on PAL is not available in PROWESS but information on HML and MUL is. Some new firms also entered the passenger car industry in the 1990s, but data is not available in PROWESS on any new firm except Daewoo Motors until 1997.[6] Most of the new entrants' data started appearing in PROWESS from 2000 onwards. Hence, the analysis of the second period is restricted up to the year 2000.

The justification for restricting the analysis of the second period up to 2000 lies in the nature of liberalisation. The policy changes experienced in the early 1990s were largely in the form of external liberalisation. The process of external liberalisation in the car industry came to a halt in 1997, when the GoI imposed restrictions on the import of certain components used in the production of cars and linked foreign entry with certain conditions (GoI 1997; Chandrasekhar 2002). The restrictions continued until March 2001. April 2001 was the period when the operating environment around the passenger car industry changed significantly along with the import and foreign investment policies. Thus, one should not treat all the policy changes after 1990 as one homogeneous type of liberalisation. The specific nature of policy changes after 2000 renders the two periods, 1991–2000 and 2000 onwards incomparable. Therefore, we intend to analyse the latter period separately in the next chapter.

Given the varying nature of liberalisation experienced by India's car industry since the early 1980s, the present study plans to analyse the influence of different forms of liberalisation on technology development. Analysis of this chapter covers the period from 1981 to 2000. It is sub-divided into two phases: (1) 1981–90 and (2) 1991–2000.

Methods Used: It is almost impossible to estimate every activity that leads to addition to the technology base of firms through quantitative indicators. Moreover, development of the technology base is not the result of only direct efforts of firms. It is also influenced by a number of indirect variables such as learning by doing, learning by innovating etc. These indirect factors are considerably influenced by the policy environment around the industrial sector because policy regimes not only influence the nature of technology import but also regulate the various aspects of collaborations, as India's experience suggests, which ultimately determines the speed of learning and the process of indigenisation.[7]

Given the availability of data, the present study uses various indicators to analyse elements of technology and changing usage of raw materials. These indicators will facilitate us in differentiating the technology acquisition strategy of firms and their strategy to develop technology. This understanding is significant because not all spending of firms on various elements of technology would lead to technology development, as manufacturing firms direct some spending towards import of technology. Import of technology can possibly be treated as a positive contributor to technology development, if increasing imports of technology are accompanied with increasing in-house R&D in order to indigenise the imported technology. In this process, the import of technology, measured in terms of expenditure, is likely to fall over a period of time. On the other hand, repeated imports of technology in various forms are a *'technology acquisition strategy'* but not a *'technology development strategy,'* as it may have adverse implications for indigenous technology development. This is so because manufacturers would remain continuously dependent on imported technology in order to exploit the local market by offering products equipped with modern technology. The growing variety of technologically advanced products would encourage those firms which were earlier performing in-house R&D to make use of imported technology in order to ensure their survival in the era of competition. In this process, the dependence on imported technology will increase and in-house

R&D is likely to fall in the following years. This is very likely in the case of India as the GoI has gradually liberalised the restrictions on the imports of technology.

The indicators discussed in what follows have been used to understand the technology development and the technology acquisition strategies of firms.

1   *Technology Intensity:* This indicator is used to provide a broader picture of the efforts of firms towards technology development/ acquisition. It is broader in the sense that it combines expenditure on both in-house R&D and imports of technology. This index will facilitate an understanding of the change in spending of firms under different policy regimes. It is calculated by dividing total expenditure on technology in all forms by total sales, multiplied by 100.[8]

This index is computed for each firm as well as jointly for all the selected firms. For the joint analysis, we have taken aggregate spending on technology of all the selected firms and divided it with aggregate sales value. In the case of individual firms, the index is calculated using variables of each firm.

2   To understand the technology strategies of firms, investment on different components of technology have been separately analysed. As mentioned earlier, in PROWESS, data related to technology is available under three sub-heads: (a) in-house R&D; (b) disembodied imports of technology and (c) imports of technology in embodied form. For the purpose, three indices have been constructed and computed both for individual firms and the industry.

a   **R&D Intensity:** It is computed by calculating spending in in-house R&D as percentage of sales value.

b   **Index of Disembodied Technology:** Expenditure on disembodied technology import includes payments in the form of royalty, fees for technical services and lump-sum payments. Disembodied technology brings technology in the form of blueprints, licensing etc. It is calculated by dividing expenditure on imports of disembodied technology by total sales, multiplied by 100.

c   **Index of Embodied Technology:** Import of embodied technology includes purchase of machinery and other capital equipment. It is considered as embodied technology because imported machinery and capital goods are generally equipped with advanced technology. Bringing these capital goods into use in the production process improves efficiency. Due to this feature, its import is termed as embodied technology imports. It is estimated by measuring expenditure on imports of capital goods as a percentage of sales value.

Based on these indicators, the present study attempts to examine the following issues: (1) the efforts of firms towards technology development/acquisition; (2) the differences in the technology development and technology strategies of firms in the same industry under the same policy regime; (3) the role of policy changes in influencing the technology strategies of firms. The quantitative information (expenditure on R&D, import of technology) will be linked with qualitative information since technology development is not only a function of direct efforts of firms, but accumulation of technology also takes place through production experience and integration with raw material suppliers.

3 **Composition of Raw Material:** This index reveals the changing composition of imported and local raw material in the production of passenger cars. It is important to assess the changing composition of raw material (domestic versus imported) used in final production because the process of indigenisation of manufacturing activity is believed to be an important source of learning for the manufacturers which ultimately plays a significant role in the process of development of a technology base. Contrary to this, the manufacturers with high usage of imported content may not positively contribute to the local technological base because the aim of these manufacturers is to: (a) exploit market potential of the host country through high usage of import content; (b) offer a wider variety of passenger vehicles. Import content is estimated by dividing expenditure on imported raw material by total expenditure on raw material (spending on indigenous and imported raw material) multiplied by 100. Indigenous content is calculated by subtracting import content from 100.

4.3 Empirical analysis

To start with, it would be significant to provide a brief background on the state of technology development that the Indian passenger car industry had achieved until the early 1980s. This would help us understand the influence of the change in policy regime on the strategy of firms to develop technology during the era of liberal trade and investment. The performance in a particular policy regime cannot be appreciated in isolation from what prevailed before.

4.3.1 State of technology until 1980

As is evident from the literature, the state and progress of technology in India's passenger car industry during the first three decades of India's independence was poor. Scholars have identified the industry as one of the technology-stagnant industries (Dore 1984; Narayana 1989; Mohanty et al. 1994; Kathuria 1996; Narayanan 1998; Pingle 1999; Tyabji 2000; Sagar and Chandra 2004; Singh 2004; Pradhan and Singh 2008; Ranawat and Tiwari 2009). It was argued that this technological stagnancy was the net outcome of a complex set of developments. First, the car industry had performed significantly well on the front of indigenisation, as firms had replicated imported models of passenger cars almost with 100 per cent local content until the early 1970s. The process of replication obviously contributed to the firm's learning capability, which is a by-product of production experience (Lall 1986, 1987). However, once they replicated early models produced with local content, the old manufacturers in the car industry (HML and PAL) did not make any serious attempts to upgrade those models in line with changing consumer choices in the country and growing availability of technically advanced cars in the international market. Instead, until the early 1980s these firms were supplying the same models of cars (with just some cosmetic changes) that they had acquired from international firms under technology collaborations in the 1950s. Second, the poor efforts towards technology development are also evident as the resources diverted towards in-house R&D by incumbent firms were almost negligible (Gumaste 1988; Narayana 1989; Mohanty et al. 1994). Whenever these firms had undertaken in-house R&D, the only motive was to resolve problems in the process of indigenisation or for the specific purpose of making Western technology suitable to Indian conditions (Narayanan 2006). According to Mohanty et al. (1994) these firms had intensified their efforts towards technology development and started formal in-house R&D on a continuous basis only after the entry of MUL into the car industry. In the middle of the 1980s, the R&D intensity of HML and PAL was as low as below 0.5 per cent and 1 per cent of sales value respectively, whereas the R&D intensity of international firms belonging to USA and Japan varied between 3 to 5 per cent of sales value in the late 1970s (Table A.4 in annexure). The huge gap in R&D spending between Indian firms and firms from developed countries indicates that technology in India was far behind the latest technology available in the international market at that time.

This evidence raises the question as to why old firms operating in India's car industry until the early 1980s did not upgrade technology and introduce new models over a period of approximately three decades. To attempt an answer, two sets of issues have been analysed based on the existing literature. First, an attempt is made to understand the long-term strategies of firms with regard to technology development as well as technology acquisition. Second, the development of the car industry and the incentive structure provided by the policy environment is also discussed.

To start with, as argued in the literature, India's automobile industry was developed in isolation from the international market, as the government granted near complete protection by imposing a ban on imported vehicles along with restrictions on the entry of foreign investors. Further, the mandatory requirement of industrial licensing under the IDRA 1951 ruled out the possibility of new entry and the product-specific licensing policy, which was implemented with the onset of the 1957 foreign exchange constraint, eliminated the chances of competition among existing manufacturers in the industry as one manufacturer was permitted to produce only one type of model against a specific license. This implied that firms were required to get additional licenses to produce a different product. As a result of such regulations, competition was muted in India's car industry and manufacturers enjoyed a captive domestic market for their products without any potential threat. Given the absence of any potential threat, the manufacturing firms neither had any incentive nor showed any willingness to develop technology as it involved risk and resources (Venkataramani 1990; Kathuria 1996; Narayanan 1998; Gulyani 2001; Saripalle 2012). According to available accounts, the absence of competition was one of the most significant factors behind the technology stagnancy observed by this industry over a period of almost three decades (World Bank 1987; Gumaste 1988; Narayana, Mridul and Chandan 1992; Kathuria 1996; Pingle 1999; Narayanan 2004; Singh 2004). It is competition that pressures business firms to continuously upgrade their technology in line with the changing nature of demand within the economy and in the international market in order to stay competitive. In a competitive market, a manufacturer will go out of business if it offers products equipped with outdated technology.

Instead of developing technological capability, the passenger car manufacturers in India were involved in unproductive activities that added to the inefficiency. The passenger car firms (HML and PAL) were controlled by the influential business groups of that time. These business houses were generally involved in influencing the state policies to their favour due to their nexus with political leaders (Frankel 1978; Chenoy 2015; Tyabji 2015).

Further, these manufacturers were not making an effective utilisation of licensed capacity. The installed capacity of these manufacturers remained below licensed capacity even when the demand for cars outstripped its supply (Narayana 1989; Kujal 1996).[9] Maintaining large excess demand was a well-planned strategy of the car manufacturers because it permitted manufacturers to sell cars with outdated technology and also allowed them to extract quasi-rents. Existence of large premiums created a deep vested incentive for shortages to persist.[10]

Thus, it is worth highlighting the fact that the government's policies had a lot to do with the poor conditions of the industry as the government could not discipline the manufacturers. Instead of disciplining the manufacturers and pressuring them to make an effective use of allocated capacity in order to increase output, the focus of the government was mainly placed on administering the prices and strictly regulating the imports of technology as the government branded cars as a wasteful luxury (World Bank 1987; Pingle 1999). The government classified the passenger car industry in that group of industries where neither technical nor financial collaboration was permitted after the mid-1960s until the late 1970s. Inflexibility in the government's policies with regard to technology imports is clear from the fact that, while car manufacturers approached the government several times during the 1960s and 1970s for permission to enter into technical collaborations with foreign firms with a view to upgrading the technology of cars, the government turned down their request every time.

Given the discussion, it is clear that the car manufacturers did not have any strategy to develop technological capability until the early 1980s. Once the passenger car manufacturers replicated the imported models with local raw material they did not make any attempt (through R&D spending) to upgrade their technology base.

If the car manufacturers thought at all of upgrading the existing models, their strategy was to acquire technology from international firms through technical collaborations, which the government did not allow, rather than to upgrade models through in-house R&D. Hence, the technology in the car industry remained stagnant until the entry of MUL. It indicates that manufacturers did not make any attempt to develop technology within the country.

These developments had not only placed the Indian passenger car industry several decades behind international technology standards, but the prices of passenger cars were also much higher than international prices of same product (Venkataramani 1990). As stated by an Ad Hoc committee appointed by the government in 1960 that

> if all the services performed within the Hindustan Motors Ltd. were free of any payment . . ., if no provision had to be made on account of depreciation of machinery, and investors got no returns for their money whatever the reduction in the consumer price of the Hindustan cars would be about 30 per cent and the vehicle would still be not cheaper than the Morris Oxford is in the U.K.
>
> (GoI 1960: 20)

It is worth pointing out that the difference in prices was the result of a number of factors, not all of which were under the control of the manufacturers. The high price of automobiles in India was largely caused by the sub-optimal scales of production[11] and the high tax imposed by the government in order to discourage luxury consumption.[12] It was also due to the unwillingness of manufacturers to upgrade technology which ultimately reduces the cost of production.

4.3.2 Technology development from 1981 to 2000

The modernisation of the passenger car industry was critical to improving fuel efficiency as continuous oil shocks experienced by the global economy during the 1970s had adversely affected the BoP of oil importing countries including India (Ahluwalia 1986; Karmokolias 1990; Jalan 1991). Given this, emphasis was placed on improving the fuel efficiency of motor vehicles. Accordingly, the GoI considerably liberalised the imports of technology and provided a number of incentives to encourage in-house R&D under its technology policy of 1983 along with allowing new entry into the industry. It was expected that the firms arrive at a balance between in-house R&D and imports of technology which would facilitate the development of indigenous technological capability. Accordingly, it was hoped that the technology stagnancy would end and, subsequently, manufacturers would supply technologically advanced vehicles in the country. To what extent did India succeed in modernising its industry and developing local technology under liberal policy regime? What are the costs and benefits of a liberal policy regime for indigenisation? The following analysis is aimed at analysing these issues.

Technology Intensity: Table 4.1 provides a broad picture of the trends in the technology intensity of passenger car firms and the industry as a whole. Figures on average technology intensity suggest that total spending on technology witnessed a sharp increase after the mid-1980s. During the period1980–81 to 1984–85, average technology intensity was just 2.72 (i.e. 2.72 per cent of total sales turnover) for all firms taken together and then it jumped sharply to 10.90 in the following five years (1985–86 to 1990–91). Not just average, the individual spending on technology by each firm also increased steadily. A much faster increase was observed in the case of PAL, the technology intensity of which rose from 3.66 in 1980–81 to 1984–85 to 27.33 in the following five years. Even after spending so much on technology, PAL could not survive in the phase of intense competition and finally disappeared from India's car industry in the 1990s.

Table 4.1 also indicates that during the 1990s, there were variations in terms of spending of firms towards technology development and acquisition. For instance, technology spending of HML varied between 1 per cent of sales turnover to 5 per cent during the 1990s, whereas in the case of MUL, technology spending varied between 1 to 12 per cent of sales turnover. The five-year average suggests that spending of HML and MUL fluctuated around 2 per cent and 5 per cent of sales turnover, respectively, during the 1990s. A new entrant during the 1990s, Daewoo Motors, spent as much as 62.38 per cent of total sales turnover on technology acquisition and development during the second half of the 1990s. In general, this provides a hint that the spending of firms on technology remained substantial after the country relaxed its regulatory environment.

It is worth noting that Table 4.1 presents only a broad overview of the behaviour of firms related to spending on technology under

Table 4.1 Technology intensity of car firms (percentages)

Year	HML	PAL*	MUL	Daewoo Motors	Average of selected firms
1989–90	1.11		1.04	–	1.07
1990–91	2.32	–	3.52	–	3.17
1991–92	5.12	–	2.91	–	3.28
1992–93	1.12	–	8.24	–	6.51
1993–94	1.01	–	11.63	–	9.12
1994–95	1.08	–	1.56	10.77	1.71
1995–96	1.24	–	3.94	5.14	3.63
1996–97	1.10	–	0.91	200.41	19.87
1997–98	3.87	–	2.04	35.02	3.54
1998–99	2.52	–	5.19	42.55	6.17
1999–2000	0.88	–	10.33	1.63	7.98
Average technology intensity					
1980–81 to 1984–85	2.19	3.66	–	–	2.72
1985–86 to 1990–91	3.17	27.33	7.64	–	10.90
1990–91 to 1994–95	1.92	–	5.40	–	4.60
1995–96 to 1999–2000	1.86	–	4.71	62.38	8.36

Source: CMIE PROWESS 4.14; Mohanty et al. (1994), Narayanan (1998, 1999).

Notes
(1) Due to non-availability of firm-level data with CMIE before 1989, the evidence for the period of 1980–81 to 1989–90 has been taken from the existing literature.
(2) * PAL data is not available with CMIE PROWESS.
(3) – indicates non-availability of data.

different policy regimes, in the presence of foreign competition. To analyse the differences in the nature and mode of technology acquisition of firms under a changing regulatory environment, we have further analysed the trends in investment of the selected firms related to various elements of technology acquisition and development. As mentioned in the section setting the analytical background, under the liberal policy regime, firms can either develop technology through in-house R&D or acquire it from the international market. The spending in in-house R&D not only adds to new technological capability but also facilitates absorption, assimilation and upgradation of imported technology. In the long run, it minimises the dependence on imported technology and such behaviour can be termed as the technology development behaviour of firms. On the contrary, imports of technology may not add to technology development if firms are repeatedly using imported technology and such behaviour can be termed as the technology acquisition strategy of firms. To understand the difference in technology acquisition strategy and efforts to develop indigenous technology, we now perform a disaggregated analysis for the 1980s and 1990s.

Disaggregated Analysis:Table 4.2 shows R&D intensity of the selected passenger car firms. It suggests that spending in in-house

Table 4.2 R&D intensity of car firms (percentages)

Year	HML	PAL*	MUL	Daewoo Motors	Average of selected firms
1983–84	0.11	1.30	–	–	0.54
1985–86	0.29	0.72	–	–	0.47
1986–87	0.36	0.92	0.12	–	0.36
1987–88	0.42	0.63	0.11	–	0.31
1988–89	0.38	0.72	0.06	–	0.31
1989–90	0.29	0.48	0.04	–	0.21
1990–91	0.27	1.30	0.36	–	0.36
1991–92	0.40	2.00	0.32	–	0.34
1992–93	0.45	1.20	0.26	–	0.33
1993–94	0.41	–	0.20	–	0.25
1994–95	0.42	–	0.17	0.06	0.16
1995–96	0.42	–	0.11	0.03	0.15
1996–97	0.34	–	0.14	0.07	0.16
1997–98	0.56	–	0.13	1.00	0.22
1998–99	0.53	–	0.15	1.95	0.28
1999–2000	0.35	–	0.22	0.44	0.26
Average R&D intensity					
1985–86 to 1989–90	0.35	0.65	0.09**	–	0.30
1990–91 to 1994–95	0.39	–	0.22	–	0.26
1995–96 to 1999–2000	0.43	–	0.15	0.52	0.22

Source: CMIE PROWESS 4.12 and 4.14; Gumaste (1988), Mohantyet al. (1994).

Notes
(1) Same as Table 4.1.
(2) ** indicates average for 1986–87 to 1989–90.

R&D activities of firms remained very low throughout the reference period and further declined during the 1990s as compared to the1980s. In general, it varied between 0.2 and 0.5 per cent of sales turnover. The interesting case here is MUL, the market leader with more than 75 per cent market share during the second half of the 1990s. The firm has not only invested the lowest percentage of resources among all selected firms but also decreased its investment on R&D during the late 1990s. Its investment in in-house R&D decreased from 0.22 per cent of sales (1990–91 to 1994–95) to as low as 0.15 per cent (1995–96 to 1999–2000). The behaviour of the market leader and in general low investment on R&D by all the firms indicate that, under the changing policy environment, firms had no strategy to develop indigenous technology. The trends illustrated in Tables 4.3 and 4.4 indicate that, in general, firms incurred

Table 4.3 Import of disembodied technology of car firms (% of sales)

Year	HML	PAL*	MUL	Daewoo Motors	Average of selected firms
1989–90	0.57	–	0.68	–	0.64
1990–91	0.62	–	0.80	–	0.75
1991–92	0.69	–	0.94	–	0.88
1992–93	0.65	–	1.27	–	1.12
1993–94	0.53	–	0.58	–	0.57
1994–95	0.47	–	0.35	0.89	0.39
1995–96	0.58	–	0.37	0.01	0.37
1996–97	0.47	–	0.44	0.00	0.40
1997–98	0.69	–	1.23	0.66	1.14
1998–99	0.68	–	1.44	0.70	1.29
1999–2000	0.49	–	1.81	0.46	1.47
Average import of disembodied technology					
1980–81 to 1984–85	1.17	2.17	–	–	1.53
1985–86 to 1990–91	0.60	0.88	2.64	–	1.64
1990–91 to 1994–95	0.57	–	0.71	–	0.68
1995–96 to 1999–2000	0.58	–	1.12	0.31	0.98

Source: Same as Table 4.1.

Note: Same as Table 4.1.

Table 4.4 Import of embodied technology of car firms (% of sales)

Year	HML	PAL*	MUL	Daewoo Motors	Average of selected firms
1989–90	0.49	–	0.17	–	0.28
1990–91	1.44	–	2.32	–	2.06
1991–92	4.03	–	1.64	–	2.21
1992–93	0.02	–	6.67	–	5.05
1993–94	0.07	–	10.85	–	8.05
1994–95	0.19	–	1.10	9.82	1.17
1995–96	0.24	–	3.46	5.10	3.11
1996–97	0.29	–	0.34	200.33	19.31
1997–98	2.62	–	0.67	33.36	2.18
1998–99	1.31	–	3.60	39.90	4.60
1999–2000	0.05	–	8.30	0.73	6.25
Average import of embodied technology					
1980–81 to 1984–85	0.86	0.69	–	–	0.80
1985–86 to 1990–91	2.35	25.60	4.90	–	8.95
1990–91 to 1994–95	0.95	–	4.47	–	3.71
1995–96 to 1999–2000	0.85	–	3.44	61.74	7.19

Source: Same as Table 4.2.

Note: Same as Table 4.1.

more expenditure on disembodied and embodied modes of technology acquisition as compared to in-house R&D. Average spending of all firms on imports of disembodied technology during the 1980s was more than 1.5 per cent of sales turnover, which declined to below 1 per cent in the 1990s but still remained higher than the corresponding figure for R&D investment (Tables 4.2 and 4.3).

Import of technology was not only in disembodied form. Firms imported technology in the form of capital goods and machinery as well, which is termed embodied technology imports. The removal of restrictions on the imports of capital goods encouraged manufacturers to import machinery and other capital goods which are equipped with advanced technology (Joseph and Veeramani 2001). The spending on this form of technology has been quite significant since the mid-1980s and generally remained higher than disembodied technology imports (Table 4.4). The high spending on different forms of import of technology indicates that the dependence on technology imports of firms has not only increased in the initial years of the post-reform period to cope-up with the changing situation but became a persistent feature. This evidence suggests that firms were repeatedly importing technology.

The evidence presented in Tables 4.3 and 4.4 measures the dependence of selected passenger car firms on technology imports. The behaviour of firms varied significantly over time. In the case of HML and PAL, from 1980–81 to 1984–85, average expenditure on disembodied imports was higher than in the next period i.e. 1985–86 to 1990–91 whereas average expenditure on import of embodied technology was very minimal until the mid-1980s. For instance, HML and PAL spent 1.17 per cent and 2.17 per cent of total sales value, respectively, during the period 1980–81 to 1984–85 on imports of disembodied technology, whereas in the same period these two firms invested 0.86 per cent and 0.69 per cent, respectively, on the imports of embodied technology (Tables 4.3 and 4.4). However, the import of embodied capital increased suddenly during the second half of the 1980s. Average spending of PAL increased to around 25 per cent of total sales turnover for the period1985–86 to 1990–91. Not only this, the new entrant of the 1980s, MUL, also invested substantial resources on embodied technology (Tables 4.3 and 4.4).

The possible reason for the high imports of disembodied technology by HML and PAL in the early 1980s was an absence of access to imported technology until the early 1980s. As mentioned earlier, HML and PAL were selling technologically obsolete models of passenger cars until the 1980s as the government did not permit them to import technology. The relaxations announced in the 1980s suddenly provided an opportunity to these firms to technologically upgrade their products through technical licensing agreements with foreign firms. Accordingly, they signed a number of technical agreements with foreign firms during the first half of the 1980s, which directly added to disembodied technology imports of the firms. Forming a series of technical agreements with foreign firms was a technology acquisition strategy of the manufacturers in order to improve their competitiveness in line with emerging market conditions. MUL's entry in the early 1980s posed strong competition to and marginalised the indigenous firms in their market position by offering low priced and fuel efficient cars in India. Therefore, besides upgrading the technology of existing passenger car models, HML and PAL also introduced a number of new technologically advanced passenger cars until the middle of the decade with a view to maintaining their position in the market. For instance, HML launched Contessa in January 1984 and then Contessa Classic in 1985. Similarly, PAL's technology tie-up with Fiat in 1981 and with Nissan in 1986 resulted in the introduction of new products in the car market. Due to these numerous technical agreements, the import payments for disembodied capital in the form of technical fees and licensing increased and remained high in the early 1980s. This increase in technology payments without a corresponding increase in R&D, however, does not mean that the technology capability of the passenger car industry was improving, because these firms used import of technology as a preventive strategy in order to save their market position. These firms did not increase their R&D spending in the wake of growing imports of technology when in-house R&D was critical to the process of indigenisation and assimilation of imported technology.

However, the imports of embodied technology sharply increased during the second half of the 1980s. The changing nature of technology imports (i.e. from disembodied to embodied) is largely associated with the changes in state policy. In the middle of the 1980s, along with the announcement of its minimum economic scale scheme wherein manufacturers were encouraged to increase production capacity, the government also eased the restrictions on the imports of capital goods as it expanded the OGL list and reduced the tariff rates (Joseph and Veeramani 2001; Panagariya 2004). Given this, the manufacturers imported large volumes of capital goods in order to build a modern manufacturing base. Accordingly, PAL increased its production capacity from 28,600 to 50,000 units of vehicles per annum. Similarly, HML expanded production capacity through high imports of capital goods. Due to this, the spending of firms especially PAL drastically increased in the form of embodied capital. These imports in the second half of the 1980s led to a sharp increase in the payments for embodied technology.

Post 1990: The distinguishing feature noticed during the 1990s is that the spending of MUL and Daewoo Motors, the new entrant during the 1990s, for technology imports was huge whereas the spending of HML initially declined but again marginally increased in the late 1990s (Tables 4.1, 4.3 and 4.4). For instance, average spending of MUL during the 1990s for the imports of embodied technology fluctuated around 4 per cent of sales. In the case of Daewoo, the spending on imports of embodied technology during the second half of the 1990s was as high as 61.74 per cent of sales (Tables 4.3 and 4.4). Such large dependence of these firms on technology imports was motivated by the desire to exploit the pre-existing pent-up demand in the car industry.

The policy changes of the 1990s released the pent-up demand that had accumulated and remained unrealised under the protective policy regime that existed until the early 1990s. The release of this pent-up demand due to the liberalisation process initiated in the early 1990s is manifested in terms of high production growth observed by the passenger car industry during the 1990s. In this period (1993–94 to 1999–2000), the car industry in India grew at a rate of 18.58 per cent per annum. Within this period, the growth during the initial four years of liberalisation was quite high as compared to the following four years. For instance, in the second period (1996–97 to 1999–2000), growth was 12.31 per cent per annum whereas growth was as high as above 23 per cent in the early years (1992–93 to 1995–96). This difference indicates that it was the pent-up demand that boosted growth in the early years. Once that demand had been met, the industry experienced a fall in its growth rate.

To exploit the growing market, Daewoo expanded production capacity as it was new in the industry. By the late 1990s, the production capacity of this firm increased to 87,000 units. Correspondingly, the firm had signed a number of agreements with international automotive component vendors in order to ensure supply of components and parts (*The Economic Times* 1997). As a result of this, the firm introduced a number of import-intensive cars in the market during the late 1990s. The company initially launched the Cielo range of cars (Cielo, Cielo GLX and Cielo GLE) in July 1995 and then entered into the small car market. It launched a small car, Matiz, in October 1998 and a mid-size car, Nexia, in April 1999. In addition, the company also upgraded its existing products and increased their variety (Cielo's upgraded version – GLX a luxury model of Cielo). Evidence indicates that the share of imported components in Daewoo's products in the early years of its entry ranged between 83 to 85 per cent of the total value of vehicles (Okada 2004). The high import content was composed not only of components but of SKD/CKD kits too. This was to be expected since, as a result of a change in policy, Daewoo signed an MoU with the government that allowed it to import CKD/SKD kits to manufacture small car (Matiz) for the Indian market. Daewoo Motors was the third JV to sign an MoU with the Indian government. The actions of Daewoo Motors led to another development in the industry. The firm's entry in the market and introduction of new cars in different segments of the industry, including a small car (namely, Matiz), directly challenged the market leadership of MUL which remained unchallenged before that. To compete with the new entrant, MUL followed an aggressive strategy that required it to introduce a number of new cars (Esteem, Upgraded model of Maruti 800, Zen etc.) during the second half of the 1990s. To launch new cars, MUL had to spend a large volume of resources on technology imports both in embodied and disembodied forms (Tables 4.3 and 4.4). This is the main reason why MUL recorded a sharp rise in the imports of disembodied technology in the late 1990s as compared to the early 1990s. Similarly, HML also launched Opel Astra for Indian consumers by forming a JV with General Motors. Further, in 1998, HML entered into a technological tie-up with Mitsubishi Motors Corporation to produce Mitsubishi products (Lancer, Pajero, Cedia, Montero, Outlander and Evo X).

From the above discussion, it can be concluded that, in the changing economic environment, (1) the passenger car manufacturers did not have any strategy to develop technology indigenously. The car manufacturers have repeatedly depended on imported technology in different forms. The repeated imports of technology without any increase in in-house R&D reflected the strategy of car firms to exploit the pent-up demand accumulated under the restricted policy environment by launching a variety of technologically advanced passenger cars in different segments. This was especially true of MUL and Daewoo Motors. (2) The transition was visible in the case of the indigenous firms as well. These firms not only signed a number of JVs with international firms but the nature of JVs also changed from technical (in the 1980s) to both technical and financial in the 1990s. This transition noticed in the case of indigenous firms was from one aimed at developing technology indigenously to one seeking to flood the domestic market with modern cars in order to prevent market loss by using international brand names, irrespective of the implications for the BoP of the country. Hence, it can be argued that the policy changes did resolve the technology problem as the supply of cars equipped with latest technology increased. This happened at the expense of indigenous manufacturing and technological capability. It implied that the government did not succeed in changing the strategies and motives of firms even after introducing a series of regulatory relaxations/changes during the second half of the 1990s.

Indirect Imports of Technology: It is evident that firms in the car industry are increasingly relying on technology imports in the post-reform period. It remains to be seen whether firms have increased or decreased dependence on imported components and parts as well. This is important because technology imports include imports not only of embodied and disembodied technology but of components and raw materials as well. Increasing reliance on imported components also would mean that indigenous technology is not developing because, as argued in the literature, technology improvement in the automobile industry is associated not only with vehicle manufacturers but also with the level of technological advancement in the manufacture of components and raw materials used in the manufacture of finished vehicles (Karmokolias 1990; Khare 1997; Okada 2004; Parhi 2008).[13] The analysis in the previous chapter clearly indicated that, with the change in policy regime, it became difficult for old manufacturers to retain their market share and for new entrants to get a reasonable share in the market. In the case of firms with a small market share as well as new entrants, it can be expected that the growing intensity of competition and rapidly increasing variety of technologically advanced cars would have forced them to increase imports of components and raw material. For small firms, this is expected because ancillary production realises economies of scale at a very large volume of production (Narayana 1989; Karmokolias 1990). So, a small market share in passenger car production would limit upstream demand and not permit ancillary firms to achieve economies of scale. Due to this, it is difficult for these manufacturers to convince ancillary firms to develop components and parts according to their requirements, as production of a new kind of component would involve huge costs. On the other hand, firms with large market size can easily make the ancillary manufacturers meet their requirements. Given this, the manufacturers with small market shares face challenges to procure required components at minimum cost. Further, technology and design in the passenger car industry change frequently. The changes in design require new kinds of components. Established firms that have already developed networks with ancillary units[14] have captive suppliers who, generally, prefer not to manufacture for firms outside the network, especially for small-sized manufacturers. Networking helps ancillary units because they can get technological support from assembling units, because help from assembling units facilitates entry into new components production, which adds to learning, and networking with large firms reduces market risk.

Other than industry-specific factors, the changing policy environment since the early 1990s involved a number of relaxations on imports, which would have encouraged imports of raw material and components (Kesavan 2001; Panagariya 2004). For instance, out of 5021 H.S. Tariff lines (6 digits), in July 1991, 4000 lines (80%) were subject to import licensing. By December 1995, more than 3000 tariff lines covering raw materials, intermediates and capital goods were made free from the import licensing requirement (GoI 1996–97). In addition, the government reduced the excise duty from 66 per cent in 1991–92 to 40 per cent in 1993–94 and import duties on CKD to 50 per cent in the middle of the 1990s (Mukherjee and Sastry 1996).

Table 4.5 presents the trends in usage of raw materials and components for the period 1980–81 to 2000–01. In general, it is observed that the policy changes during the 1980s and afterwards halted the process of indigenisation of manufacturing activities, which was the core objective of policy measures initiated in the 1950s. This is evident from the rising share of the imported raw material in total raw material consumption (Table 4.5). Old established firms, which had successfully indigenised production activities to the extent of nearly 100 per cent during the 1970s, also increased the import content in final vehicle manufacturing (Table 4.5). For instance, in 1989–90 the import content of HML and PAL increased to 41.1 per cent and 22 per cent, respectively. The primary reason behind the increasing usage of imported raw material was fresh collaborations and the subsequent introduction of new types of modern cars by HML and PAL.

Contrary to the experience of HML and PAL, the new entrant in the car industry of the 1980s, MUL, increased the local content of its products. Local content increased from just 14.7 per cent in 1984–85 to 60.5 per cent in 1989–90. However, it is worth noting that the growing indigenisation in the case of MUL was an outcome of the agreement signed between the GoI and Suzuki (Japan) at the time of formation of the JV. As per the agreement, the management of MUL was expected to indigenise its vehicle components to the extent of 95 per cent by 1988–89 (Venkataramani 1990). Relative to this, the process of indigenisation achieved was well below the target.[15]

Table 4.5 Trends in imported and indigenous content (percentages)

Year	HML		PAL*		MUL		Daewoo Motors	
	Import	Indigenous	Import	Indigenous	Import	Indigenous	Import	Indigenous
1980–81	30.12	69.88	18	82	–	–	–	–
1984–85	34.59	65.41	19	81	85.3	14.7	–	–
1989–90	41.10	58.90	22	78	39.5	60.5	–	–
2000–01	47.95	52.05	–	–	33.23	66.77	58.60	41.4

Source: Same as Table 4.2.

Notes
(1) Same as Table 4.1.
(2) CMIE PROWESS provides data on indigenous and import content from 1999–2000 onwards.

Post 1990: MUL continuously reduced its usage of imported raw material, whereas other manufacturers increased the import content in the production of their vehicles (Table 4.5). In actual fact, MUL attracted large ancillary units into India during the 1980s to procure components and other raw materials from within India (D'Costa 2005; Singh 2015). Hence, imports of MUL got converted into domestic procurement and showed up in increasing indigenisation. Further, the market share of MUL was very large so as to allow indigenisation of production of components without fear of raising costs. As argued in the literature, there is a trade-off between indigenisation of production activities and the costs of production (Baranson 1968; Agarwal 1987). It is true especially in those cases where production size is small. As Narayana (1989: 4) argues,

> though many of the developing countries may reap economies by setting up vehicle assembly units of relatively smaller sizes, it becomes an entirely different matter when they proceed to indigenise the production of components; for it is then that the economies involved in forging, casting and pressing become incompatible with the smaller scales.

So, if other manufacturers such as HML and PAL with a small market share would have manufactured internally, then, first, they would not have been on par with international standards and, second, indigenisation of production activities would have raised their costs of production. To maintain their position (which got weakened with the entry of new firms), these manufacturers were forced to manufacture technologically advanced products at low prices. They could achieve this objective by importing components and raw material. Increase in import content is reflected in the continuously declining share of indigenous raw material so much so that in 2000–01, HML was using 47.95 per cent of imported content in the production of its cars. Similarly, the new entrant of the 1990s, Daewoo Motors, with a small market share was also heavily depending on import content (58.60 per cent).

This suggests that it is not only the direct import of technology which increased after liberalisation, but indirect dependence in the form of imports of components and parts also increased as HML and PAL continuously increased the usage of imported raw material and the other two JVs also significantly depended on imported components, CKD kits and technology both to launch new cars and upgrade existing ones. This would mean that the move towards a liberal policy has adversely affected technology development in the automobile industry in India and defeated the efforts to develop a truly indigenous industry.

4.4   Why indigenous car manufacturers could not survive: a discussion

One important question arises as to why indigenous firms could not maintain their position even after a series of collaborations with foreign firms? Research in India's context argues that the restrictive policy environment adopted in India up to the 1980s did not provide the incentives needed for these firms to develop their technological base (Dore 1984; Agarwal 1987; Narayana 1989; Narayana et al. 1992; Mohanty et al. 1994; Kathuria 1996; Narayanan 1998, 2001, 2004; Sagar and Chandra 2004). But this argument may not be completely true, as India has succeeded in developing a diversified industrial base as well as achieving an edge in technology in a number of industries primarily due to the indigenisation policy and other protective measures initiated in the early decades of India's independence (Lall 1984, 1987; Chandrasekhar 1999; Pingle 1999). Even within the automobile industry, Indian firms (such as Tata, M&M; Bajaj, Punjab Tractor etc.) developed remarkably good manufacturing and technological capabilities during the phase of indigenisation. Thus, the varying performance of firms within the automobile industry suggests that the policy regulations are not the only ones to be blamed. Besides the policy regime, there might be some firm-specific factors which would have played a critical role in the success or failure of firms. According to Nelson and Winter (1982), certain differences can exist between firms in the same industry under the same economic environment which are associated with variation in technological capabilities which firms had acquired over a period of time. This is the 'evolutionary approach' of Nelson and Winter, which emphasises the inherent heterogeneity among firms.

To understand the role of firm-specific factors, it is important to understand the efforts of these firms towards technological development in an evolutionary perspective. The emergence of a technological base is the outcome of systematic efforts of a firm over a long period of time.[16] Bell, Scott-Kemmis and Satyarakwit (1982) argue that systematic efforts of firms towards technology development include gaining experience through production (learning-by-doing) and by accumulating other technical knowledge.[17] In their view, learning through experience in production is important in the process of technical change, but it remains inadequate on its own. This argument is further supported by Tyabji (2000) with evidence from Indian industry. Tyabji (2000) analysed the process of industrialisation and innovation in India and supported the above view by highlighting two characteristics of firm-level technology development: (1) learning to make and (2) learning to make better. According to Tyabji (2000: 86), 'there is a difference between the expertise required to make a commodity and that needed to make it better or cheaper, i.e., innovate.' Learning to make is a function of time, with automatic additions to knowledge through production experiments, whereas learning to make better requires resources and long-term commitment from the organisation.

Given this understanding, it is interesting to note that firms which manufactured passenger cars (HML and PAL) in India before 1980 succeeded in *'learning to make'* (experience of production), which was evident from the degree of indigenisation of components and other raw materials used in the manufacture of passenger cars (Table 2.4 in Chapter 2). But, these firms did not do well in terms of developing knowledge from other sources especially through in-house R&D (World Bank 1987; Gumaste 1988; Narayana 1989; Kujal 1996; Tyabji 2000; Pradhan and Singh 2008). The investment in in-house R&D of passenger car firms was almost absent until the entry of MUL (Gumaste 1988; Mohantyet al. 1994). If these firms had undertaken R&D at all that was purpose-specific in order to resolve particular problems. On the other hand, international firms had achieved an edge in technology by investing large resources in in-house R&D. For instance, investment in R&D by General Motors and Ford Motors was 3.9 per cent and 4.5 per cent, respectively, of total sales turnover in the 1980s. Similarly, R&D investment of Japanese manufacturers ranged between 2.9 to 4.0 per cent of total sales turnover (Table A.4 in annexure).

This suggests that, due to the imbalance between the two elements of knowledge development (learning and other sorts of technical knowledge), old established firms failed to exploit the technological base developed through production experience. The inadequate technological base pushed these firms into a series of technical agreements with foreign firms in the 1980s and JVs with foreign firms in the 1990s to defend their market position. As argued in the literature, such technology strategies would ultimately fail in the absence of local technological capabilities. It happens even in the phase when imports of technology are free since, in the absence of local capabilities, imported technology cannot be fully exploited. Lack of absorption becomes clear from the fact that: (1) these firms continuously depended on foreign firms either in the name of technical assistance or financial JVs either to marginally upgrade the existing products or to launch new products; and (2) all the designs of cars offered by HML and PAL were acquired from international partners, and this remains true for HML till recently (for instance, HML recently developed SUVs and cars based on models from Mitsubishi). This implies that, even after sixty years of production experience, the old indigenous firms did not develop indigenous design capability.

Based on the above discussion, one can argue that, along with the policy environment, factors internal to manufacturers also play an important role in the development of the technology base of firms. It was the internal efforts of this firm that differentiated it from its counterparts in India under the same policy regime.

But one should not also conclude that the policy regime around the industrial sector was not at all responsible for the demise of a number of car manufacturing firms. It is worth noting that the regulatory policy regime failed to achieve its desired goals on many other fronts (Chandrasekhar 1994; Pingle 1999). One of the main reasons was that leading industrialists enjoyed a close relationship with the national leadership during the independence struggle and even after that (Pingle 1999; Frankel 1978, 2004; Tyabji 2015). Due to the nexus between national leaders and leading industrialists, government decisions, in general, were influenced by industrialists, which would have obviously affected the long-term objectives of policy. Not only this, the leading industrial groups were operating in almost all categories of business (Hazari 1966). In the words of Chandrasekhar (1999: 230) 'the representative unit of Indian oligopoly was most often composed of a number of legally independent firms, operating in completely unrelated areas, that were controlled by a single, central decision-making authority.' This happened because the government was not able to discipline the manufacturers in line with the overall objectives of the policy for the economy.

In sum, changing policy regimes played a considerable role in influencing the technology strategies of firms. This conclusion is significant, because after 2000, there were major changes in the policy environment. The chapter that follows examines the influence of these developments on technology acquisition and the technological development strategies of firms in the passenger car industry after 2000.

Notes

1 Basant (1997: 1683), 'It is widely recognised now that a firm's technology strategy is influenced by the "technology regime" in which it operates. The regime is broadly defined by a combination of variables capturing industrial structure, nature of technical knowledge (e.g., complexity and cumulativeness of the relevant together) and the policy environment.'

2 Scott-Kemmis and Bell (1988) argued that technological capabilities are critical not only to acquire technology but also to understand know-why character in contrast to know-how.

3 For a detailed discussion on various sources of technology, see studies by Lall (1987, 1992), Ernst, Ganiatsos and Mytelke (1998), Narayanan (1998), Mani (2011), Kale (2012).

4 Kale and Little (2007) highlighted the case of India's pharmaceutical industry and stated that imitation and reverse engineering played a key role in developing basic technological capabilities. By developing new processes, firms manufactured patent protected medicines at lower prices. This study, thus, argues that the firms in developing countries can acquire technological capabilities through learning and imitation processes.

5 Incremental innovations are neither published and patented nor formally recognised even within the innovating firm (Lall 1982; Rosenberg 1982).
6 During the 1980s, HML, PAL and MUL accounted for almost 100 per cent of the car market. In the 1990s, HML, MUL and Daewoo were accounting for more than 90 per cent of the car production in India.
7 See Bell (1984), Desai (1984), Fransman and King (1984), Basant (1997), Tyabji (2000).
8 Technology Intensity = (Expenditure on Technology)/(Total Sales)*100
9 It is argued that the administered prices were not lucrative; the profits of firms decreased significantly in the late 1960s and early 1970s (Narayana 1989).
10 The strategy of the manufacturers to maintain excess demand gave birth to an underground market as there were large bogus allottees. The situation developed because premiums were offered to allottees by persons who wanted to avoid the huge waiting period to get a new car (Venkataramani 1990). Not only this, unlike contemporary times when a newly purchased car would begin to depreciate in value from the moment it comes out of showroom, until the 1980s the buyer of a car was actually selling it at a premium after some usage (Bhargava and Seetha 2010).
11 The economies of scale are assumed to be critical in the process of supplying low-cost products. In the words of Karmokolias (1990: 6) 'the total unit cost of a small car produced at 100,000 units per year . . . is estimated to be 80 per cent greater than if the same car is produced at a volume of 400,000 units per year.'
12 The World Bank (1987: 9) highlighted that 'the cumulative indirect taxes levied at various stages of manufacture, together with post-manufacture taxes such as excise duty and sales taxes and octroi, are estimated to add some 50 % to the ex-factory cost of cars.'
13 The probability of technology advancement in main vehicle manufacturing largely depends on ancillary units. As reported by Karmokolias (1990: 20), ancillaries 'have assumed a great deal of the responsibility for research, design, manufacturing, and stock maintenance.'
14 According to Parhi (2008: 6) 'this was primarily due to "follow sourcing" strategies of the global manufacturers present in India who encouraged their group companies or suppliers to create manufacturing base in India, often in the form of joint venture Indian suppliers.'
15 MUL claimed that delay in the process of indigenisation was mainly because of the inadequacies of domestic ancillary units. Japanese experts in the Board of Directors of MUL stated that indigenous ancillary units were lacking in terms of technology and failed to supply components confirming to certain specifications. Due to these constraints, MUL had to spend a large amount on the imports of raw material and components in the initial year. According to the available account in annual report (1983–84) of MUL, indigenous raw material used in production accounted for only 1.9 per cent of total sales value. Repudiating the argument of Suzuki, the ACMA president claimed that the Indian automobile ancillary units had attained a significant level

of sophistication, which enabled them to manufacture components according to the requirement of Japanese firm (Hamaguchi 1985). But MUL was not willing to procure from them. Adding to this, some ancillary units argued that MUL manipulated the criteria to select suppliers in such a way that only Japanese suppliers could fulfil requirements (Hamaguchi 1985; Gumaste 1988). The intention of MUL was to attract large ancillary units from abroad, especially from Japan, which entered by forming JVs with local ancillary units in order to manufacture components for MUL.

16 Refer to the writings of Nelson and Winter (1982), Rosenberg (1982), Dosi, Freeman and Nelson (1988) among others.

17 Other technical knowledge can either be acquired from specialised research institutes or developed within the firm through in-house R&D activities.

Chapter 5

Technological development of the passenger car industry since 2000

This chapter is an attempt to explore the implications of the changing policy regime after 2000 on the process of technological development in the passenger car industry. It is worth noting that the analysis performed in this chapter is not directly comparable with that in the previous chapter. To start with, out of the six firms selected for analysis in this chapter, only two firms (HML and MUL) are the same as in the previous chapter, whereas four other firms (Hyundai, General, Honda and Ford) were not included in the empirical analysis of the previous chapter. These firms started production in India only in the late 1990s. Secondly, in the previous chapter, firms included for analysis were either fully indigenous or JVs between Indian and foreign firms, but in the present chapter, except for HML all other selected firms are subsidiaries of foreign firms. Given the nature of ownership, we compare the investment in in-house R&D of foreign subsidiaries in India and their parent firms outside India. Third, trends in usage of import content in the production of luxury cars are also analysed.

Empirical investigation of this issue is important because the analysis in the previous chapter suggests that policy changes during the 1980s and 1990s have adversely affected indigenous technology development in the passenger car industry, as investment in in-house R&D witnessed a downward trend. Further, firms have reduced their reliance on indigenous inputs in the manufacture of passenger cars. Surprisingly, research during the last decade or so on the passenger car industry claimed that India's car industry has performed remarkably well in terms of technological development (Narayanan 1998, 2004; Sagar and Chandra 2004; Parhi 2008; Mani 2011; Kale 2012; Tiwari and Herstatt 2014).

To understand the validity of the above claim, it is important to understand the changing economic environment around the passenger car industry, especially with respect to the access to imports of raw material, intermediates, components and capital goods, on the one hand, and the nature of the operations of foreign firms in India, on the other. Since April 2001, that policy environment has drastically changed, with far-reaching implications for the pace of technology development and acquisition. Besides lifting all quantitative restrictions and regulations imposed by the GoI during the second half of the 1990s, 100 per cent FDI was allowed in 2002. Further, customs duty, as well as excise duty, was significantly reduced after 2000. Basic customs duty on components was reduced from 40 per cent in 1999–2000 to 20 per cent in 2004–05 and then to 10 per cent in 2014–15 (SIAM 2012a, 2016a). Similarly, the rate of excise duty on small cars has also reduced to 13.5 per cent (including 1 per cent national calamity contingent duty) in 2014–15. Further, imports of CBU and CKD units, which were earlier subject to import license requirements, were tarrified.

The explicit goals of the economic reforms announced after 2000 were to develop India as a manufacturing hub of small cars by attracting large inflows of foreign investment into the industry and also to encourage firms to invest more in in-house R&D (GoI 2002, 2006; GoI and SIAM 2016). In actual fact, the reform process helped the passenger car industry to attract a large number of foreign firms in the form of subsidiaries, but could not realise other objectives of the policy changes. Rather than investing more in in-house R&D, firms operating in the industry remained engaged in technology imports in all forms. This led to a further decline in in-house R&D activities of firms manufacturing passenger cars in India.

5.1   Approach of the study

For empirical analysis, data is collected from the CMIE PROWESS electronic database version 4.12 and 4.14. Though there are a large number of firms operating in India's passenger car industry, this analysis is confined to six passenger car firms namely HML, MUL, Hyundai Motor, General Motors, Honda Cars and Ford India. These firms accounted for more than 87 per cent of total car production in India in 2009–10. The selection of firms is constrained by the availability of information in the dataset used for empirical analysis. The CMIE PROWESS electronic database does not provide information on the other car manufacturing firms and, even if information for some other firms is available, it is for a limited number of years.[1] Given that constraint, the analysis is limited to the six firms mentioned for the period of 2000–01 to 2013–14.

To understand the process of technology development strategy and technology acquisition strategy of firms, indices estimated in this chapter are the same as in the previous chapter.

5.2 Empirical analysis

We have estimated technology intensity (total spending on technology as percentage of sales value) for the passenger car industry, which provides a broader indication of the efforts towards technology development and technology acquisition. Firm-wise technology intensity is also estimated to highlight the variation in technology orientation among selected firms. Disaggregated analysis similar to Chapter 4 has also been performed to delve deeper into the trends. In addition, an attempt is made to examine the import content in production.

5.2.1 Technology intensity

Table 5.1 presents the trends in technology intensity for the selected firms and average technology intensity of the industry. In general, the technology intensity of the passenger car industry witnessed an upward trend from 2000–01 to 2013–14. In 2000–01, the technology intensity of the industry was just 3.21 per cent. It rose to 5.56 per cent in 2006–07 and further to 8.93 per cent in 2013–14. The point to emphasise here is that resources devoted for technology development and technology acquisition were much higher towards the end of the decade as compared to early years. For instance, during the period 2000–01 to 2004–05, average spending of all firms towards technology acquisition and technology development was 3.08 per cent of total sales turnover, which increased sharply during the following five years (5.59 per cent) and then further jumped to 7.84 per cent during the period 2010–11 to 2013–14.

The rise in average technology intensity of the industry was not uniformly spread across all firms selected for the analysis. Firm-wise analysis suggests that there is considerable variation in the technology intensity of firms during the reference period (Table 5.1). Among the selected firms, HML is the only firm which not only invested the least in technology from 2000–01 to 2013–14, but

Table 5.1 Technology intensity of car firms (percentages)

Year	HML	MUL	Hyundai Motor	General Motors	Honda Cars	Ford India	Average of all firms
2000–01	0.98	4.85	0.23	0.66	4.70	1.34	3.21
2001–02	1.04	2.94	0.61	2.04	4.22	1.09	2.24
2002–03	1.46	1.92	5.14	8.09	4.66	1.74	2.91
2003–04	1.59	1.21	9.63	9.02	5.63	2.07	4.22
2004–05	1.32	2.01	4.31	2.89	2.12	3.29	2.73
2005–06	1.47	1.81	6.57	2.77	5.58	8.44	3.96
2006–07	0.25	2.42	14.03	3.42	2.36	2.56	5.56
2007–08	0.80	6.41	10.03	6.23	6.36	–	7.31
2008–09	0.73	8.38	4.57	5.61	13.81	–	7.18
2009–10	0.69	4.40	2.15	13.03	3.35	–	3.99
2010–11	0.77	7.47	4.84	–	–	–	6.49
2011–12	2.77	8.80	4.76	–	7.03	–	7.21
2012–13	7.48	8.91	5.44	–	15.26	–	8.08
2013–14	–	9.54	5.32	2.16	11.35	17.12	8.93
Average technology intensity							
2000–01 to 2004–05	1.23	2.48	4.71	4.13	3.85	2.04	3.08
2005–06 to 2009–10	0.75	4.97	6.41	6.81	6.14	4.91**	5.59
2010–11 to 2014–15	2.52#	8.73	5.12	2.16*	9.35$	17.12*	7.84

Source: CMIE PROWESS Version 4.12, 4.14 and 8.10.

Notes
(1) – refers non-availability of data.
(2) ** refers average for the period 2005–06 to 2006–07;
* indicates one year figure;
$ indicates average for 2011–12 to 2013–14;
# indicates average for 2011–12 to 2012–13.

also reduced its spending sharply until 2009–10 while spending on technology of other selected manufacturers, with some fluctuations, recorded an increase throughout the reference period (2000–01 to 2013–14). Further, though the direction of change is similar, there are substantial differences among the other five firms as well (Table 5.1). Technology intensity of Hyundai, General Motors and Honda was higher than the average technology intensity of all firms taken together from 2000–01 to 2009–10. Except General Motors, it remained significantly high in the following years. In the case of other firms such as MUL and Ford India, technology intensity remained lower than the average technology intensity of all firms until 2009–10, but a sharp increase was recorded in their average technology spending in the following years. In the case of MUL, average technology spending as per cent of sales jumped from 4.97 per cent during the period 2005–06 to 2009–10 to 8.73 per cent in the following four years (2010–11 to 2013–14).

The evidence presented in Table 5.1 reveals the overall efforts of firms towards technology acquisition and technology development. This, however, is not sufficient to reflect on the efforts of firms towards technology development or technology acquisition as well as the change in technology strategies of the firms. For that, disaggregated analysis is warranted.

5.2.2   Disaggregated analysis

The disaggregated analysis of the changes in technology intensity helps in highlighting the changing importance of technology development through in-house R&D as well as technology acquisition through imports.

R&D Investment in India: Trends in R&D intensity of passenger car firms operating in India are presented in Table 5.2. Average R&D intensity of all firms varied between 0.2 to 0.4 per cent from 2000–01 to 2012–13, which is very low when compared with the total technology intensity of all firms (Tables 5.1 and 5.2). Moreover, the value of five-year average investment in R&D also declined during the period 2005–06 to 2009–10 and then recorded an increase (0.40 per cent of sales turnover) in the following four years. The average spending on R&D was 0.27 per cent of sales turnover during the period 2000–01 to 2004–05; it declined marginally (0.22 per cent) during the following five years of the decade. Falling investment on R&D is contrary to the trend observed in the case of overall spending on technology during this period (2005–06 to 2009–10). In this period, except HML, technology intensity of all other firms increased by 30 per cent to 180 per cent (Table 5.1).

Inter-firm comparison highlights another aspect of investment in R&D. Hyundai presents an extreme trend when one compares technology intensity and R&D intensity (Tables 5.1 and 5.2). Hyundai, in general, remained on top in terms of aggregate spending on technology until 2007–08, but it appeared at the bottom in terms of R&D spending. The average R&D intensity of this firm stayed at around 0.05 per

Table 5.2 R&D intensity of car firms (percentages)

Year	HML	MUL	Hyundai Motor	General Motors	Honda Cars	Ford India	Average of all firms
2000–01	0.31	0.29	0.00	0.29	0.10	0.13	0.23
2001–02	0.49	0.32	0.02	1.26	0.21	0.19	0.30
2002–03	0.56	0.24	0.06	2.74	0.34	0.43	0.27
2003–04	0.78	0.25	0.07	0.99	0.07	0.66	0.27
2004–05	0.51	0.27	0.05	0.35	0.04	1.26	0.26
2005–06	0.37	0.26	0.04	0.78	–	0.62	0.23
2006–07	0.23	0.31	0.04	0.67	–	0.55	0.23
2007–08	0.18	0.18	0.03	0.61	–	–	0.15
2008–09	0.46	0.28	0.06	0.66	–	–	0.21
2009–10	0.42	0.34	0.05	1.18	–	–	0.27
2010–11	0.60	0.46	0.04	–	–	–	0.30
2011–12	0.83	0.57	0.05	–	–	–	0.35
2012–13	1.67	0.52	0.06	–	–	–	0.34
2013–14	–	0.52	0.09	0.86	–	1.45	0.46
Average R&D intensity							
2000–01 to 2004–05	0.50	0.27	0.05	0.76	0.12	0.61	0.27
2005–06 to 2009–10	0.33	0.28	0.05	0.79	–	0.58**	0.22
2010–11 to 2013–14	0.84#	0.52	0.06	0.86*	–	1.45*	0.40

Source: Same as Table 5.1.

Note: Same as Table 5.1.

cent during most of the reference period (Table 5.2). Another interesting case is that of Honda, which invested little in R&D (0.12 per cent) until 2004–05 and then completely stopped in-house R&D activities. The investment in R&D of the market leader (MUL) remained fluctuating around 0.3 per cent of sales turnover until 2009–10 and observed a meagre increase in the following years.

International R&D of Foreign Firms: Contrary to the record of foreign subsidiaries operating in India, the investment in in-house R&D by parent firms outside India not only was significantly higher but also showed an upward trend from 2000 to 2014 (Table 5.3). For instance, the investment in R&D by the parent firms of General Motors India, Ford India, Honda Cars India and MUL varied

Table 5.3 R&D intensity of international firms (percentages)

Year	General Motors Company	Honda Motor	Hyundai Motor Company	Suzuki Motor Corporation	Ford Motor Company
2000	3.57	4.75	–	–	4.82
2001	3.50	5.03	–	–	5.65
2002	3.37	–	–	2.70	5.73
2003	3.34	–	–	3.00	5.42
2004	3.37	5.50	–	3.45	5.03
2005	3.47	5.41	2.99	3.67	5.21
2006	3.23	5.15	2.85	3.27	5.02
2007	4.50	4.98	2.70	2.91	4.86
2008	5.37	4.90	2.75	3.10	5.65
2009	5.13	5.63	2.45	3.83	4.63
2010	5.41	5.40	2.15	4.41	4.19
2011	4.86	5.46	1.71	3.99	4.14
2012	4.63	6.54	2.10	4.37	4.35
2013	4.75	5.67	2.12	4.63	4.59
2014	–	5.35	2.39	4.33	5.08

Source: Annual reports (various years) of respective firms.

between 2 and 7 per cent of sales (Table 5.3). Interestingly, Honda has done negligible investment in R&D in India, whereas the R&D intensity of the parent firm of this company was as high as 6.54 per cent in 2012. Similarly, the market leader in India's car industry (MUL) invested around 0.3 to 0.5 per cent of sales value whereas R&D intensity of the parent firm of MUL increased from 2.70 per cent in 2002 to 4.63 per cent of sales value in 2013 (Tables 5.2 and 5.3).

These numbers suggest that the subsidiaries of international firms operating in India's car industry did not show any interest in developing technology in the country, as is evident from their low investment in R&D. Not developing technology in the host country is perhaps the outcome of a strategy of foreign firms to confine their innovation activities in the home country. This is evident from the fact that the parent firms of foreign subsidiaries operating in Indian industry have continuously invested very hugely on R&D outside India (Table 5.3).

Based on the evidence, it is clear that the policy measures announced by the GoI specifically to attract investment in R&D in the automobile industry under 'Auto Policy, 2002' and AMP (2006–16) did not motivate foreign subsidiaries to develop technology in India.

To understand why firms do not invest in R&D, it is important to examine two underlying factors: (1) the nature of and motives behind R&D activities performed by international firms in the host economy and, (2) the changing character of demand in developing countries, including India, under globalisation.

First, evidence suggests that the international firms have carried out R&D activities in the host countries (Behrman and Fisher 1980; Reddy 1997). But the nature of R&D activities varies across nations as it is influenced by the long-term motives of international firms as well as host country specificities, including the policy environment. The study by Ronstadt (1977) indicated that a major part of R&D performed by foreign firms in the host country was adaptive in nature. R&D of this kind helps firms to adapt products and processes available in the international market or with the parent firm according to demand conditions in the host country. Other than adaptive R&D, there were only a very few cases where foreign affiliates created technology outside the parent country (Ronstadt 1977; Narula 2005; Pearce 2005). This happened in contexts where the nature of demand in the host country was very different from other markets, but the market's potential was huge (Reddy 2005; UNCTAD 2005). Additionally, in recent years, studies revealed that international firms have started shifting innovation activities to developing countries (Reddy 1997, 2000; Pearce 1999, 2005; Narula 2005; Mrinalini and Sandhya 2008 Mrinalini, Nath and Sandhya 2013 and many more). But most of the studies also argued that this shift is solely with the objective of exploiting skilled manpower and scientific infrastructure. This suggests that, generally, foreign firms are not interested in investing in R&D in the host country.

Second, with growing integration across countries, market heterogeneity between developed and emerging countries is shrinking (Reddy 1997, 2000). Alternatively, the consumer preferences across the countries are converging and demand for luxury goods specifically is getting standardised. The standardisation of demand can influence the pace of technology development in the host country in general and R&D activities of international firms in particular. As mentioned earlier, this is so because most of the R&D performed by international firms is devoted to adapt international products and technology according to local market conditions. Convergence of demand would contribute negatively to the R&D efforts of international firms, as subsidiaries of foreign firms can sell products available in international markets or with parent firms without any major modification for the local market.

Hence, it can be argued that the changing nature of demand under the free import regime would have been one of the underlying factors behind falling R&D in India's passenger car industry. This is more likely in the case of an industry wherein more than 85 per cent cars are manufactured by the subsidiaries of foreign firms in the recent years. Rather than developing technology through in-house R&D, these firms preferred to import technology from and limit technological development with the parent firm in the parent country (Tables 5.3, 5.4 and 5.5). Subsidiaries of leading international firms

Table 5.4 Import of disembodied technology of car firms (% of sales)

Year	HML	MUL	Hyundai Motor	General Motors	Honda Cars	Ford India	Average of all firms
2000–01	0.42	1.22	–	–	4.29	1.05	1.27
2001–02	0.52	1.50	–	–	3.92	0.89	1.52
2002–03	0.50	1.42	1.37	–	3.78	0.92	1.45
2003–04	0.46	0.77	2.01	–	2.64	1.01	1.27
2004–05	0.31	1.10	2.75	1.25	1.99	0.90	1.58
2005–06	0.22	1.20	2.70	1.12	3.14	1.10	1.79
2006–07	0.00	1.72	2.68	2.36	2.12	1.16	1.99
2007–08	0.57	2.10	2.60	1.12	3.32	–	2.27
2008–09	0.24	2.93	1.89	0.48	4.35	–	2.48
2009–10	0.11	2.82	1.68	0.92	3.22	–	2.32
2010–11	0.12	4.98	2.12	–	–	–	3.95
2011–12	0.19	5.28	1.90	–	5.41	–	4.04
2012–13	0.36	5.37	1.54	–	5.92	–	4.08
2013–14	–	5.46	1.70	1.03	5.02	0.99	3.76
Average import of disembodied technology							
2000–01 to 2004–05	0.43	1.18	2.19&	1.25*	2.89	0.95	1.43
2005–06 to 2009–10	0.23	2.31	2.17	1.14	3.21	1.13**	2.22
2010–11 to 2014–15	0.18#	5.29	1.79	1.03*	5.34$	0.99*	3.94

Source: Same as Table 5.1.

Notes
(1) Same as Table 5.1.
(2) & indicates average for 2002–03 to 2004–05.

invested very negligible amounts in in-house R&D (Table 5.2). Given the growing pace of economic integration and subsequent changes in demand due to growing exposure to international products,[2] the process of technology development in India may slow down even further as foreign investment is allowed in almost all manufacturing industries. A study by Altenburg, Schmitz and Stamm (2008) states that India has successfully attracted production activities of international firms, but it failed to attract R&D activities of these firms, as these are still confined to the parent country.

Imports of Disembodied Technology: Disembodied technology refers to that form of technology that firms receive through licensing and technical services against lump-sum payments, technical fees and royalties. Table 5.4 presents the trends in import of disembodied technology by passenger car firms. Results indicate that spending on disembodied technology imports increased remarkably during the period under consideration. Spending on the import of disembodied technology for all firms was 1.27 per cent of total sales turnover in 2000–01, it reached 1.99 per cent in 2006–07 and further rose to 4.08 per cent in 2012–13. Similarly, average spending on disembodied technology during the period 2010–11 to 2013–14 was around three times the spending during the period 2000–01 to 2004–05 (Table 5.4). If we include payments for services along with royalty payments, then it touched 5.77 per cent in the period 2010–11 to 2013–14 (Table A.5 in annexure).

Substantial differences in terms of spending on disembodied technology across car producers have been observed from 2000–01 to 2013–14. Honda is not only spending the highest on the imports of disembodied technology, but its average spending also remained higher than the average spending of the industry (Table 5.4). Similarly, other firms, namely MUL, General Motors, Hyundai and Ford India also spent substantial amounts on the imports of disembodied technology. It is worth noting that the expenditure of all firms, except HML, on disembodied technology remained high and even increasing in the case of MUL and Honda. The substantial change has been noticed in the case of MUL and Honda after 2009. It could be because the GoI has eliminated the ceiling limit for royalty payments after 2009. HML has directed lesser resources towards imports of disembodied technology and remained at the bottom of the list from 2000–01 to 2013–14 (Table 5.4). From 2000–01 to 2004–05, average spending of HML was 0.43 per cent of sales value, which fell to 0.23 per cent in the period 2005–06 to 2009–10 and to 0.18 per cent during the recent years.

What made firms spend enormously on imports of disembodied technology? The sudden increase in the imports of disembodied technology must be analysed in the context of: (1) the rapid expansion of the car market; and (2) the growing competition and resultant reduction in product life.

First, the CAGP of production in the passenger car industry in India was 19.32 per cent per annum from 2001–02 to 2010–11 (Table 3.9 in Chapter 3). In terms of volume, production of cars in India increased from 186.48 thousand units in 1992–93 to 577.15 thousand units in 1999–2000 to 2537.17 thousand units in 2010–11. Rapid expansion of the industry attracted large number of fully owned subsidiaries of foreign firms, which started production of passenger cars in India. For instance, in 2000–01 eight firms were manufacturing cars in India and the number increased to thirteen in 2006–07 and currently more than 15 firms are manufacturing cars in India (SIAM 2006a, 2016a). The competition among the new entrants to get a foothold in the market encouraged them to offer a variety of passenger cars which were not available until then, i.e. the early years of the previous decade. Growing heterogeneity in the available cars in India divided the passenger car industry into six sub-segments (such as small, compact, mid-size, executive, premier and luxury) with multiple models in each segment.

These developments triggered cut-throat competition in the passenger car industry in general and especially in compact and mid-size segments, which ultimately intensified the price war. As a response to these changes, existing firms (especially MUL, Honda and Hyundai) also introduced a number of new models at competitive prices as well as increased the variety of existing models of passenger cars. For instance, since 2005 MUL launched Swift, Grand, Vitara, Ritz, Alto (Alto K10, Alto 800) etc. This has obvious implications for the imports of disembodied technology. As these firms were subsidiaries of international firms, they would obviously import technology from the parent firms or other subsidiaries, leading to the sudden jump in the payments for technology during the second half of the 2000s. According to the UNCTAD (2005) more than 80 per cent of royalty payments made by foreign subsidiaries against technology imports went to parent firms.

Second, the growing intensity of competition has shortened the life span of technology. This is true in the case of rapidly growing industry such as passenger cars where designs and technology change very frequently. This is evident from the fact that manufacturers are continuously replacing models of cars with new designs and modern technology. This development has obviously put pressure on manufacturers.

To cope with the changing market situation, the manufacturers in India are depending on imported technology as in-house R&D requires large resources as well as long gestation periods. As noticed earlier, major R&D activities of these subsidiaries are locked with parent firm, hence, the foreign subsidiaries use that technology to compete in the host country. It is strategically good too for foreign firms to locate R&D at one place as it postpones leakage and also enables the parent firm to realise economies of scale in innovations.

Imports of Embodied Technology: The trends in spending on the import of embodied technology are provided in Table 5.5. Import

Table 5.5 Import of embodied technology of car firms (% of sales)

Year	HML	MUL	Hyundai Motor	General Motors	Honda Cars	Ford India	Average of all firms
2000–01	0.25	3.34	0.23	0.37	0.31	0.16	1.99
2001–02	0.03	1.12	0.59	0.78	0.08	0.01	0.78
2002–03	0.39	0.26	3.72	5.36	0.54	0.39	1.20
2003–04	0.35	0.18	7.55	8.03	2.92	0.39	2.73
2004–05	0.50	0.64	1.51	1.29	0.10	1.14	0.89
2005–06	0.88	0.34	3.84	0.87	2.44	6.72	1.95
2006–07	0.01	0.39	11.31	0.39	0.25	0.85	3.33
2007–08	0.06	4.12	7.39	4.50	3.05	–	4.88
2008–09	0.03	5.16	2.61	4.48	9.46	–	4.49
2009–10	0.16	1.23	0.42	10.93	0.13	–	1.40
2010–11	0.06	2.03	2.68	–	–	–	2.09
2011–12	1.75	2.95	2.82	–	1.62	–	2.82
2012–13	5.46	3.01	3.85	–	9.34	–	3.66
2013–14	–	3.55	3.53	0.27	6.33	14.68	4.71
Average import of embodied technology							
2000–01 to 2004–05	0.30	1.03	3.06	2.83	0.85	0.49	1.48
2005–06 to 2009–10	0.19	2.38	4.20	4.89	2.93	3.20**	3.15
2010–11 to 2013–14	1.49#	2.92	3.27	0.27*	3.62$	14.68*	3.37

Source: Same as Table 5.1.

Note: Same as Table 5.1.

of embodied technology occurs through the import of capital goods such as plant and machinery. The spending on these imports for the industry as a whole and for individual firms except HML has, with some fluctuation, consistently increased during the last twelve years (2000–01 to 2013–14). But the increase was sharper after 2004–05 as compared to the early years of the decade (Table 5.5). For instance, average spending of all selected firms increased from 1.48 per cent of sales for the period 2000–01 to 2004–05 to 3.15 for the period 2005–06 to 2009–10 and further increased to 3.37 per cent for the period 2010–11 to 2013–14. The rise in import of embodied technology occurred in tandem with the rise in import of disembodied technology (Tables 5.4 and 5.5).

A firm-wise analysis reveals significant variations in terms of spending on the import of embodied technology. Average spending by Hyundai and General Motors was substantial and higher than the average spending of all selected firms during the reference period. Other firms (Ford, Honda and MUL) also spent significant amounts on embodied technology; only HML invested a very meagre amount. For instance, the average spending of HML on embodied capital for the period 2005–06 to 2009–10 was 0.19 per cent of sales turnover whereas average investment of all the firms in the same period was 3.15 per cent. Further, the import spending on embodied technology of HML varied between 0.01 per cent and 0.88 per cent in the period 2000–01 to 2010–11, whereas average spending of the industry varied between 0.78 per cent and 4.88 per cent during the same period (Table 5.5). The low investment by HML on all forms of technology development and technology acquisition (R&D, disembodied and embodied) could be the fundamental reason behind the non-competitiveness of this firm, which is manifested in its falling market strength. In a globalised world, technology is assumed to be the key input for a firm to compete successfully in the market. It helps a firm to offer technically advanced products at minimum possible prices and also allows to introduce new products according to changing demand conditions. The competitiveness of a firm is not only a function of the existing technology base of the firm but it also depends on upgradation of existing technology on a continuous basis.

The sudden jump in the import of embodied technology after 2005 can be understood in the context of rapid expansion in installed capacity of car manufacturers owing to high growth in car demand. As discussed earlier, the installed capacity of the passenger vehicles industry increased from 1.88 million in 2005–06 to 4.2 million units in 2011–12 and further reached to 4.96 million units in 2014–15. According to SIAM, by the end of 2017 the installed capacity of the industry would reach to 6.96 million units. It is possible, as Maruti Suzuki, Honda Cars and Ford India have been expanding their production base. This large increase in the production capacity occurred mainly in the compact and mid-size car segments, which are largely controlled by a few leading firms namely, MUL, Hyundai and Honda (Singh 2015). The jump in production capacity would obviously increase spending on fixed capital (plant and machinery). Given the liberal import regime and dominance of foreign firms in the industry, imported machinery and capital goods were used to build additional production capacity. Due to this, the import payments on embodied technology increased substantially over the recent years.

But why were imports of embodied technology fluctuating over the reference period? The reason behind the fluctuations in imports may be the nature of embodied technology. As embodied technology comes in the form of capital goods and machinery, these goods are not replaced every year because machinery and other capital equipment are a part of fixed capital. Large imports of embodied capital in one year will obviously reduce the required import of machinery and plant for the next few years until the imported capital has to be replaced or new machinery has entered or has become available in the market with exceptionally advanced technology.

Based on the above discussion, it is possible to argue that, unlike what the extant literature suggests, the policy changes during the last one and a half decades have halted the process of indigenous technology development in India's passenger car industry. It is reflected in a decline in R&D activities and growing imports of technology. Unwillingness to develop technology on the part of foreign subsidiaries is largely because the innovation activities of these firms are still tied up with the parent firms. Sizeable investment in in-house R&D by parent firms and negligible investment in R&D by foreign subsidiaries in India indirectly implies the continuous dependence of the latter on the former to get access to modern technology. This dependence would increase further, because market power got transferred from the hands of indigenous firms to the subsidiaries of international firms; and because proper policies which could regulate the activities of these firms and encourage them to promote R&D activities in India were absent.

5.2.3 Indirect imports of technology

Raw material usage indicates the composition of components and raw material procured by firms from internal sources as well as from external sources (imports). There are various reasons to expect change in raw material and components usage to be directly related to policy changes, as GoI not only removed the local content requirement but also eliminated the foreign exchange neutrality norm imposed in 1997. After 2000, customs duty imposed on imports of components, CBU and CKD kits have also been brought down significantly and the licensing requirement for the imports of CKD/SKD goods has been scrapped (GoI 2002; Singh 2015; SIAM 2016a). Given these factors, it is important to examine the trends in the imports of raw material, intermediates, components and capital goods. The following section analyses the implications of changing technology strategies for the usage of imported components and CKD kits for the production of passenger cars.

Composition of Raw Material Usage: Table 5.6 presents the changing distribution of raw material and components procured by passenger car firms from India and abroad to manufacture cars. In general, it is worth noting that the use of imported content in final production has consistently declined from 2000–01 to 2013–14. Average share of imported raw material in total raw material (imported plus indigenous) of all firms was 36.95 per cent in 2000–01, which declined to 29.20 per cent in 2004–05 and further fell to 14.41 per cent in 2010–11. Reverse trends were noticed after 2010–11, as imported content increased to above 20 per cent in 2013–14. Five-year average figures also indicate that the import content has declined over time. It was 33.14 per cent for the period 2000–01 to 2004–05, which reduced to around 18 per cent in the period 2010–11 to 2013–14.

The firm-wise analysis points to a considerable variation across the firms in terms of reduction in import content in the manufacture of passenger cars (Table 5.6). Given the varying degree of usage of

Table 5.6 Trends in imported and indigenous content (percentages)

Year	HML Imported content	HML Indigenous content	MUL Imported content	MUL Indigenous content	Hyundai Motor Imported content	Hyundai Motor Indigenous content	General Motors Imported content	General Motors Indigenous content	Honda Cars Imported content	Honda Cars Indigenous content	Ford India Imported content	Ford India Indigenous content	Average of all firms Imported content	Average of all firms Indigenous content
2000–01	38.67	61.33	33.39	66.61	31.29	68.71	67.34	32.66	46.21	53.79	32.22	67.78	36.95	63.05
2001–02	32.53	67.47	27.96	72.04	42.22	57.78	61.93	38.07	50.01	49.99	25.63	74.37	32.31	67.69
2002–03	29.25	70.75	26.07	73.93	35.29	64.71	56.83	43.17	48.18	51.82	25.47	74.53	30.17	69.83
2003–04	22.83	77.17	20.46	79.54	33.97	66.03	72.17	27.83	52.50	47.50	30.71	69.29	30.51	69.49
2004–05	16.69	83.31	19.72	80.28	37.10	62.90	41.42	58.58	51.36	48.64	40.10	59.90	29.20	70.80
2005–06	21.80	78.20	18.80	81.20	34.54	65.46	33.80	66.20	49.31	50.69	44.81	55.19	29.11	70.89
2006–07	27.38	72.62	12.71	87.29	34.82	65.18	31.85	68.15	49.80	50.20	43.86	56.14	26.36	73.64
2007–08	36.42	63.58	10.99	89.01	31.16	68.84	90.90	9.10	46.60	53.40	–	–	23.57	76.43
2008–09	46.33	53.67	11.84	88.16	25.36	74.64	47.59	52.41	47.52	52.48	–	–	20.68	79.32
2009–10	42.21	57.79	12.94	87.06	21.60	78.40	52.94	47.06	42.85	57.15	–	–	20.97	79.03
2010–11	53.96	46.04	10.86	89.14	19.72	80.28	–	–	–	–	–	–	14.41	85.59
2011–12	54.88	45.12	10.72	89.28	22.37	77.63	–	–	42.55	57.45	–	–	17.07	82.93
2012–13	–	–	12.12	87.88	26.13	73.87	–	–	34.92	65.08	–	–	18.94	81.06
2013–14	–	–	9.19	90.81	23.06	76.94	49.08	50.92	24.41	75.59	40.54	59.46	20.23	79.77
Average imported and indigenous content														
2000–01 to 2004–05	27.99	72.01	24.93	75.07	36.05	63.95	55.10	44.90	50.35	49.65	32.10	67.90	33.14	66.86
2005–06 to 2009–10	34.83	65.17	13.05	86.95	27.37	72.63	50.21	49.79	47.22	52.78	44.40**	55.60**	24.25	75.75
2010–11 to 2013–14	54.42#	45.58#	10.70	89.70	23.04	76.96	49.08*	50.92*	33.96$	66.04$	40.20*	59.80*	17.99	82.01

Source: Same as Table 5.1.

Note: * Same as Table 5.1.

import content for car production by selected manufacturers, we have classified them into three groups. Firms which have: (1) significantly reduced import content, (2) marginally reduced import content, and (3) registered an increase in import content. Among the first set of firms are MUL and Hyundai, the two car manufacturers that have substantially increased the use of indigenous raw material in the production of cars (Table 5.6). In the case of MUL and Hyundai, the average use of indigenous raw material with reference to total raw material cost was 75.07 per cent and 63.95 per cent respectively from 2000–01 to 2004–05, which increased to 89.70 per cent and 76.96 per cent respectively during the period 2010–11 to 2013–14. As a corollary, the imported raw material content of MUL and Hyundai declined from 24.93 per cent and 36.05 per cent respectively during the period 2000–01 to 2004–05 to 10.70 per cent and 23.04 per cent respectively in the period 2010–11 to 2013–14. To understand why MUL and Hyundai succeeded in the process of indigenisation, we must first understand the initial strategy, long-term behaviour and market strength of these firms.[3]

The second set of firms include General Motors and Honda, which have registered marginal decline in the use of imported raw material from 2000–01 to 2013–14. But their use of imported raw material still remained significantly high. The third set of firms, namely HML and Ford, recorded an increase in the use of imported raw material during the same period. Evidence presented in Table 5.6 clearly suggests that MUL ranks last in the list in terms of use of imported raw material and Hyundai Motor ranks last but one, whereas the other selected firms are characterised by a high import content in the manufacture of final vehicles.

Given the above evidence, it appears that, rather than internal innovation, it is the liberal economic environment which enabled firms to continuously launch new passenger cars based on high import content. We can expect this trend to be even stronger in the case of those firms that are manufacturing high-end cars (BMW, Mercedes-Benz India etc.). This is so because the market size for high-end cars is very small given their price. The demand for high-end cars mainly comes from the elite section of the population in a developing country. Given these facts, it is very likely that firms would have started offering completely assembled passenger cars to exploit the market for luxury cars. The following sub-section analyses the activities of these firms.

5.2.4 Import content in high-end cars

Over the last decade, demand for luxury goods in general and high-end cars (premier and luxury cars) in particular has increased in India. Combined production of premier and luxury cars, which stood at 3999 in 2001–02, increased to 5422 in 2005–06 and to 13610 in 2010–11 (SIAM 2006a, 2012a). The increase in production is more than 3.4 times the production level in 2001–02. Correspondingly, the number of manufacturers increased from four in 2001–02 to eight in 2010–11 and further to eleven in 2012–13.[4] Given the limited volume of production and the large number of manufacturers, these firms would have found it difficult to achieve economies of scale to manufacture products in India. Thus, they might have offered completely assembled products based on imported components. It is worth noting that selling assembled passenger cars proves to be much cheaper than developing indigenous cars or importing final cars since the tariff on imports of complete cars is much higher than that on the sum total of components, including CKD/SKD kits (Singh 2015). Thus, firms can easily sell assembled products through imports.

The major constraint in analysing the import content and nature of imports (i.e. raw material, CBU/CKD etc.) is the paucity of data. The CMIE PROWESS dataset did not cover any information on the firms manufacturing luxury cars in India. SIAM's annual publications provide some information, but the information is scattered and available only for some years and for some firms. Based on the data available with SIAM publications, we can get a clue, but it is difficult to perform any detailed comparative analysis as would have been possible with the CMIE PROWESS data.

Information collected from the SIAM publication entitled *Profile of the Automobile Industry in India* suggests that almost all firms manufacturing premier and luxury cars use imported raw material, components, CKD kits and CBU units to manufacture passenger cars in India. Due to the high import content, import payments of these firms were quite substantial. For instance, import spending of Skoda was 65 per cent of sales turnover in 2007–08 and it increased to 150 per cent in the following year (2008–09). Similarly, import spending of Mercedes-Benz India Pvt. Ltd. remained above 55 per cent of sales turnover in the recent years (Table 7.8 in Chapter 7). The evidence suggests that Mercedes-Benz India used around 95 per cent imported CKD kits when it entered India in the early 1990s

(Okada 2004). In recent years, it has declined to around 70.14 per cent. Another firm (BMW India Pvt. Ltd.) introduced a variety of luxury cars in India in 2011–12 and 2012–13. Most of the BMW cars were assembled based on CKD and CBU kits (Singh 2015). According to CMIE, the import content in BMW's products was as high as 92.47 per cent in 2012–13. These numbers suggest that the firms operating in the high-end car segment exploited the market by offering import-intensive passenger cars.

From the above discussion, it is clear that except for two manufacturers (MUL and Hyundai), all firms operating in India's car industry are largely depending on imported components, including CBU and CKD kits. Given the unregulated entry of foreign subsidiaries and growing competition, the process of indigenisation may halt further in the near future because, *first*, the life cycle of passenger car technology is getting shorter. According to Lee (2013), foreign firms are getting specialised in short-cycle technologies, which may pose a challenge for the survival of indigenous firms. And second, firms operating in high-end segments (Volkswagen, BMW, Mercedes-Benz etc.) started launching compact and mid-sized cars equipped with luxury features, which may pose a challenge for market leaders operating in these segments. Given the trends, it is high time for the state to intervene. The government should come-up with certain policy measures which regulate entry as well as encourage subsidiaries of foreign firms to use local content. In the absence of state intervention, India will not only destroy its indigenous manufacturing and technology capability, which had been built over time through direct state intervention, but this pattern of development has serious implications for BOPs of the country as well.

5.3   Observations and implications

The empirical analysis performed in this chapter highlighted the changes observed in the passenger car industry especially in terms of technology development from 2000–01 to 2013–14. First, though the spending of firms on technology has significantly increased since 2000, a large chunk of total spending for technology development is directed towards imports of technology (investment on R&D remained as low as around 0.3 per cent of total sales value from 2000–01 to 2012–13). This indicates that passenger car manufacturers, especially the subsidiaries of foreign firms, are repeatedly importing technology to manufacture new models and upgrade existing models of cars. This is so because technology development activities of foreign subsidiaries operating in India are confined to parent firms as investment in R&D by parents firms varied between 2 to 7 per cent of sales value since 2000 and these trends are moving upwards over time. Given this, these firms can easily access modern technology developed by the parent firm or a subsidiary operating in a third country. The limited R&D performed by these firms in the host country is necessary to adjust imported technology and other products according to local scale of production and availability of raw material. Second, it is interesting to note that the import content varied considerably between high-end (including premier and luxury cars), middle-sized (including mid-size and executive cars) and small-sized cars (including compact cars). Indeed it is difficult to establish a direct link between the type of cars and import content used in manufacture. But the empirical analysis performed above enables us to trace the varying degree of import content across different firms manufacturing different types of cars in India. Third, firms manufacturing high-end and middle-size cars not only imported components and raw materials but also imported SKD/CKD kits in large volumes during the last decade, which they used to offer assembled passenger cars.

Given the results of this chapter, it is apparent that those who claimed that India's passenger car industry has achieved an edge in technology do not find support in the empirical evidence. Measuring technology development based on product innovations and the variety of passenger cars available presents a completely misleading picture in the context of India's passenger car industry.

These developments observed in the passenger car industry during the last one and a half decades can have adverse effect on local technology development. Further, if the outflow of foreign exchange on account of imports in different forms is occurring without a corresponding increase in export earnings, it will contribute to an increase in the BoP deficit. The following chapter intends to analyse the implications of the development trajectory of the passenger car segment for the BoP.

Notes

1 In CMIE PROWESS, data on passenger car production by Tata is not available separately, and all the information is grouped under the commercial vehicle segment and hence cannot be included.

2 The demonstration effect is very strong in developing countries. This is especially true in the case of high and upper-middle income households. The growing income of these households allows them to enjoy luxury life. To differentiate them, they prefer to use imported branded products manufactured by multinational firms in India or other parts of the world. This leads to strong convergence of demand between emerging economies and developed countries.

3 For detailed discussion on the initial objective and long-term strategy of MUL and Hyundai, see Chapter 8.

4 It includes Nissan Motor India, Skoda Auto India, Volkswagen India, Toyota Kirloskar, Honda Cars India, Hyundai Motor India, BMW India, Mercedes-Benz India, Tata-JLR, Volkswagen-Audi and Volkswagen Porsche.

Chapter 6

Foreign presence and balance of payments (1981–2000)

The empirical analyses presented in the previous chapters suggest that spending of passenger car manufacturers on technology acquisition has been increasing in response to the changing economic environment since the middle of the 1980s. The distinguishing features of the trajectory of technology acquisition were that: (1) firms largely exploited external sources, as reflected in their imports of disembodied and embodied technology; and (2) firms with small market shares were offering import-intensive passenger cars.

Given this, the present chapter extends the empirical analysis by analysing the impact of foreign entry on the trade performance of the passenger car industry. This is important as foreign firms are increasingly dominating the industry and the official expectation is that foreign firms would ease the BoP impact of imports of technology and inputs by improving export performance. This expectation is justified on the following grounds. First, foreign firms are seen as equipped with modern technology and other intangible assets (managerial skills; brand name, etc.) that allow them to compete successfully in the international market. Second, foreign investors are seen as searching for attractive locations to source production for the world market. Thus, it is hoped that enhanced foreign presence in the post-reform period would enhance India's competitiveness in the world market and bring much needed improvement in the country's external balance.

The passenger car industry provides a good case to test this hypothesis. As mentioned earlier, it is one of those industries in India where foreign firms have been dominating since the middle of the 1990s.[1] To what extent have these foreign firms facilitated car exports from India? This is the issue which we are investigating in this chapter.

The empirical analysis in this chapter does not lend support to the hypothesis that increasing foreign presence increases exports of host country. It supports the argument that the kind of foreign investment that India's passenger car industry has attracted with the onset of economic reforms initiated since the early 1980s has remained 'payments negative' in nature. This character is evident from the fact that exports of foreign firms were neither substantial nor increasing significantly during the last two decades of the 20th century, whereas their imports were substantial and increasing steadily in the expansionary phase of the domestic market. The high import intensity in the absence of exports would obviously have negative consequences for the BoP of the country.

6.1 Analytical background

The importance of foreign investors for the export performance of the host country is an extensively studied area of research in the context of developing countries and thinking in this area has advanced considerably over time (Nayyar 1978; Jenkins 1979; Subrahmanian and Pillai 1979; IIFT 1981; Lall 1985, 1996; Chandrasekhar 1997; Chandrasekhar and Ghosh 2002; Kumar 2007; Singh 2015). Contrary to the perception which developing countries earlier had with respect to the motives underlying investment by foreign firms in developing countries (wherein it was believed that foreign investment aims at gaining control of the host country's market and other scarce resources) and their negative BoP effects, it is now believed that the main objective of foreign investment is to find low-cost destinations, given their higher costs of production in home countries. If this holds true, then it is very likely that the foreign firms entering in the developing countries would not solely aim at serving the local market, as international firms were doing under the import-substitution regime. Rather, these firms would choose those locations of production which would help them to serve the world market too. It is expected that foreign investment of this kind would not have negative implications for the BoP of developing countries, as such foreign investment would deliver export revenues and a positive relationship between exports and foreign investment.

The expectation of a positive contribution of foreign investment to the exports of a developing country is based *inter alia* on the market power associated with foreign investors which enable them to perform better in terms of exports as compared to their local counterparts (Lall 1985; Moran, Graham and Blomstrom 2005; Narula and Lall 2006; Rugman and Doh 2008; Dunning and Lundan 2008). These advantages include: first, an international network, access to globally established marketing channels and distribution networks, and access to global information, as these firms operate simultaneously in a number of countries and serve diverse markets; second, core competencies and capabilities in the form of ownership of new technologies, managerial skills, product differentiation and familiarity with aggressive advertising strategies etc. All these are the firm-specific advantages, which are moveable and internal to the firms, that foreign firms have acquired through long production and marketing experience and through purposeful investment in research and development activities over a long period of time. These advantages are over and above what local firms have in the market. As a result, these firms are expected to exploit locational advantages to a much greater degree as well as to perform better than non-multinational or local firms.

Given the access to such tangible and intangible assets and the changed motives of foreign investors, it is hoped that the presence of foreign firms in developing countries would be instrumental in promoting exports from the host countries and stimulating local firms to produce better quality products and enter the export market (Rugman and Doh 2008; Kumar and Joseph 2007). A number of East and Southeast Asian countries have already succeeded in expanding their manufactured exports by serving as hosts to international firms for production activities (Ernst et al. 1998; UNCTAD 1999;[2] Joseph 2006). The experience of China in recent times also supports the idea of an emerging nexus between foreign presence and the promotion of manufactured exports since foreign-owned enterprises in China accounted for as much as 55 per cent of the country's merchandise exports (Kumar 2007). It is worth highlighting that the contribution of foreign firms to China's exports increased from 40 per cent to 55.4 per cent between1996 and 2008 (Chandrasekhar 2013). A study by Long (2005) pointed out that China was an ideal production location for foreign manufacturers to manufacture goods for export purposes because wage levels in China were 47.8 percentage points lower than wage levels in the United States and 29.9 percentage points lower than in Japan.

These instances of success have led to fundamental changes in the development strategy of almost all the developing countries since the early 1980s. Notable shifts have been witnessed in policies related to external sector liberalisation, which has a special significance in the development strategy of any economy. Besides trade liberalisation, the major focus of these economies is to attract higher FDI, which is contrary to the earlier attitude of developing countries towards FDI (Lall 1996; Subrahmanian et al. 1996; J. Singh 2009, 2014). Apart from fiscal incentives, export promotion zones or special economic zones have been established in these countries to attract higher export-oriented FDI. As a result, developing countries have succeeded in attracting large inflows of foreign investment (Singh et al. 2011; UNCTAD 2013). For instance, the share of developing countries in world FDI increased from 14 per cent in 1980 to 27 per cent in 2001, 35 per cent in 2005 and further to 42 per cent in 2015 (UNCTAD 2017).

Indian Experience: The nexus between foreign investment and export performance has also received considerable attention in India (Nayyar 1978; Subrahmanian and Pillai 1979; IIFT 1981; Lall 1985; Kumar and Siddharthan 1994, 1997; Sharma 2000; Aggarwal 2002; Chandrasekhar and Ghosh 2002; Verma 2009; Singh 2015). The underlying objective of almost all these studies was to understand the varying export performance of foreign and domestic firms in manufacturing industries in India. The empirical literature on the issue at hand is much debated, and it has produced considerable disagreement among researchers. A set of researchers infers the positive association between FDI inflows and the exports of the host country (Lall 1985; Kumar and Siddharthan 1994; Sharma 2000; Aggarwal 2002). But results remained statistically insignificant or weakly significant (at 10 per cent or above). Contrary to this view, other scholars[3] did not support the positive nexus between foreign presence and exports of the host country. Results did not highlight any statistically significant difference in the export performance of two set of firms (domestic and foreign). A study by Chandrasekhar and Ghosh (2002) analyses the contribution of foreign firms to the BoP of the country by analysing the trends in exports and imports of foreign firms. Results indicate that the net contribution of foreign firms remained positive (foreign exchange earnings greater than spending) for some years in the early 1990s, but the growing integration with the world economy has changed the trends, as after 1993 the foreign exchange spending on imports outstripped export earnings and this gap has been widening since then. In the same line, Verma (2009) also analysed the implications of foreign firms for the BoP and observed that foreign firms remained net importers under liberalisation. In general, almost none of the existing studies strongly support the virtuous nexus between foreign presence and export performance of India. It suggests that the underlying objective of foreign firms entering India is not to use available comparative advantages in order to manufacture products for the world market. These firms entered the host country to exploit the domestic market, as foreign firms have expanded manufacturing capacity only in the phase of rapid expansion of the domestic market (Chandrasekhar and Ghosh 2002; Singh 2015).

India's experience as compared to China and the Newly Industrialised Countries highlights that there is no unidirectional relationship between foreign presence and the host country's exports. Varying behaviour of foreign firms across countries could be because of several reasons, as development strategies and the institutional environment across countries vary considerably (Evans 1995; Ernst et al. 1998). According to Long (2005), there is no automatic relationship between foreign presence and the host country's exports; it is the institutional set-up of the host country which influences the motives of foreign firms. In general, foreign firms are not driven by the motive of undertaking export-production in host countries. The fundamental focus of foreign players is to retain their competitiveness and earn high profits.

In the light of this literature, the present chapter is an attempt to analyse the nexus between foreign investment and India's export performance with reference to the passenger car industry. The issue is critical, as successive Indian governments, inspired by the experience of China and the Newly Industrialised Countries and in view of the changing understanding of the motives and long-term objectives of foreign firms, are continuously abolishing restrictions on the entry of foreign firms and their operations (Singh 2015; GoI 2002, 2016a; GoI 2016b, 2017).

6.2 Data sources and methodology

Data Sources: Empirical analysis is conducted using firm-level data collected from PROWESS. The information collected from this source is related to foreign exchange spending and earnings. The earnings and spending of foreign exchange are not only limited to imports and exports of goods; they also cover payments/earnings from royalties and technical fees, dividends and interest on borrowings. As mentioned earlier, the PROWESS data is available from

1989 onwards, but the analysis of this study starts in 1981. For previous years, information available with 'The Automobile Industry: Statistical Profile' published by the AIAM has been used for the analysis. It is worth noting that the AIAM publications do not provide information either on imports of goods or earnings from and spending on other services.

Selection of Firms and Methods Used: For the selection of firms, we continue with the methodology of Chapter 4. The selected firms are HML, PAL and MUL for analysis during the 1980s and HML, MUL and Daewoo Motors for the 1990s.

On account of data constraints, the analysis performed for the period of the 1980s is limited only to the export performance of firms, whereas, in the 1990s, the analysis of foreign exchange flows of the selected firms is undertaken separately for: a) transactions in goods[4] only; and b) all foreign exchange transactions,[5] including trade in goods as well as non-goods.

Trade in goods: Trade in goods includes transactions of firms in tangible goods. For this, we have calculated export intensity and import intensity for both individual firms as well as industry.

- *Export Intensity*: It measures the earnings from exports of goods as percentage of total sales turnover.[6]
- *Import Intensity*: It is calculated by dividing spending on imports of goods by total sales and multiplied by 100.[7]
- *Ratio Index*: It estimates spending on imports of goods as percentage of export earnings.[8] The index indicates the changing extent of mismatch between imports and exports of goods. If import payments exceed export earnings, then the value of index goes above 100 and vice versa.

Total transactions: This includes trade in Goods and Non-Goods and includes all kinds of foreign exchange transactions of firms. This is important because firms' transactions are not limited to trade in goods, but a significant volume of payments are also accounted for by royalties, technical fees, other services, dividends and interest payments.

- *Foreign Earnings Index*: it is calculated by dividing total foreign exchange earnings by total sales and multiplied by 100.[9] Total foreign exchange earnings incorporate foreign exchange earnings from the export of goods and earnings from other sources.

- *Foreign Spending Index*: it measures total foreign exchange spending as percentage of total sales.[10] Total foreign exchange spending includes payments for the import of goods and payments in terms of royalty, technical fees, dividends etc.
- *Net Contribution Index*: it is defined as percentage of total foreign exchange spending to total foreign exchange earnings.[11] If the value is above 100, then spending is higher than earnings and vice versa.

6.3 Empirical analysis

The analysis effectively starts from 1989–90 onwards, as the information for the period before 1989 is not available with CMIE PROWESS.[12] Before undertaking an empirical analysis for the 1990s, a brief background related to the 1980s is provided.

The analysis for the 1980s is restricted to the export performance of three manufacturers (HML, PAL and MUL) as their combined production of cars was more than 98 per cent of the total production in India in the mid-1980s. Further, these three firms had collaborations with foreign firms (Table A.1 in annexure).

6.3.1 Trade performance of firms during the 1980s

Table 6.1 presents the trends in export performance of three leading firms which were operating in the car industry during the 1980s. The exports of firms did not record any significant change during the reference period. Average export intensity of the selected firms was 1.27 per cent from 1980–81 to 1984–85, which increased to 1.33 per cent in the following five years (1985–86 to 1989–90). Similar trends were observed at the individual firm level. For instance, the exports of HML were 3.07 per cent of total sales value in 1980–81, which declined to 2.17 per cent in 1985–86 and then reached to 2.53 per cent in 1989–90. The export intensity of PAL remained below 0.5 per cent until 1987–88. The export performance of MUL was also very poor, even when this firm had acquired a dominant position in the car industry after the mid-1980s. The question arises as to why foreign collaboration of domestic firms could not promote their exports from India. The factors behind poor export performance of MUL and the two other firms (HML and PAL) remained different, as these firms entered during a different time period under a different policy regime. The policy regime in which

Table 6.1 Export intensity of car firms (percentages)

Year	HML	PAL	MUL	Average of selected firms
1980–81	3.07	0.45	–	2.27
1981–82	3.16	0.33	–	2.17
1982–83	1.17	0.29	–	0.86
1983–84	0.89	0.23	–	0.65
1984–85	0.91	0.40	–	0.70
1985–86	2.17	0.18	–	1.34
1986–87	1.69	0.16	0.03	0.55
1987–88	1.52	0.34	0.37	0.70
1988–89	1.85	0.72	0.81	1.07
1989–90	2.53	1.54	2.74	2.39
Average export intensity				
1980–81 to 1984–85	1.79	0.34	0.00	1.27
1985–86 to 1989–90	1.99	0.76	1.20*	1.33

Source: Mohanty et al. (1994), AIAM (1995).

Note: *indicate average export intensity for 1986–87 to 1989–90.

a firm grows is likely to influence the long-term motives, strategies and behaviour of manufacturers.

The poor export performance of HML and PAL can be attributed to several factors. First, these firms have been supplying cars to Indian consumers under the protective regime since the late 1940s. The sole purpose of old indigenous firms to sign collaborations with foreign firms was to supply upgraded passenger cars to domestic consumers only in the wake of growing competition within the domestic economy as they lost their market to MUL. The change in policy and subsequent collaborations with foreign firms would not have automatically changed the orientation of manufacturers.

Second, technologically superior products along with competitive prices and high quality have greater potential to find acceptability in the international market. As discussed earlier, the passenger cars offered by Indian indigenous firms (HML and PAL) until the middle of the 1980s were neither technologically advanced nor price competitive, as these firms were selling the same models of cars until the early 1980s, which they had acquired from international firms during the 1950s.[13] Due to the technology gap, these firms could not mark their presence in the international market, hence the market of HML and PAL products was largely limited to the domestic economy. Whatever exports these firms had were mainly confined to countries in the Middle East and neighbouring developing countries in the South Asian region (such as Sri Lanka and Malaysia) and Africa (World Bank 1987; Narayanan 2006). In these countries, similar road and load conditions, driving habits and hot and humid weather conditions, combined with geographical proximity, created a demand for Indian automobiles.

Unlike HML and PAL, the poor performance of MUL was not because of technological backwardness, as the passenger cars and Multi Utility Vehicles launched by MUL in the 1980s were equipped with Suzuki technology. Thus, it was the underlying motives of MUL which restricted this firm to selling vehicles in the domestic economy rather than to competing in the international market. These underlying motives of MUL are evident. First, a survey was conducted by the Indian Market Research Bureau in the late 1981 on the MUL's request to explore the pattern of domestic demand for cars in India, as a prelude to the start of production in the early 1980s. Second, MUL entered at a time when India's passenger car industry was characterised by a huge shortage in the supply of cars in general and technologically advanced cars in particular, which was reflected in the growing waiting list of car purchasers (Okada 1998; Bhargava and Seetha 2010). Thus, the aim of this firm was to increase output in order to overcome the excess demand as well as to exploit the untapped domestic (pent-up) demand by launching new types of technologically advanced cars. Third, at the time of the JV between the GoI and Suzuki (Japan), no commitment was taken from the JV to use India as a production base for world market. The focus was to manufacture fuel-efficient cars by increasing the usage of local content. Given all this, it can be argued that the entry of foreign firms in any form until the early 1990s was aimed only at exploiting the domestic market and any relationship between foreign presence and exports of goods manufactured in India was almost non-existent.

Foreign Exchange Spending of Car Manufacturers:[14] The foreign exchange spending of all the three firms had drastically increased during the 1980s, which led to a huge drain of foreign exchange resources. These firms made large payments against technical collaborations in the form of royalties and technical fees. For instance, the average foreign exchange spending of PAL increased from 2.86 per cent of sales value in the period 1980–81 to 1984–85 to 26.48 per cent of sales value in the period 1985–86 to 1990–91 (Tables 4.3 and 4.4 in Chapter 4). In the same period, the foreign exchange earning of the firm remained below 1 per cent of sales value (Table 6.1). In addition, the import content in the production of HML and PAL products had significantly increased which added to the outflow of foreign exchange. The share of imported content in the total raw material usage rose to above 41 per cent in the case of HML and around 29 per cent in the case of PAL in 1989–90 (Table 4.5 in Chapter 4). Increase in the usage of imported content mainly occurred on two accounts. First, growing foreign presence automatically led to imports of components and parts from firms related to the foreign technology supplier. Second, HML and PAL, on account of entry of MUL, were pressured to launch technically advanced cars in collaboration with foreign firms.

Similar trends were observed in the case of MUL. The combined imports of MUL in disembodied and embodied form of technology remained more than 7 per cent of total sales during the second half of the 1980s whereas the export earning of this firm remained below 1 per cent until 1988–89 (Tables 4.3 and 4.4 in Chapter 4 and Table 6.1). As pointed out in Chapter 4, MUL initially offered assembled cars based on imported SKD/CKD kits and components from Japan. Foreign exchange payments against the imports of components of the new JV (MUL) were as high as Rs. 4.62 crores in 1983–84 (Hamaguchi 1985; Gumaste 1988). The share of indigenous raw material used in the production of cars by MUL was only 1.9 per cent of total sales value. Alternatively, the import content of MUL was as high as 85.3 per cent of total raw materials consumption in 1985. This implies that the foreign exchange spending of the firm was much higher than foreign exchange earnings. Another factor adding to the import payments of MUL was huge imports from Japan at the time when Japanese Yen appreciated significantly in the mid-1980s. Due to these factors, the gap between earning and spending widened significantly in the second half of the 1980s (D'Costa 1995).

These developments suggest that the policy of liberalisation contributed negatively to the BoP position of the country during the 1980s. Not only this, the import content of the old firms also increased. Thus it appears that the import relaxations initiated in the 1980s led to large foreign exchange outflows against various kinds of imports without much increase in foreign exchange earnings.

6.3.2 Foreign entry and BoP during the 1990s

The nature of foreign presence changed in the 1990s as the government permitted manufacturers to start production activities in India in collaboration with domestic firms. Hence, it can be expected that foreign firms would have delivered export revenue in the new economic environment owing to various incentives and relaxations announced by the GoI.

Trade Performance of Firms: Table 6.2 shows the trends in export intensity and import intensity for the period 1989–90 to 1999–2000, at industry level as well as firm level. It is observed that the import intensity of the passenger car industry has always remained higher than its export intensity. Moreover, the export intensity increased in the initial years of the 1990s only, whereas the trend remained declining after wards. As compared to this, import intensity of the industry recorded an increasing trend (Table 6.2). The downward trend in export intensity and increase in import intensity implies that the gap between spending and earning of foreign exchange has increased over the reference period (1989–90 to 1999–2000). Trends remained similar when we calculate five-year averages with a view to dealing with the effects of annual fluctuations. As compared to the first five years of the 1990s, export intensity of the industry declined during the second half of the 1990s, from 6.36 per cent to 5.86 per cent, whereas import intensity increased from 17.92 per cent to 22.08 per cent in the corresponding period. The consistent rise in the import intensity provides grounds to argue that the import content in the production of cars in India had jumped in the post-liberalisation period.

Further, the increase in exports in the early 1990s is not of much significance, as this temporary improvement in export intensity would have occurred in response to various export incentives announced by the government during that time. Exports were incentivised by the two downward adjustments in the value of the rupee with respect to major currencies of the world, on the 1st and 3rd July 1991. For instance, on July 1, 1991, the rupee was devalued against four major currencies (US Dollar, Pound Sterling, Japanese Yen and Deutsche Mark) by 8.7 to 9.7 per cent and further on

Table 6.2 Export and import intensity of car firms (percentages)

Year	HML		MUL		Daewoo Motors		All firms	
	Export intensity	Import intensity	Export intensity	Import intensity	Export intensity	Import intensity	Export intensity	Import intensity
1989–90	2.55	15.60	3.36	19.73	–	–	2.99	18.33
1990–91	1.10	10.00	4.06	16.65	–	–	3.18	14.68
1991–92	0.76	9.78	12.56	16.98	–	–	9.75	15.26
1992–93	0.67	8.65	7.52	19.81	–	–	5.86	17.11
1993–94	1.56	6.56	7.65	26.65	–	–	6.42	21.81
1994–95	1.47	7.43	7.31	20.28	21.09	29.4	6.59	18.14
1995–96	1.57	7.33	7.00	19.15	8.05	84.93	6.28	22.19
1996–97	2.22	7.01	7.86	13.38	1.85	228.81	6.58	33.02
1997–98	2.10	11.14	5.25	11.64	12.67	45.82	5.12	12.90
1998–99	9.97	20.1	4.98	15.20	32.07	78.00	6.81	18.36
1999–2000	5.80	13.78	3.22	25.14	15.46	26.56	4.86	23.51
Average export and import intensity								
1990–91 to 1994–95	1.17	8.26	7.84	20.68	–	–	6.36	17.92
1995–96 to 1999–2000	4.73	12.45	5.51	17.10	12.05	97.16	5.86	22.08

Source: CMIE PROWESS 4.12.

Note: – indicates non-availability of data.

July 3, 1991 the rupee was devalued by 10 to 11 per cent against five currencies (French Franc, US Dollar, Pound Sterling, Japanese Yen and Deutsche Mark). As a result of this, currencies of these nations appreciated against the Indian currency by around 21 to 23 per cent which made exports from India cheaper in these nations (GoI 1992–93). It could be argued that the downward adjustment of the Indian rupee was a critical factor behind the sudden jump in exports in the early 1990s. Other than the downward adjustment in the exchange rate, the GoI also announced the Export Promotion Capital Goods Scheme which facilitated easy imports of capital goods for exporters.

Firm-level analysis shows significant inter-firm variation in performance with respect to export and import intensity. It is surprising that MUL, which happened to be the dominant firm in terms of market share and which had systematically increased indigenisation of its production activities during the 1990s (Table 5.6 in Chapter 5), later experienced a decrease in export intensity during the reference period.[15] Average exports of this firm declined to 5.51 per cent of sales value in the period 1995–96 to 1999–2000, from the level of 7.84 per cent of sales value in the period 1990–91 to 1994–95 (Table 6.2). MUL's exports as a share of sales were less than half of another JV, Daewoo Motors, which entered in the 1990s. The export intensity of Daewoo was 12.05 per cent as compared to MUL's 5.51 per cent during the period 1995–96 to 1999–2000. The export intensity of Daewoo was better than that of other firms selected for the analysis, and for the year 1998–99 it even increased to as high as 32 per cent.

Corresponding to the high exports by Daewoo, though for a short time, the import intensity of Daewoo was extremely high (Table 6.2). In the second half of the 1990s, the average import intensity was as high as 97.16 per cent of sales value, which was 8 times the export intensity.

The sudden jump in the export intensity of Daewoo can be understood as a strategy of and compulsion for this firm. As a first step, Daewoo started production on a large scale to be able to produce at lowest possible cost. This firm started production facilities at Surajpur (U.P.) with an initial production capacity of 70,000 units of passenger cars per annum and later increased it to one lakh (D'Costa 2005). In line with expanding production capacity, Daewoo also signed a series of agreements with international automotive component vendors in order to ensure the supply of components and parts equipped with modern technology (Singh 2015). As part of its aggressive production strategy, Daewoo launched a number of models in India falling under different sub-segments. It initially launched the Cielo range of cars (Cielo, Cielo GLX and Cielo GLE) and then entered into the small car (Matiz), mid-size (Nexia, Nubira-II and the Lanos-II) and luxury (Magnus car with a 2.0L engine) segments. In addition, the company also upgraded its existing products (Cielo's upgraded version – GLX, a luxury model of Cielo). The focus of the firm was not only on competing with the market leader, MUL, but also on supplying cars to other countries from India. The export strategy of Daewoo was evident, as the firm was well aware that it was difficult to make an effective use of the large installed capacity by only serving Indian market as new entrants in the late 1990s (Hyundai and Tata) along with MUL flooded India's car market by introducing passenger cars in different segments. In addition, the passenger cars launched by Daewoo were meeting Euro-II emission norms and that was the major hurdle for exporting firms. But the competitive strategy of the firm did not survive for long as the parent firm of Daewoo India ran into financial trouble which adversely affected the performance of Daewoo Motors India.

Second, it was a compulsion for Daewoo to export as it signed an MoU with the DGFT in 1997 to import 60,000 CKD/SKD kits to manufacture Matiz and Ceilo cars. As part of an MoU signed with DGFT, Daewoo was forced to increase its exports in order to neutralise its import payments. Though the firm's exports increased after 1996–97 but were still far behind the target as there was a huge gap between import payments and export earnings of the firm.

Trends in imports to exports ratio are presented in Table 6.3. The import intensity of all the firms not only remained higher than export intensity but the gap widened over time, even in the case of MUL (Table 6.3). The average import intensity of MUL was 263 per cent (or 2.63 times) higher relative to its export intensity from 1990–91 to 1994–95, and this gap increased further to 310 per cent (3.1 times) during the second half of the 1990s (1995–96 to1999–2000) (Table 6.3).

The widening gap between export and import intensity especially in the case of the two leading international firms which entered through JVs (MUL and Daewoo) with Indian firms points to the nature and motive of foreign investment attracted by India in response to the 1991 policy changes. With the onset of economic

Table 6.3 Ratio of imports to exports (percentages)

Year	HML	MUL	Daewoo Motors	All firms
1989–90	612.03	556.21	–	614.83
1990–91	909.56	407.30	–	461.63
1991–92	1284.63	134.69	–	156.52
1992–93	1289.08	259.12	–	291.97
1993–94	421.21	348.43	–	339.83
1994–95	504.69	277.42	139.43	275.15
1995–96	468.14	273.71	1055.62	353.59
1996–97	315.13	170.12	12338.65	501.69
1997–98	531.03	221.82	361.53	251.75
1998–99	201.69	304.65	243.26	269.67
1999–2000	237.64	779.99	171.76	484.17
Average				
1990–91 to 1994–95	706.21	262.79	–	281.76
1995–96 to 1999–2000	263.24	310.19	806.61	376.96

Source: Same as Table 6.2.

Note: Same as Table 6.2.

reforms, especially the liberalisation of the import regime, the unmet (pent-up) demand, which existed under the earlier protectionist regime but was not getting released on account of the restricted import regime, was unleashed. With a view to exploit the benefit of the accumulated demand, foreign JVs started offering import-intensive passenger cars, which is reflected in increases in import payments throughout the 1990s.[16] Those who were already supplying import-intensive cars could increase import content in the production of finished goods. These foreign firms found it relatively cheaper to serve the domestic demand for their goods by making small investments in the production process to sell assembled products. Even for that purpose, these JVs imported capital goods to establish modern assembly facilities to exploit future demand (Table 4.4 in Chapter 4). The large imports in the form of raw material and capital goods caused a large outflow of foreign exchange without a corresponding increase in exports. It resulted in the negative contribution of foreign firms to India's BoP as the gap between earnings and spending increased during the reference period (Table 6.3).

To avoid developing India as a mere assembling centre for passenger cars, in the second half of the 1990s, GoI imposed various restrictions, including an increase in compulsory use of indigenous content, the condition that firms bring in a minimum foreign equity of US$ 50 million within the first three years of the start of operations, and the condition that car manufacturers sign an MoU with DGFT to import CKD/SKD kits. Many car firms had signed an MoU with DGFT wherein they agreed to balance import and export payments as well as increase use of local content. But no foreign firm fulfilled the commitment signed in MoU until the time the government scrapped the conditions imposed in the mid-1990s under the pressure of many developed countries through WTO.

Total Foreign Transactions of Firms: We now turn to an analysis of the BoP performance of firms on the basis of their total transactions. Total transactions of firms include foreign exchange earnings from and spending on all sources. Based on the total transactions of firms, their net contribution can be estimated. Once we added the payments in foreign currency for royalties, technical services, dividends etc. to the payments for import of goods, the extent of the deficit increased by more than 1 percentage point relative to total sales (compare Table 6.2 with Table A.6 in annexure). It means the outflow of foreign exchange was not only on account of the import of goods; repatriation of profits and other transactions of firms also accounted for 1 to 2 per cent of total sales turnover (Table A.6 in annexure).

However, earnings of foreign exchange were mainly on account of the export of goods. It is evident from the fact that there is no difference between total foreign exchange earnings (from, export of goods + other sources) and foreign exchange earnings from the export of goods only of selected firms (compare Table 6.2 and Table A.7 in annexure). On account of this, the mismatch between earnings and spending of foreign currency further widens, which directly contributes to increased external sector vulnerability.

Table 6.4 presents the trends in ratio of total foreign exchange spending to total foreign exchange earnings of selected passenger car firms. The ratio of total spending to total earnings (goods + services) is quite high, as compared to the ratio of imports to exports of goods. It suggests that payments for non-goods (royalties, technical

Table 6.4 Ratio of total foreign exchange spending to earnings (percentages)

Year	HML	MUL	Daewoo Motors	All firms average
1989–90	585.77	613.90	–	605.73
1990–91	637.02	450.34	–	477.82
1991–92	1256.81	151.60	–	174.66
1992–93	1375.20	288.24	–	319.52
1993–94	224.07	366.02	–	348.93
1994–95	405.90	290.84	141.02	284.48
1995–96	409.77	285.72	1060.18	363.16
1996–97	343.62	178.03	12369.55	510.65
1997–98	567.98	249.80	361.43	277.85
1998–99	209.68	339.45	246.15	292.26
1999–2000	246.75	845.74	178.94	520.23
Average				
1990–91 to 1994–95	495.05	282.43	–	292.15
1995–96 to 1999–2000	274.33	335.75	810.42	397.52

Source: Same as Table 6.2.

Note: Same as Table 6.2.

fees, profits repatriations etc.) accounted for a considerable out-flow of foreign exchange. The outflow of foreign exchange not only increased, but the gap between outflow and inflow has also widened from 1989–90 to 1999–2000. It is evident as the ratio of average foreign spending to average foreign earnings increased from 292.15 per cent during the period 1990–91 to 1994–95 to 397.52 per cent during the period 1995–96 to 1999–2000 (Table 6.4). It seemed likely to increase further because of two reasons: (1) foreign JVs (both MUL and Daewoo) were continuously expanding their equity share through purchase of equity of local partners. For instance, Suzuki's equity share in its joint venture increased from 26 per cent in 1982 to 50 per cent in 1992 and further to 54.2 per cent in 2002 (Table A.1 in annexure). Similarly, Daewoo held 51 per cent of equity capital in 1994, which increased to above 91 per cent in 1997 (Khare 1997). The expansion in equity share of foreign partners would automatically increase their share in profit and in other earnings which these firms are free to repatriate and (2) the imports of technology by MUL and Daewoo has been increasing continuously.

6.4   Discussion and implications

The foregoing analysis related to trade and foreign transactions clearly indicates the absence of any kind of relationship between foreign presence and export promotion in India's car industry either in the 1980s or 1990s. Rather than easing BoP constraints by bringing in more inflows of foreign exchange through exports, it added to the external vulnerability of the country. The numbers indicate that in the period when foreign entry into the car industry was liberalised the net outflow of foreign exchange increased drastically. For instance, net outflow of foreign exchange for all firms stood at about Rs. 2948.90 million in 1989–90 and reached to Rs. 6596.70 million in 1994–95 and rose sharply to Rs. 25942.70 million in 1999–2000. The increase in average foreign exchange outflow for all firms taken together during the second half of the 1990s (1995–96 to 1999–2000) was 4.2 times the outflow in the previous five years (1990–91 to 1994–95) (Table 6.5). Similar trends were noticed in the case of individual firms but the extent of the outflow varied significantly among the selected firms. The increase in average spending of foreign exchange between 1990–91 to 1994–95 and 1995–96 to 1999–2000 was to the extent of 2.2 times for HML, and 2.9 times for MUL (Table 6.5). As discussed earlier, the large outflow of foreign exchange by Daewoo occurred as the firm got approval from DGFT to import 60,000 CKD/SKD kits to manufacture Matiz and Ceilo. Further, Daewoo imported capital goods in order to build modern assembling facilities in India and supplied importintensive passenger cars in order to exploit accumulated pent-up demand.

The trends in relation to sales turnover also confirmed that net outflow of foreign exchange has continuously increased during the 1990s. For instance, net outflow of foreign exchange accounted for 12.39 per cent of total sales of all firms in 1994–95, which increased to 20.42 per cent in 1999–2000. Though the trends in outflow fluctuated on a year-to-year basis, an interesting point to note is that the average outflow was significantly higher in the period 1995–96 to 1999–2000 as compared to the previous five years (1990–91 to 1994–95) (Table 6.5). The increase observed between these two averages for all firms was to the tune of 5 percentage points relative

Table 6.5 Net foreign exchange earnings of car firms*

Year	HML		MUL		Daewoo Motors		Average of selected firms	
	Rs. million	% of sales	Rs. million	% of sales	Rs. million	% of sales	Rs. million	% of sales
1989–90	−822.90	−13.42	−2126.00	−17.91	0.00	–	−2948.90	−16.38
1990–91	−573.00	−8.99	−2165.80	−14.33	0.00	–	−2738.80	−12.74
1991–92	−602.70	−9.94	−1262.20	−6.50	0.00	–	−1864.90	−7.32
1992–93	−627.40	−9.02	−3125.90	−14.39	0.00	–	−3753.30	−13.09
1993–94	−367.00	−4.18	−5751.00	−20.34	0.00	–	−6118.00	−16.51
1994–95	−617.00	−6.26	−5853.90	−13.95	−125.80	−8.92	−6596.70	−12.39
1995–96	−758.00	−6.24	−8401.50	−13.00	−4668.40	−77.69	−13827.90	−16.70
1996–97	−692.60	−5.52	−4776.20	−6.14	−21557.60	−227.53	−27026.40	−27.07
1997–98	−1292.10	−9.95	−6531.80	−7.86	−1320.50	−34.32	−9144.40	−9.15
1998–99	−1734.90	−10.96	−9420.70	−11.95	−1745.30	−46.98	−12900.90	−13.11
1999–2000	−1685.00	−8.51	−22693.00	−24.04	−1564.70	−12.21	−25942.70	−20.42
Average net foreign exchange earnings								
1990–91 to 1994–95	−557.42	−7.33	−3631.76	−14.36	0.00	0.00	−4214.34	−12.70
1995–96 to 1999–2000	−1232.52	−8.41	−10364.64	−12.99	−6171.30	−86.03	−17768.46	−17.49

Source: Same as Table 6.2.

Notes
(1) Same as Table 6.2.
(2) * Net inflow = Total earnings − Total spending.

to total sales turnover, which is quite significant. Similarly, net out-flows of foreign exchange remained substantial, though varying, in the case of each selected firm (Table 6.5). These developments had obvious consequences for local firms which faced threats to their survival. To save themselves, these local firms also adopted a defensive strategy[17] by forming JVs with international firms, which further added to the foreign exchange outflow. Given the circumstances and the behaviour of manufactur-ers, it would be difficult to expect these entities to contribute to an easing of India's BoP constraint.

As discussed in the analytical section, changes have been observed with respect to the nature and motives of foreign investors with evi-dence of relocation of production activities to developing countries with a view to serving international market. That is expected to result in net inflows of foreign exchange and to ease the BoP con-straint. But contrary to this understanding, the nature and motives of foreign investment that India has attracted during the 1980s and 1990s has mainly been that of catering to India's huge domestic market and exploiting its future potential.

Given this, it would be significant to analyse the experience of this industry from 2000 onwards, when the government freed the entry of and eased the conditions on the operations of foreign firms.

Notes

1 For instance, the share of foreign firms in India's car production has been varying between 85 to 90 per cent in the recent years (Table 3.3 in Chapter 3). Except Tata, all other indigenous firms either have already stopped car production or are serving a meagre market (less than 0.5 per cent of total market demand).

2 According to UNCTAD (1999: 232) multinational firms 'would account for two-thirds to three-quarters of world exports, and more than a third of world exports would be between affiliated firms.'

3 See Nayyar (1978), Subrahmanian and Pillai (1979), IIFT (1981), Kumar (2000), Chandrasekhar and Ghosh (2002), Verma (2009).

4 Transactions in goods include earnings from and spending on raw material, finished goods and capital goods.

5 Foreign exchange earnings include export of goods and services, earn-ings from dividend, interest and other earnings. Similarly, total foreign spending includes import of goods, interest payments, dividend, pay-ments in the form of royalty/technical know-how and others payments (including payment for services).

6 *Export Intensity = (Export Earnings)/(Total Sales)*100*

7 *Import Intensity = (Spending on imports of goods)/(Total Sales)*100*

8 *Ratio Index = (Spendind on imports of goods)/(Export Earnings)*100*
9 *Foreign Earnings Index= (Total foreign exchange earnings)/(Total Sales)*100*
10 *Foreign Spending Index= (Total foreign exchange spending)/(Total Sales)*100*
11 *Net Contribution Index= (Total foreign exchange spending)/(Total foreign exchange earnings)*100*
12 Though we have collected data from some other sources (such as AIAM publications and from published research), the latter were lacking both in terms of coverage of foreign transactions of firms and consistency over time. Hence, it is difficult to undertake a comparable analysis for the 1980s and 1990s.
13 According to the World Bank (1987), the passenger cars offered by HML (Ambassador) and PAL (Padmini) in the 1980s were not even available in the international market at that time.
14 As mentioned earlier, we don't have complete firm-wise information on import payments. So, this section is developed on the basis of existing literature as well as information traced from other sources.
15 Indigenisation is crucial since it helps these firms in exploiting location-specific advantages of the host country, which subsequently strengthens their competitiveness. In addition, a high degree of indigenisation reduces the external vulnerability of firms in terms of stable raw material prices. In the absence of access to indigenous raw material and components, any change in the international market (in terms of price, exchange rate etc.) will ultimately influence the cost of production through import payments. It has implications on the competitiveness of the firms.
16 Under Export-Import Policy (1992–1997), the government allowed free imports of capital goods except those which were listed under negative list. In addition, India announced the Export Promotion Capital Goods Scheme which facilitated easy import of capital goods for exporters.
17 HML, which was a local firm, formed a JV with General Motors in the mid-1990s as its market position got eroded in the wake of growing variety of passenger cars launched by internationally known firms.

Chapter 7

Contribution of foreign firms to balance of payments since 2000

Net importers or exporters?

This chapter investigates the impact of foreign firms on trade performance in India's passenger car industry during the period 2000–01 to 2013–14. The analysis performed in this chapter is different from that in the previous chapter (which addressed the same issue for the period of the 1990s) in four respects: (1) The number of firms selected in this chapter is greater, and all selected firms, except HML,[1] are fully owned subsidiaries of foreign firms. (2) The policy environment around the passenger car industry has drastically changed since April 2001, enabling manufacturers to import all components and CKD/CBU units, which were subject to licensing earlier. (3) Regulations applying to the operation of foreign firms in India's passenger car industry, under Public Notice No. 60 of December 1997, were also removed in April 2001 and foreign investors were permitted to increase equity up to 100 per cent through the automatic route under Auto Policy 2002. And (4) the analysis is extended to sub-segment-wise export performance using SIAM data. This facilitates an understanding of the competitiveness of India in particular types of cars.

As part of the strategy of developing India as an export hub for small cars by attracting large inflows of foreign investment, the GoI announced a rationalised basic custom duty structure, wherein there were differentiated duties for CBU/CKD and imports of components (GoI 2002, 2006; Narayanan and Vashisht 2008). Custom duty for CBU was set at 60 per cent in 2001–02, which did not change until 2010–11. Custom duty for CKD and imports of components were set at 35 per cent in 2001–02, which was reduced to 10 per cent in 2010–11. Further, the government divided CKD imports into two groups, (a) CKD in pre-assembled form and (b) CKD not in pre-assembled form, wherein custom duty was set at

30 per cent in the first category and 10 per cent in the second group in 2010–11, which remained the same until recently (SIAM 2016a). Similarly, GoI also followed a differentiated excise duty structure for the car segment since 2007. Excise duty on small cars declined from 17 per cent (including 1 per cent National Calamity Contingent Duty) to 11 per cent in 2010–11 and then increased to 13.5 per cent in 2015–16 (SIAM 2016a). In the case of cars and utility vehicles with an engine capacity of 1500–1900cc, excise duty was set at 25 per cent plus fixed Rs. 15000 in 2008–09 and it was raised to 28 per cent in 2014–15.

It was hoped that the differentiated custom duty would discourage assembly of cars in India by discouraging the use of imported CKD/CBU kits and encouraging the use of indigenous raw material along with the low tariff components. The differentiated excise duty was also aimed at discouraging the demand for high-end products, which are developed using high import content. In this process, indigenous manufacturing capabilities of firms were expected to develop.

Based on the analysis in this chapter, it is argued that the nature and objective of foreign firms in general remained market seeking. The exports of a large number of fully owned subsidiaries of foreign firms remained close to zero, whereas the import intensity of these firms varied between 25 to 50 per cent and more so in the case of firms which manufactured luxury cars.

7.1   Data sources and methodology

For empirical analysis, data has been taken from two major secondary sources: (1) CMIE PROWESS electronic data; and (2) annual publications of SIAM. As mentioned earlier, PROWESS covered only listed firms. Given the constraints of PROWESS dataset, the analysis of this chapter is confined to six passenger car firms (see Chapter 5).

To supplement the analysis based on the PROWESS data, the information published by SIAM in two annual publications (namely Profile of the Automobile Industry in India and Statistical Profile of Automobile Industry in India) are used. Unfortunately, the data available in SIAM's annual documents are not as comprehensive as in the CMIE data. The information on foreign transactions of firms is not published in either of the two annual publications. The data related to exports of firms is useful for the present analysis.

The indices used in this chapter are the same as in the previous chapter.

7.2   Empirical analysis

The empirical analysis in this section intends to address the following issues: The *first* part examines trade performance of firms. The *second* part analyses the total foreign transaction of firms. The *third* part of the empirical analysis examines the export performance by taking the sub-segments as well as firms as the unit of analysis.

Trade Performance of firms: Table 7.1 shows the trends in both export as well as import intensity of the passenger car firms for the period of 2000–01 to 2013–14. In general, export as well as import intensity of the industry observed an upward trend until the end of the first decade of the 21st century, but the increases observed were sharper in the case of exports as compared to imports, which led to a reduction in the gap between import spending and export earnings. For instance, export intensity of all firms taken together increased from 2.79 per cent of sales turnover in 2000–01 to 10.06 per cent in 2005–06 and further to 18.91 per cent in 2013–14, whereas the corresponding change in import intensity was from 17.01 per cent to 20.36 per cent and then to 17.91 per cent. Since 2009–10, the car industry remained a net exporter (Table 7.1). Similarly, five-year averages also indicated that the export intensity of the industry increased from 7.12 per cent in the period 2000–01 to 2004–05 to 17.85 per cent during the period 2010–11 to 2013–14, whereas, correspondingly, import intensity declined marginally. It remains to be seen what the contribution of each individual firm was, as the average may be inflated by high exports of one or two firms. If all firms have experienced an increase in exports by this margin, then it would be a healthy sign for the BoP position of the country.

Firm-wise comparison of export and import intensity did not show very encouraging trends. Except Hyundai, all other firms remained net importers during the reference period. Not only this, these firms did not observe any significant change on the export front, whereas they observed a sharp increase in import intensity during the reference period (except MUL, which recorded marginal improvements in export intensity along with a reduction in import intensity, but it still remained a net importer) (Table 7.1).

Until 2009–10, the performance of three firms, namely HML, General Motors and Honda remained very disappointing. In 2009–10, export intensity of HML, General Motors and Honda remained

Table 7.1 Export and import intensity of car firms (percentages)

Year	HML Export intensity	HML Import intensity	MUL Export intensity	MUL Import intensity	Hyundai Motor Export intensity	Hyundai Motor Import intensity	General Motors Export intensity	General Motors Import intensity	Honda Cars Export intensity	Honda Cars Import intensity	Ford India Export intensity	Ford India Import intensity	Average of selected firms Export intensity	Average of selected firms Import intensity
2000–01	0.81	15.49	2.41	17.58	4.06	14.18	0.00	29.54	0.50	19.85	8.65	14.77	2.79	17.01
2001–02	0.84	12.22	2.16	12.09	3.20	16.73	0.07	27.75	0.51	20.67	18.76	12.23	3.17	14.20
2002–03	1.11	12.34	6.74	11.67	4.27	17.92	0.09	46.37	0.71	18.15	16.05	16.09	5.92	14.32
2003–04	1.08	10.08	8.46	10.82	16.11	26.18	0.04	42.94	0.50	30.69	10.76	15.66	9.41	18.10
2004–05	0.90	8.26	7.28	12.75	25.25	22.56	0.03	24.73	0.44	27.07	8.89	25.51	10.78	17.96
2005–06	0.20	13.03	3.86	10.64	27.76	31.76	0.02	20.13	0.09	30.33	5.53	31.27	10.06	20.36
2006–07	0.38	18.53	3.31	8.11	28.31	34.83	0.01	19.27	0.04	28.53	4.30	24.78	9.42	19.92
2007–08	0.04	25.87	3.49	10.62	30.03	27.34	0.07	39.19	0.03	30.84	–	–	10.32	20.42
2008–09	0.08	28.01	6.41	12.69	46.02	20.50	0.33	47.30	0.03	38.48	–	–	19.68	20.18
2009–10	0.01	24.52	14.10	9.24	44.26	14.29	0.00	49.16	0.53	27.32	–	–	22.35	14.83
2010–11	0.02	35.85	8.62	9.42	34.47	17.72	–	–	–	–	–	–	16.24	11.82
2011–12	0.16	33.67	9.38	10.86	32.67	20.17	–	–	3.99	30.17	–	–	17.32	15.49
2012–13	0.16	127.38	9.29	11.79	35.66	22.80	–	–	9.86	31.35	–	–	18.31	17.02
2013–14	–	–	8.43	10.05	37.71	22.40	0.01	30.07	8.30	21.40	36.18	36.79	18.91	17.91
Average export and import intensity														
2000–01 to 2004–05	0.92	11.97	5.68	12.87	13.69	20.78	0.04	31.06	0.51	25.05	12.19	17.61	7.12	16.61
2005–06 to 2009–10	0.14	22.54	7.26	10.26	37.84	23.31	0.09	37.51	0.15	30.95	4.79**	27.38**	15.55	18.71
2010–11 to 2013–14	0.09#	49.06#	8.92	10.56	35.27	21.00	0.01*	30.07*	6.35$	25.95$	36.18*	36.79*	17.85	15.68

Source: Same as Table 5.1.

Note: Same as Table 5.1.

0.01 per cent, 0.00 per cent and 0.53 per cent, respectively. Correspondingly, the import intensity of these firms remained 24.52 per cent, 49.16 per cent and 27.32 per cent, respectively. It indicates that these firms have spent very high amounts on imports without any change in exports. The gap between export and import payments has widened over time. For instance, the import payments of General Motors and Honda were 408 times and 40 times of export earnings, respectively, in 2001–02, which increased to 14556 times and 51 times of export earnings, respectively, in 2009–10 (Table 7.2).

Ford India initially had high export intensity but over time it has also become a net importer.[2] MUL did not show a huge gap in export and import intensities but it also remained a net importer throughout. Therefore, the average of all firms taken together was providing a misleading picture of the industry as the high export intensity of Hyundai had inflated the average figure for export intensity of industry and showed a declining gap with import intensity. Otherwise, at the individual firm level (except Hyundai), import intensity remained higher than export intensity during the reference period.

In recent years, the picture has turned more worrisome as Hyundai's exports started declining, which is the sole good performer in the industry. HML, MUL and General Motors continue to perform on the same lines and remained net importers. Honda showed an increasing trend of exports but it also remained a net importer by a huge margin. Overall, the gap between export and import intensities of HML, General Motors and Honda is still too huge to be offset by higher exports of Hyundai and it has severe implications for BoP of the country.

There could be several reasons behind the better performance of Hyundai as compared to other firms. The most important one is the initial objective and long-term strategies of the foreign firms, which determine the outcome (see Chapter 8).

Except for Hyundai, which entered as a fully owned subsidiary of the parent firm in 1996, all other firms (MUL, Ford, Honda and General Motors) initially entered India as JVs with small stakes. For instance, General Motors formed a JV with Hindustan Motors in 1994, Ford signed a 50:50 JV with M&M, Honda with Shriram Group and Suzuki with Maruti. At the time of entry, Hyundai aimed to develop India as a manufacturing base to serve the local market and to supply CKD kits and components to the parent plant in South Korea and other subsidiaries of parent companies located in 14 countries (Gulyani 2001; Tewari 2001; Park 2004).[3] On the other hand, if we look at the case of other selected firms,

Table 7.2 Ratio of imports to exports (percentages)

Year	HML	MUL	Hyundai Motor	General Motors	Honda Cars	Ford India	Average of selected firms
2000–01	1919.72	729.26	349.15	0.00	3939.06	170.75	608.89
2001–02	1448.13	559.30	522.81	40794.00	4092.31	65.20	447.96
2002–03	1110.79	173.15	419.30	53094.44	2545.21	100.27	241.75
2003–04	931.72	127.96	162.48	99054.76	6088.71	145.51	192.31
2004–05	920.91	175.09	89.37	87905.88	6101.29	287.12	166.62
2005–06	6380.53	275.68	114.39	110116.67	32116.96	565.61	202.50
2006–07	4823.55	244.92	123.03	212050.00	78180.57	576.68	211.39
2007–08	68959.38	303.95	91.05	59996.61	122364.23	–	197.92
2008–09	33757.81	198.04	44.56	14205.33	133230.89	–	102.55
2009–10	450750.00	65.57	32.28	145641.67	5130.80	–	66.34
2010–11	221953.85	109.23	51.42	–	–	–	72.82
2011–12	21448.39	115.82	61.67	–	755.14	–	89.42
2012–13	78351.22	126.94	63.94	–	317.97	–	92.96
2013–14	–	119.17	59.41	267780.43	257.88	101.71	94.70
Average							
2000–01 to 2004–05	1296.19	226.46	151.73	81685.09	4901.48	144.49	233.33
2005–06 to 2009–10	16035.37	141.31	61.59	40667.65	20210.64	571.56**	120.32
2010–11 to 2013–14	55051.02#	118.43	60.00	267780.43*	334.33$	101.71*	88.94

Source: Same as Table 5.1.

Note: Same as Table 5.1.

including MUL,[4] their strategies neither explicitly nor implicitly emphasised the objective of developing India as a base for world market production. These firms have aggressively launched a variety of technically advanced cars with high usage of import content with the intent to capture market share in the large Indian market for modern cars. It suggests that the initial intention of these firms, except Hyundai, was to exploit the promising market. Evidence suggests that local profits were more attractive than what these firms would have earned in the international market, where the competition was much higher (Chandrasekhar and Ghosh 2002).[5] Over time, these firms reduced the share of local partners in JVs and steadily converted themselves into subsidiaries of parent firms. Given the evolution of MUL, Ford, General Motors and Honda,

> it should be expected that any increase in the equity stake of the foreign investors in existing joint ventures or purchase of a share of equity by them in the domestic firms would not automatically change the orientation of the firm. That is, the aim of such FDI investors would be to benefit from the profits earned in the Indian market. As a result, in such cases FDI inflows need not be accompanied by any substantial increase in exports, whether such investment leads to modernization of domestic capacity or not.[6]
> (Chandrasekhar and Ghosh 2002: 133)

The strategy of Hyundai would have also been influenced by profitability considerations, which are the outcome of the policy environment and depend on a firm's competitive strengths. Hyundai entered India at a time when the policy environment was liberal, and India's car market was flooded with technologically advanced cars launched by Daewoo, MUL, General Motors etc. D'Costa (2005) points out that large-scale entry into the industry in the middle of the 1990s and subsequent expansion in the manufacturing capacity led to a fall in capacity utilisation in the industry. Thus, rather than depending completely on the local market to exploit scale economies in production and earn profits, given Hyundai's international competitiveness, it was strategically sound and possibly more profitable for it to export to other markets from India. Given the surrounding policy environment and aggressive strategy of Hyundai to start production at a large scale (initial installed capacity of Hyundai was 1,20,000 units per annum), these factors would have additionally motivated this firm to use India as a base for world production.

7.2.1 Total foreign transactions of firms

To understand the actual contribution of foreign firms to the BoP, we estimate total foreign exchange earnings and spending which include, besides export and import of goods, earnings from exports of services, interest earnings, other sources of foreign exchange and foreign exchange expenditures such as dividend, interest payments, spending on travel, royalty and technical fees etc. Once we include the foreign exchange spending of passenger car firms under these categories, foreign exchange expenditure increased by 3 to 7 per cent of sales value for all firms taken together (Table A.8 in annexure). Correspondingly, the inclusion of earnings of foreign exchange from these sources showed a negligible impact on total foreign exchange earnings, especially until 2004–05, after which it increased by just around 1 per cent of sales value (Table A.9 in annexure). This suggests that earnings from 'exports of non-goods' remained much lower than spending on 'imports of non-goods.' This led to a further widening of the gap between foreign exchange earnings and spending (Tables 7.2 and 7.3).

This gap is likely to increase further as foreign investors are reducing spending in in-house R&D and increasing use of imported technology and raw material in their manufacturing activities during the last decade and a half (see Chapter 5). Growing import of technology is obviously associated with outflow of foreign exchange in terms of royalties and technical fees. From 2010–11 to 2013–14, the royalty and technical fee payments almost tripled as compared to the payments for the same from 2000–01 to 2004–05 (Table 5.4 in Chapter 5). It is so because abolition of the ceiling for royalty payments in 2009 provided a free hand to firms to import as much as they want.

Trends in spending to earnings ratio have varied substantially across the firms. Hyundai is the only firm which started contributing positively to the BoP since 2008–09. Alternatively, total foreign exchange spending of Hyundai has been less than its total foreign exchange earnings since 2008–09. But the same does not hold true for any of the other firms selected for this analysis. The ratio is quite substantial and increasing over time in the case of firms like HML and General Motors until 2013–14 and in the case of firms like Honda and Ford until 2009–10 (Table 7.3).

The trends in net foreign exchange earnings both in relative and absolute terms are presented in Table 7.4. On the basis of five-year averages for all firms taken together, spending amounted to more than earnings until recently but the gap between earnings and

Table 7.3 Ratio of total foreign exchange spending to earnings (percentages)

Year	HML	MUL	Hyundai Motor	General Motors	Honda Cars	Ford India	Average of selected firms
2000–01	1908.64	815.78	370.30	8603.21	4825.21	201.87	663.71
2001–02	1495.78	668.35	526.57	6225.46	4898.14	84.21	508.76
2002–03	1126.28	200.10	536.40	6252.65	3122.17	119.65	295.98
2003–04	938.27	141.74	172.67	1784.77	6628.36	172.41	204.33
2004–05	897.78	196.59	106.33	904.94	6587.36	289.25	180.65
2005–06	6525.66	319.44	127.29	405.55	35543.60	546.09	213.06
2006–07	4863.55	313.01	130.39	482.21	85089.14	606.34	221.67
2007–08	54392.86	386.32	100.35	646.77	136221.95	–	207.75
2008–09	28888.16	256.73	53.34	384.74	150423.58	–	113.56
2009–10	49237.84	89.28	45.99	873.76	5895.78	–	82.43
2010–11	59408.16	175.99	66.64	–	–	–	102.74
2011–12	15055.97	186.35	74.40	–	908.32	–	119.45
2012–13	21129.41	197.57	78.04	–	385.96	–	123.21
2013–14	–	197.02	74.48	1936.80	298.43	108.76	121.94
Average							
2000–01 to 2004–05	1296.64	257.36	172.25	1702.67	5500.00	165.19	256.72
2005–06 to 2009–10	14787.02	181.80	72.59	550.25	22602.29	577.53**	134.00
2010–11 to 2013–14	24289.58#	190.07	74.00	1936.80*	392.31$	108.76*	118.09

Source: Same as Table 5.1.

Note: Same as Table 5.1.

Table 7.4 Net foreign exchange earnings^

Year	HML Rs. million	% of sales	MUL Rs. million	% of sales	Hyundai Motor Rs. million	% of sales	General Motors Rs. million	% of sales	Honda Cars Rs. million	% of sales	Ford India Rs. million	% of sales	Average of selected firms Rs. million	% of sales
2000–01	-2659	-15	-15647	-17	-3631	-12	-1590	-31	-1706	-24	-926	-9	-26159	-16
2001–02	-1456	-12	-11350	-12	-5018	-15	-2309	-31	-2058	-24	315	3	-21876	-13
2002–03	-1281	-12	-6211	-7	-8257	-21	-1391	-67	-2113	-22	-330	-3	-19581	-12
2003–04	-832	-10	-3931	-4	-7288	-12	-3927	-41	-5203	-33	-1047	-8	-22228	-10
2004–05	-1078	-8	-9495	-7	-1322	-2	-4253	-23	-7545	-29	-2961	-18	-26654	-9
2005–06	-726	-13	-12813	-8	-7303	-8	-3217	-16	-10243	-33	-5071	-28	-39373	-13
2006–07	-1477	-18	-12314	-7	-9718	-9	-4170	-17	-14873	-31	-6281	-23	-48833	-13
2007–08	-2280	-27	-21225	-10	-139	-0.1	-12793	-35	-16743	-34	–	–	-53180	-12
2008–09	-2188	-28	-23544	-10	41337	23	-11726	-37	-18490	-43	–	–	-14610	-3
2009–10	-1818	-25	4870	1.5	54928	26	-16320	-46	-15394	-31	–	–	26266	4
2010–11	-2906	-36	-26587	-7	26373	12	–	–	-13986	-36	–	–	-17106	-3
2011–12	-2004	-34	-31879	-8	22148	9	–	–	-12579	-32	–	–	-24314	-4
2012–13	-3218	-128	-44491	-9	23906	9	–	–	-13104	-28	–	–	-36906	-5
2013–14	–	–	-40181	-8	29179	10	-13388	-33	-16359	-18	-3063	-3	-43812	-4
Average														
2000–01 to 2004–05	-1461	-12	-9327	-9	-5103	-11	-2694	-32	-3725	-28	-990	-8	-23300	-12
2005–06 to 2009–10	-1698	-23	-13005	-6	15821	11	-9645	-33	-15149	-34	-5676 **	-25**	-25946	-6
2010–11 to 2013–14	-2709#	-49#	-35785	-8	25402	10	-13388*	-33*	-14007	-26	-3063*	-3*	-43550	-5

Source: Same as Table 5.1.

Notes
(1) Same as Table 5.1;
(2) ^ Net inflow = Total earnings – Total spending.

spending has declined substantially after 2007–08. Alternatively, on an average, net foreign exchange outflow of all firms stood at 12 per cent of sales turnover during the period 2000–01 to 2004–05, which declined to 6 per cent in the period 2005–06 to 2009–10 and then reduced to 5 per cent in the following four years (2010–11 to 2013–14). As noted earlier, the foreign exchange spending of all firms except Hyundai remained higher than foreign exchange earnings. Once we exclude Hyundai from this analysis, the net outflow of foreign exchange increased significantly (increase varied to the tune of 2.5 to 6.0 per cent of sales) (compare Table 7.4 and A.10 in annexure). It also is reflected in five-year average figures.

The inter-firm variation clearly indicates that Hyundai is the only exception whereas all other firms have continuously drained the country of foreign exchange resources until recently (Table 7.4). The negative earnings were increasing in terms of value and remained substantially high in terms of percentage share of sales of all firms. In recent years, General Motors and Honda had negative earnings to the tune of 33and 26 per cent of sales turnover. Although, data for General Motors and Ford is not available for all the years, but observing their consistently high negative net foreign exchange earnings, nothing positive can be hoped for in the years with missing data. If we check the total average, it becomes clear that excluding Hyundai's contribution further widened the gap between earnings and spending and that too increasingly over time (Table A.10 in annexure).

7.2.2   Firm-wise and sub-segment-wise analysis

Up to now, our analysis was based on six selected firms.[7] It is important to mention here that our previously selected six firms accounted for more than 90 per cent of total production in India as late as 2000–01 and 80 per cent of total production of cars in India in 2013–14. Therefore, exclusion of other firms is not likely to change our previous results but analysing the performance of the remaining firms would provide more insight into the trends relating to the external performance of car firms in India.

Therefore, we have extended our analysis by including information on some more firms using the SIAM data. As discussed earlier, this data is not as comprehensive as CMIE data, as it covers information on specific indicators related to total production and exports and no information is available on imports.[8] The positive thing is that it covers a large number of firms operating in the passenger car industry. Based on this information, Table 7.5 presents the export contribution of 13 firms operating in the car industry to total industry exports as well as the export intensity of the car industry as a whole. In general, exports of passenger cars increased from 2001–02 to 2013–14. In 2001–02, exports of the car industry were to the tune of 9.84 per cent of total production of cars in India, which almost doubled to 18.24 per cent in 2010–11 and further stood at 23.73 per cent in 2013–14. Despite this, car exports did not exceed one fourth of the total production of cars in India. In other words, more than 75 per cent of cars produced in India were sold in the domestic market itself.

Export Contribution of Firms: To assess the importance of different firms in terms of contribution to total industry exports, percentage share of each firm in total exports of the car industry is calculated. The important point which emerges from Table 7.5 is that out of all the firms, the contribution of 8 firms towards total exports of the car industry remained either zero or close to zero (less than 0.5 per cent) from 2001–02 to 2011–12. The situation did not change much even until recently. In 2013–14, 6 firms contributed either zero or close to zero per cent, 4 other firms contributed just between 1–6 per cent. It supports our earlier findings that their motive was and still remains that of exploiting a growing domestic market.

Substantial variation has been noticed across firms in terms of their contribution to the industry performance. Just three firms, namely, Hyundai, Nissan and MUL were contributing approximately 90 per cent of the total exports of the car industry in 2012–13. This means the contribution of the other 10 firms was meagre. Based on their contribution to industry exports, the firms can be divided into four groups. Firms which have (1) contributed significantly to total industry exports throughout the reference period, (2) contributed significantly in the initial years and then observed a downturn, (3) observed some increase in contribution to industry's exports in recent years, (4) contributed nil to the total industry exports.

Among the first set of firms are MUL and Hyundai, the two car manufacturers that have substantially contributed to the industry exports throughout the reference period. The combined contribution of these two firms increased from around 72 per cent for the period 2001–02 to 2005–06 to more than 90 per cent for the period 2006–07 to 2010–11 (Table 7.5). The second group of firms includes Ford India and Tata Motors, which contributed significantly to the total exports of industry in the early years of the previous decade but observed a significant downturn after 2006–07. For instance, the contribution of Ford and Tata to the total industry was 61.72 and 4.41 per cent respectively in 2001–02, which declined to 5.55 and 1.04 per cent in 2013–14. The third set of firms, including Nissan, Toyota and Volkswagen, witnessed a marginal increase in their contribution to industry's exports during the last two to three years. Until 2010–11, the export contribution of Toyota and Volkswagen remained zero, which increased to 4.95 and 6.05 per cent respectively in 2013–14. The last group includes firms like Fiat, General Motors, Honda, HML, M&M and Skoda, which made negligible contribution to the total industry exports (Table 7.5).

It indicates that, except for two firms (Hyundai and MUL), the export performance of other firms has remained inconsistent. For instance, the rising contribution of Toyota and Volkswagen in the last two years is a positive sign but it is difficult to predict the sustainability of their contribution. Evidence indicates that firms which contributed significantly to the exports of the industry in the initial years of the 21st century have shifted their focus to the domestic market over time.

The two dominant firms (Hyundai and MUL) also performed very differently from each other, as Hyundai's contribution was much larger than MUL's during the major part of the reference period. Moreover, the dominance of Hyundai in export contribution in the industry remained consistent and also increased significantly over time, while MUL's contribution has varied over time but did not change much. For instance, export share of Hyundai in the car industry increased by almost 4.4 times from 2001–02 (11 per cent) to 2012–13 (47.70 per cent). Further, the average export contribution of Hyundai increased from 41.82 per cent for the period 2001–02 to 2005–06 to 45.73 per cent for the period 2011–12 to 2013–14, whereas the corresponding figures for MUL were 30.62 per cent and 21.56 per cent (Table 7.5). Given the numbers, it is clear that the increase in the export intensity of India's car industry is mainly driven by the export performance of just one firm (Hyundai) since 2001. It corroborates our previous finding related to the important role of Hyundai in relation to foreign exchange earnings.

Based on the above analysis, it is clear that Hyundai is the only firm which has been exporting substantially since 2001–02 and

Table 7.5 Car exports from India, 2001–02 to 2013–14 (percentages)

Year	Export intensity of car industry	Firm-wise distribution of exports												
		Fiat India	Ford India	General Motors	HML	Honda Cars	Hyundai Motor	M&M	MUL	Nissan Motor	Skoda Auto	Tata Motors	Toyota India	Volkswagen India
2001–02	9.84	–	61.72	0.10	0.13	0.01	11.00	–	22.63	–	–	4.41	–	–
2002–03	12.61	–	39.22	0.00	0.07	0.12	12.75	–	44.84	–	–	3.00	0.00	–
2003–04	16.01	–	19.15	0.00	0.01	0.04	33.60	–	40.10	–	0.00	7.10	0.00	–
2004–05	16.73	–	14.08	0.00	0.01	0.11	51.09	–	29.65	–	0.00	5.05	0.00	–
2005–06	16.25	–	9.49	0.00	0.00	0.03	60.06	–	19.76	–	0.00	10.66	0.00	–
2006–07	15.57	–	11.93	0.00	0.00	0.02	59.94	0.00	19.59	–	0.00	8.51	0.00	–
2007–08	14.80	–	1.19	0.00	0.00	0.02	68.42	0.00	24.59	–	0.00	5.78	0.00	–
2008–09	21.86	0.18	0.20	0.04	0.00	0.02	76.42	0.49	20.76	–	0.00	1.90	0.00	–
2009–10	22.86	0.25	0.35	0.11	0.00	0.02	64.67	0.23	33.09	–	0.01	1.28	0.00	0.00
2010–11	18.24	0.30	2.72	0.09	0.00	0.02	52.09	0.43	30.40	12.36	0.00	1.58	0.00	0.00
2011–12	19.77	0.27	5.10	0.09	0.00	0.01	47.34	0.00	25.06	20.12	0.00	1.45	0.16	0.40
2012–13	22.42	0.02	5.38	0.04	0.00	0.48	47.70	0.00	21.82	18.17	0.00	1.04	4.30	1.03
2013–14	23.73	0.01	5.55	0.00	0.00	0.92	42.32	0.00	18.11	21.06	0.00	1.04	4.95	6.05
Average														
2001–02 to 2005–06	14.96	–	20.97	0.01	0.02	0.06	41.82	–	30.26	0.00	0.00	6.85	0.00	–
2006–07 to 2010–11	18.96	0.19	2.45	0.06	0.00	0.02	63.53	0.28	27.13	3.41	0.00	2.93	0.00	–
2011–12 to 2013–14	21.92	0.09	5.35	0.06	0.00	0.48	45.73	0.00	21.56	19.78	0.00	1.17	3.23	2.56

Source: Same as Figure 3.1.

Note: – indicates non-existence of firm in those years or non-availability of data.

started earning positive net foreign exchange revenues since 2009. It is, therefore, wrong to argue based on the contribution of just one firm alone, as advocates of liberalisation have done, that increased foreign presence is resulting in net inflows of foreign exchange into the country.

But how sustainable in the long run would this trend based on the contribution of just one firm be? Hyundai is a subsidiary of an international firm which has entered India to exploit locational advantage. If this firm changes its strategy on account of better advantages offered by (available in) another country, as developing countries are competing to attract more and more foreign investment, then export performance of the car industry would drastically decline which would adversely affect the BoP situation of the country, as all other firms are net importers and did not record any significant improvements in exports since their inception.

How sustainable would the Indian car industry's exports be? The question that arises is whether the increasing trends in exports of the car industry, as witnessed after 2000, would continue in the years to come. It is critical to analyse the sustainability of these trends since exports of two major firms (Hyundai and MUL), which are accounting for maximum exports of the car industry since 2001–02, have started witnessing a decline both in absolute as well as in relative terms in the recent years (Tables 7.1, 7.4 and 7.5 and SIAM 2016a). Hyundai, the only firm to emerge as a net exporter since 2007–08, has started shifting its export base outside India. In 2014, Hyundai decided to stop its exports from the Chennai plant (India) to the European market. The firm has shifted the production base of some of its export models (i10 and i20) from India to its subsidiaries located in Turkey and Czechoslovakia (Gupta 2014). Accordingly, the exports of Hyundai declined from 2.59 lakh units in 2012–13 to 1.19 lakh units in 2014–15 (SIAM 2016a). Correspondingly, the export intensity of the firm declined from 40.70 to 31.17. It is a concern for sustainability of exports of India's car industry, as Europe accounted for around 45 per cent of Hyundai Motor India's total exports before July 2014 (Mukherjee 2014).

What caused change in the exports strategy of Hyundai? The decision of the firm is shaped by a combination of factors. First, in December 2013, the European Union (EU) discontinued import duty relief, which was provided to India under the Generalised System of Preferences. Accordingly, import duty on Indian products entering into the European market increased from 6.5 to 10 per cent, which made Indian products uncompetitive in the European market (*Business Line* 2013). The concession duty was withdrawn by the EU in order to pressure India to expedite signing a free-trade agreement with the EU, the process of which was initiated in 2007 but is still pending (*Business Line* 2013; Lakshmikumaran and Sridharan 2017; Mishra 2017). Second, the incidence of a prolonged strike by a section of employees at the Hyundai plant in Chennai in 2009 adversely affected the production of some of its export market models (*Livemint* 2009; Agarwal 2010; *Business Today* 2012; Chatterjee 2016). It was realised that any such incidence in the future could jeopardise the expansion plans of the firm in Europe. Thus, the parent firm of Hyundai decided to establish a production facility near the market (Gupta 2014). Third, being the only one to use India as a base to serve the world market and to contribute positively to foreign exchange earnings, the firm was expecting special incentives from the government of India as are provided to the exporters by major emerging economies. The absence of any special favourable treatment from the Indian government also contributed to the decision of the firm to shift out. Fourth, according to a senior official of Hyundai, the company has stopped exports to Europe in order to free up production capacity to cater more to the Indian market given that the firm has been using more than 95 per cent of its installed capacity in the Chennai plant in recent years (*Livemint* 2014; Mukherjee 2014; Baggonkar 2016). To improve its market share in India, Hyundai is focusing on expanding its compact car and SUV portfolio by launching the second generation cars according to the requirement of the Indian market (Mukherjee 2014; Gupta 2014). It indicates that external as well as internal factors including growing acceptance of its products in India motivated the firm to exploit the local market.

The downturn in car exports is not only confined to Hyundai, but the exports of other firms such as Nissan, Toyota, Fiat and MUL have also recorded consistent decline after 2014–15. The declining exports of all these firms put a question mark on India's emergence as a manufacturing hub for the world market, which remains the primary objective of the government's policies initiated since the onset of liberal policy regime. The long-term motives of these firms are evident as their focus while launching new models remains to increase their presence in India. For that purpose, they are launching a number of new models on a regular basis in the rapidly growing domestic car market. It implies that foreign entrants do not have any commitment and also the pressure, owing to India's commitments to WTO agreements, to use India as a base for world market.

Given this strategy, it is very difficult to expect that the kind of FDI that India has received after liberalisation would promote India as a manufacturing base to serve the world and bring net positive foreign exchange earnings in the near future.

Sub-Segment Wise Contribution to Exports: As was noted in Chapter 3, the segmentation in the passenger car industry is increasing. Only one segment (namely compact) accounted for around 80 per cent of total cars manufactured in India in the recent past (Figure 3.1 in Chapter 3). It would therefore be useful to analyse whether India's export competitiveness also lies in this segment of the industry or not.

Based on Table 7.6 some specific characteristics with regard to the exports of the car industry can be identified. Exports of cars from India are very specific in nature as only one segment (namely compact) accounts for a very large share of total exports. The dominance of this segment has increased over the reference period as the contribution of this segment to the car industry's exports increased from 29.95 per cent in 2001–02 to 74.81 per cent in 2005–06 and to a high of 91.25 per cent in 2011–12. In terms of long-term average, more than 66 per cent of total car industry exports were confined to the compact segment from 2001–02 to 2005–06, which further increased to 87 per cent for the period 2006–07 to 2010–11. On the other hand, the export intensity of the mini and mid-size segment declined drastically in the reference period. For instance, the export share of the mid-size car segment was 63.97 per cent in 2001–02, which declined to 6.30 per cent in 2010–11. The interesting point to be highlighted is that the contribution of the mid-size segment in the industry exports started increasing after 2009–10, but around 84 per cent of the exports of the car industry are confined to the compact size segment from 2011–12 to 2013–14. These numbers indicate that exports of the car industry are very specific in nature and concentrated in the compact segment.

Exports are not only concentrated in one segment but also in one firm. Table 7.7 reveals that the export contribution of Hyundai remained substantial in both the segments (compact and mid-size) and it increased over time. The export contribution of Hyundai in the compact and mid-size segments increased from 30.60 per cent and 2.87 per cent, respectively, in 2001–02 to 51.71 per cent and

Table 7.6 Sub-segment-wise exports of car firms (percentages)

Year	Export intensity of car industry	Segment-wise distribution of exports						
		Mini	Compact*	Mid-size	Executive	Premier	Luxury	Total
2001–02	9.84	6.07	29.95	63.97	0.00	0.00	0.00	100.00
2002–03	12.61	9.51	48.04	42.41	0.00	0.04	0.00	100.00
2003–04	16.01	8.36	67.09	24.52	0.00	0.03	0.00	100.00
2004–05	16.73	5.09	75.65	19.22	0.00	0.03	0.00	100.00
2005–06	16.25	6.59	74.81	18.59	0.00	0.00	0.00	100.00
2006–07	15.57	8.75	71.39	19.86	0.00	0.00	0.00	100.00
2007–08	14.80	8.27	80.63	11.10	0.00	0.00	0.00	100.00
2008–09	21.86	4.41	86.55	9.04	0.00	0.00	0.00	100.00
2009–10	22.86	1.27	93.41	5.23	0.08	0.00	0.00	100.00
2010–11	18.24	2.79	90.87	6.30	0.04	0.00	0.00	100.00
2011–12	19.77	–	91.25	8.69	0.06	0.00	0.00	100.00
2012–13	22.42	–	83.20	16.78	0.02	0.00	0.00	100.00
2013–14	23.73	–	79.12	20.87	0.01	0.00	0.00	100.00
Average								
2001–02 to 2005–06	14.96	6.87	66.26	26.85	0.00	0.02	0.00	100.00
2006–07 to 2010–11	18.96	4.12	87.04	8.80	0.03	0.00	0.00	100.00
2011–12 to 2013–14	21.92	–	84.32	15.65	0.03	0.00	0.00	100.00

Source: Same as Figure 3.1.

Note: * since 2011–12, compact segment includes mini segment.

Table 7.7 Export share of dominant firms (% of respective segment)

Firms	2001–02	2002–03	2003–04	2004–05	2005–06	2006–07	2007–08	2008–09	2009–10	2010–11	2011–12	2012–13	2013–14
*Mini segment**													
MUL	100	100	100	100	100	100	100	100	100	100	–	–	–
Compact size													
Hyundai Motor	30.60	20.94	42.52	61.85	71.33	76.68	75.82	79.59	64.63	51.71	46.49	50.79	46.79
MUL	54.69	72.83	46.93	32.41	17.56	15.13	20.21	18.86	33.93	30.22	27.25	22.58	22.88
Tata Motors	14.71	6.24	10.55	5.73	11.11	8.19	3.98	1.30	1.15	1.39	1.47	1.09	1.20
Nissan Motor	–	–	–	–	–	–	–	–	–	13.61	18.94	15.24	17.97
Ford India	–	–	–	–	–	0.00	0.00	0.00	0.00	2.71	5.41	6.38	6.49
Toyota India	–	–	–	–	–	–	–	–	–	–	0.14	3.31	3.31
Volkswagen India	–	–	–	–	–	–	–	–	–	–	–	–	0.20
Mid-size segment													
Ford India	96.48	92.47	78.09	73.24	51.04	60.07	10.71	2.20	6.65	4.04	1.88	0.46	1.99
Hyundai Motor	2.87	6.35	20.70	22.37	36.01	26.19	65.65	83.25	82.21	81.02	56.64	32.42	25.39
MUL	0.28	0.82	1.02	0.21	0.21	0.22	0.29	0.37	2.33	2.47	2.27	18.07	0.02
Nissan Motor	–	–	–	–	–	–	–	–	–	0.00	32.67	32.73	32.80
Tata Motors	–	0.00	0.09	3.72	12.61	13.44	23.23	8.55	3.89	5.05	1.26	0.78	0.39
Toyota India	–	0.00	0.00	0.00	0.00	0.00	0.00	0.00	0.00	0.00	0.44	9.23	11.14
Volkswagen India	–	–	–	–	–	–	–	–	–	0.00	4.55	6.16	28.21

Source: Same as Figure 3.1.
Note:
(1) Same as Table 3.5.

81.02 per cent in 2010–11 (Table 7.7). In the corresponding years, the combined export contribution of two other firms (MUL and Tata), which accounted for 70 per cent of total compact car exports in the early years of the last decade, recorded a sharp decline and their contribution fell to around 32 per cent in 2010–11. Since 2011–12, the contribution of Nissan in mid-size and compact segments increased, but recent reports cite a sharp decline in the firm's exports.

According to Baggonkar (2016) Nissan's exports have continuously declined in the last three years (2014–15 to 2016–17 until August). Its share in the passenger vehicle industry exports have reduced from 19.3 per cent in 2014–15 to 12.7 per cent in 2016–17 (up to August, 2016).

Based on these numbers, it can be expected that if Hyundai further phases out its exports, as it has decided to stop serving the European market from India and supply more cars in the domestic market, then no other firm in compact and mid-size car segments seems motivated or strong enough to neutralise the negative effects of Hyundai's decline from the export market. Further, a number of firms have shifted their product line towards the compact segment during the second half of the 2000s. These firms include Ford, Toyota, Honda, Fiat and General Motors. All but one of these firms failed to export in any of the segments, which means the shift in product line was mainly driven by a strategy to exploit the local market, as most of these firms have improved their production share in recent years (Table 3.3 in Chapter 3).

Another point that emerges from Table 7.6 is that the growing production of high-end cars in India during the last decade is not an end result of an export-oriented strategy. Rather, it is mainly driven by the domestic demand structure which emerged in the context of the changing income structure and easy credit policies under globalisation. This is evident from the fact that exports in the Executive, Premier and Luxury segments were nil. All the firms operating in these three segments are fully owned subsidiaries of foreign firms, which are catering to domestic demand for these types of cars by offering assembled or highly import-intensive products.

The information on net foreign exchange earnings of selected firms operating in the high-end car market in India are presented in Table 7.8.[9] A huge mismatch is visible between export earnings and import spending of the selected passenger car firms. In the case of Mercedes-Benz India, net outflow of foreign exchange increased

Table 7.8 Net foreign exchange earnings of car firms*

Year	Mercedes-Benz India		Skoda Auto		Toyota India		Volkswagen India	
	Rs. million	% of sales	Rs. million	% of sales	Rs. million	% of sales	Rs. million	% of sales
2002–03	−853.00	−31.78	–	–	–	–	–	–
2003–04	−1471.00	−36.50	–	–	–	–	–	–
2004–05	−1661.00	−35.90	–	–	–	–	–	–
2005–06	−3908.00	64.06	–	–	−7083.90	−17.42	–	–
2006–07	−2278.70	28.49	–	–	−8233.23	−18.08	–	–
2007–08	−4161.00	−36.15	−11291.2	−65.02	–	–	−22.00	−84.58
2008–09	−7628.00	−56.76	−27920.9	−150.86	–	–	−170.70	−320.44
2011–12	−14714.82	−54.37	−29450	−55.72	−45239.34	−32.44	−21207.00	−34.75

Source: SIAM (2006b, 2010b, 2012b, 2014b, 2016b).

Notes:
(1) Due to data constraints, the information on royalties, technical fees, dividends etc. are not included. Hence, the numbers presented in this table are not comparable with CMIE PROWESS and are just an indication but not the exact amount of net outflow of foreign exchange made by these firms.
(2) *Comparison is not possible across firms. In the case of some firms, information on foreign exchange spending includes all kinds of imports (such as components, CBU/CKD etc.), whereas in other cases information is missing for some kinds of import payments.
(3) – indicates non-availability of data.

from 31.78 per cent of sales turnover in 2002–03 to 54.37 per cent in 2011–12. Similarly, net outflows of three other firms are very large both in absolute terms as well as in relation to the sales turnover of the respective firms. An interesting fact is that the inflow of foreign exchange earned by Hyundai in 2011–12 is lower than the net outflow of Toyota in 2011–12 (Tables 7.4 and 7.8). These firms are selling import-intensive passenger cars mainly because of the limited size of the high-end car market in India that does not provide any incentive to component suppliers to enter and produce components for this segment because it is not possible to realise economies of scale in a small market.

In addition, the raw materials and other components used in the production of high-end cars are very specific in nature and generally not available with local suppliers mainly engaged in the production of components for compact cars. As a result of this, it is a viable option for the manufacturers in the high-end segment to import intermediate goods for final production.

Hence, there is no near future possibility of indigenisation of manufacturing activities in these segments. Also, due to the liberal trade and investment regime, new firms are still entering the high-end car segment and they are increasing the variety of cars based on imported raw materials and CKD kits which has direct implications for net foreign exchange flows.

7.2.3 Why to worry about imports of high-end segment?

Some researchers may argue that the high percentage of import content in the high-end car segments does not have important implications for foreign exchange outflow because their production share is very small. This assertion is valid only partially. Their size seems to be very small when compared with MUL (the largest firm in the Indian car industry) in terms of number of cars produced. But if we compare these firms with MUL on the basis of sales turnover, then the size of high-end car firms is not much smaller than MUL (Table 7.9). For instance, in terms of number of units produced, the size of MUL was 252.92 times larger than the size of Mercedes-Benz India in 2001–02, which further increased to 301.03 times in 2012–13. Once the difference in size is measured in terms of sales turnover, then MUL's size is just 18.80 times that of Mercedes-Benz India in 2012–13 (Table 7.9). The same holds true for other

Table 7.9 Size difference across car firms: production vs. sales

	Year	Mercedes-Benz India	Skoda Auto	Toyota India	Volkswagen India	BMW India
Size in terms of volume of production (with respect to MUL)	2001–02	252.92		14.31	–	–
	2002–03	340.55		12.03	–	–
	2003–04	295.57	137.99	11.51	–	–
	2004–05	298.21	72.74	12.14	–	–
	2005–06	321.40	58.57	12.72	–	–
	2006–07	324.86	52.32	13.26	–	4631.49
	2007–08	262.60	53.75	14.28		363.68
	2008–09	252.77	51.09	16.63	–	319.35
	2009–10	305.10	65.99	16.22	3133.78	371.75
	2010–11	222.15	53.81	15.19	23.76	221.84
	2011–12	166.38	30.87	7.04	14.26	111.62
	2012–13	301.03	38.49	6.22	17.53	176.44
Size in terms of sales turnover (with respect to MUL)	2002–03	33.77	–	5.12	–	–
	2003–04	23.54	–	3.53	–	–
	2004–05	24.54	–	3.77	–	–
	2005–06	22.50	–	3.38	–	–
	2006–07	18.98	–	3.33	–	–
	2007–08	18.20	12.06	4.27	–	–
	2008–09	17.18	12.47	5.11	–	–
	2011–12	14.27	7.31	2.77	6.33	13.78
	2012–13	18.80	8.56	2.63	8.26	17.06

Source: Statistical Profile of Indian Automobile Industry (various issues).

firms presented in Table 7.9. It hardly bears stating that products produced by Mercedes, BMW, Skoda etc. are much costlier than products of MUL and other firms manufacturing small, compact and mid-size cars. Hence, the absolute import content of these high-end car firms is not small in magnitude, as might appear from their production share. The true picture of their size is given by sales turnover, according to which these firms are not much smaller than the largest firm in the domestic market.

Given these features, the large spending on imports by these firms (Mercedes, BMW, Skoda, etc.) raises a serious concern. These numbers suggest that the high import intensity of these firms with zero exports would contribute negatively to India's already vulnerable current account position. The trends in exports of the car industry are neither positive nor show much potential to be positive in such a large way so as to offset the large import spending, especially in the high-end car segment, and prevent serious effects on BoP. Policy intervention is warranted to deal with this situation.

7.3   Observations and implications

Unlike the experience of the 1980s and 1990s, the exports of the passenger car industry seem to have improved after 2000 as indicated by the industry level analysis. Due to high exports, the gap between foreign exchange earnings and spending has reduced towards the end of the decade.

On the contrary, the firm-level results on exports and imports of passenger car industry in India provide an altogether different picture. The increase in exports is not true of all the selected firms, whereas the imports of almost all the firms have moved upwards in the reference period. Hyundai is the only exception which has performed well on the exports front and brought positive net foreign exchange inflows into the country but only since 2008–09. The absolute decline in the exports of this firm in the recent years raises a serious concern about the commitment of the firm to use India as a base for world production.

Further, the exports of cars from India are very specific in nature as the contribution of one segment (namely compact) in total exports of the car industry has increased significantly over the years. Further, the exports from executive, premier and luxury segments remained zero throughout the reference period whereas the imports of firms operating in these segments remained very high. All these findings imply that the liberalisation measures initiated since the early 1990s in India with a view to strengthening India's external sector could not succeed in achieving the desired goal. It failed to bring relief with regard to the BoP constraint; rather, it seems to be worsening the situation in the absence of policy safeguards. The analysis in this chapter, just like in the previous one, leads us to suggest that the nature and objective of foreign firms coming to India is not of the kind India needed to ease its BoP constraint and develop indigenous manufacturing capabilities; rather, it remained market seeking in general, leading to increased external sector vulnerability and reduced exports sustainability over time.

Notes

1 HML has technical collaboration with Mitsubishi Motors Corporation, Japan, to manufacture premier passenger cars based on Mitsubishi designs. This collaboration was set up in 1998 and over the years the two firms have launched a number of passenger vehicles in the Indian market, namely, Lancer, Pajero, Montero, Cedia, Evo X and Outlander (see Table 2A in Annexure).

2 Absence of data for six years did not allow to comment anything strongly on the basis of 2013–14 figures.

3 For detailed discussion, see Chapter 8.

4 At the time of entry, MUL was aiming at exploiting the home market and was not oriented towards developing its export market. Since its inception, it focused on the requirements of domestic market even though it could have been able to compete in the world market, given its usage of advanced technology of Suzuki, and the latter's expertise in small car technology and international experience, as well as MUL's clustering or localisation strategies.

5 It is well argued in the literature that the foreign firms entering in India in any form (technical or financial collaborations) under protection were continuously confined to exploit domestic demand as protective market was offering more lucrative options. Give this consideration, a large number of firms entering in India were aiming at materialising excess profits by selling products in the local market.

6 This statement, though, not with regard to the passenger car industry, correctly justifies the point.

7 In recent years, CMIE started covering some more firms like Skoda, Toyota, Volkswagen etc., but information is either completely missing for some years or available on very few variables; hence, it is not possible to do a comprehensive analysis with these firms as done previously.

8 The analysis based on SIAM data is in terms of volume rather than value. SIAM does not publish information in value terms.

9 As mentioned earlier, the firm-level data for the high-end segment is not available in CMIE PROWESS. Hence, it is difficult to measure the extent to which these firms are using import content in car production. To get a broad indication about the trends related to foreign exchange spending of high-end car firms, we have collected scattered information published by SIAM. It is to caution that this information is indicative only, and is neither comparable across firms nor consistent over the period owing to the limitations of this data.

Chapter 8

MUL and Hyundai

Two special cases

Analysis performed in the previous chapters suggests that India's passenger car industry has observed entry of foreign firms with varying ownership structures and long-term motives. Owing to the differences, the survival strategies and performances also varied and few firms remained unique therein since their entry in the industry.[1] There are two special cases in the car industry that need to be discussed further, namely MUL and Hyundai.[2] Since the initial years of entry of MUL, it continues to hold the largest market share in India and also succeeded in indigenising the production activities to a great extent. Hyundai, in a short span of time, has achieved a high degree of indigenisation, holds the second largest market share and is also the largest exporter in the industry.

Given this, it is interesting to understand the unique performance of these firms in view of their long-term objectives and strategies in India and the underlying factors which helped them attain success in India in various ways. In this context, the present chapter tries to analyse (1) how MUL continues to hold dominant position in Indian car industry in the phase of stiff competition from new entrants; (2) what motivated Hyundai to use India as a manufacturing base to serve the world market, and what facilitated the firm to emerge as the second-largest car manufacturer in a short span of time during the phase of intense competition.

8.1 MUL: three decades of leadership

Analyses in the previous chapters made it clear that MUL's performance was different from other selected firms in many ways. First, MUL has continuously increased the usage of local content in production. It has achieved a high degree of indigenisation as the use of indigenous content increased to around 90 per cent in recent years. Second, within a short period of its entry in India's car industry, the firm attained a leadership position with a market share of 58.04 per cent in 1986–87, which further increased to 84.56 per cent in 1998–99 and then declined to 42.5 per cent in 2013–14.[3] Irrespective of the downturn in the market share, MUL has continuously maintained its leadership position. The international experience along with direct support from the government during the 1980s contributed to the success of firm during its initial years (Venkataramani 1990; Pingle 1999; Singh 2015). But even after liberalisation and entry of a significant number of new foreign players with a huge variety of highly advanced cars, MUL continues to maintain its top position in terms of market share. The firm still manufactures almost half of the total production of cars in India in the compact segment, which accounts for around 80 per cent of total car production in India. What enables MUL to retain its dominant position? To explore this, the following discussion highlights various edges that MUL have over its competitors in the car industry that facilitated MUL to retain her leadership position.

First Mover Advantage and Product Variety: The firm has first mover advantage, which has helped in creating a loyal consumer base. When MUL launched its first car in 1983, it was the only available small fuel-efficient car in India for the emerging Indian middle class. It continued until the middle of the 1990s, as the firm had no direct challenge until the entry of other firms (Daewoo, Hyundai and Tata Motors) in the car industry. The firm was able to build on first mover advantage later on, as it already had a huge customer base by the time of liberalisation of the car industry. It is visible as MUL acquired 86.44 per cent of the total market in 1997–98. Hence, when other firms were struggling to get a foothold in the market, MUL had started expanding its consumer base by increasing its product profile within the compact segment, targeting low middle and middle income consumers. During the second half of the 1990s, the firm launched Zen, Esteem, Wagon R etc., whereas other firms had only a single model of cars in the compact segment, for instance, Daewoo (Matiz), Tata (Indica), Hyundai (Santro). MUL has continuously maintained its edge in terms of product variety, as in 2014–15, the firm has a maximum number of products in the mini and compact segment as well as the mid-sized car segment (see Table 8.1).

Table 8.1 Segment-wise number of car models, 2014–15

Firms	No. of models	
	Mini and compact	Mid-sized
BMW India	0	0
Fiat India	1	0
Ford India	1	2
General Motors	3	1
HML	0	1
Honda Cars	3	1
Hyundai Motors	7	2
MUL	9	3
M&M	1	1
Mercedes-Benz India	0	0
Nissan Motor	2	1
Renault India	1	1
Skoda Auto	1	1
Tata Motors	4	2
Toyota India	1	1
Volkswagen India	1	2
Share in Production in 2013–14	**77.14**	**21.25**

Source: SIAM (2016a).

It is clear from Table 8.1 that MUL has an edge over its competitors in terms of variety of products in the low-end compact and mid-size segment. These two segments accounted for almost 98.39 per cent of India's car production and sales. As compared to Hyundai, the second largest firm, MUL has a greater variety of products in both segments. The firm has a long experience with Indian consumers and it understands them well. The company not only provides a huge variety in base models but also provides a lot of modifications in its products in each segment to cater to a range of consumer preferences and requirements.

The maintenance of a maximum variety of products in the mini and compact segment is a strategy of the firm to attract all first-time consumers who are diversified in their choices and preferences but their choices are price sensitive. Since its initial days, the firm has targeted the value-conscious middle-class segment, as a majority of India's population belonged and still belongs to that segment (NCAER 2002; Shukla 2010; Singh 2015). The firm has followed the phrase 'cars produced for the most will sell the most.' While continuing to expand its large variety of products in lower-end segments, the firm is also providing products in the higher-end segment as well.

Therefore, in totality, any first-time buyer has a huge array of options in MUL's cars, including a diverse range of base models, modifications and enhancements on base models, and varied price ranges suiting different budget needs and requirements. In other words, MUL's product portfolio is optimal, and it has affordable cars for almost everyone in the low- and high-end compact segment.

The firm not only has a great variety of models but also has the most popular variety of cars in India. The popularity of MUL cars can be judged from the fact that one or the other product of the firm remains on top in terms of sales volume and three to four models remain in the top 10 models every year (Table 8.2). In 2014–15, the count has reached five. Further, the ranking of these products has moved up in the top 10 and, since 2013–14, the top four ranks are acquired by MUL cars (Table 8.2). The optimum product portfolio has helped MUL to be able to maintain a very 'car-for-all' type of brand image over time. Unlike some other companies, which got caught in a particular image trap – for instance, people think Fiat means taxi cars, Nano means low income, Volkswagen or Skoda

Table 8.2 Ranking of top 10 car models sold in India, 2008–09 to 2014–15

Ranks	2008–09	2010–11	2013–14	2014–15
1	Alto	Alto	Alto	Alto
2	Wagon R	Wagon R	Swift	Swift
3	Indica	i 10	Dzire	Dzire
4	Swift	Swift	Wagon R	Wagon R
5	i-10	Dzire	Eon	Grand i10
6	Santro	Indica	Amaze	Eon
7	Dzire	Indigo +Indigo Marina	Grand i10	Elite i20
8	Maruti 800	Santro	i10	City
9	Indigo +Indigo Marina	i20	i20	Celerio
10	City	Figo	Indica	Amaze

Source: SIAM (2010a, 2012a, 2014a, 2016a).

are perceived as high maintenance etc. – MUL has always carried a people's car image for its products. It is evident from their wide-ranging consumer base, which equally includes farmers as well as servicemen and businessmen, students as well as retirees, people located in remote areas as well as in metro cities etc., housewives as well as working women and so on.

Post Sales Services: Given its long experience in India, MUL has built a long chain of authorised service centres and dealers across India, which makes it convenient for a consumer in a remote area to get the vehicle serviced or repaired easily. For instance, MUL had 3086 services centres in India in 2014–15, which was 2.8 times higher than the second largest car manufacturer in India, namely Hyundai (Table 8.3). Not only this, every year MUL adds about 200 sales and service stations, and around 6,000 technicians. To ensure availability of trained staff, MUL has over time built up dedicated channels to train mechanics for its cars. Until 2015–16, MUL has established ties with 100 Industrial Training Institutes (ITIs) to provide training related to automobile repair and maintenance (Modi 2016).

Table 8.3 Firm-wise dealership and service centre network, 2014–15

Firms	Dealership	Service centre
BMW India	39	–
Fiat India	100	105
Ford India	n.a.	n.a.
General Motors	231	250
HML	39	36
Honda Cars	267	–
Hyundai Motor	419	1114
MUL	1619	3086
Mercedes-Benz India	19	47
Nissan Motor	n.a.	n.a.
Renault India	161	132
Skoda Auto	76	74
Toyota India	240	43
Volkswagen India	118	111

Source: SIAM (2016b).

According to Modi (2016), every ITI is transformed into a model workshop by MUL with an investment of Rs. 20 Lakh. These workshops offer practical training on Maruti cars and assemblies under the guidance of a dedicated trainer for developing potential mechanics for their authorised service centres. Nearly 300 teachers at these institutes were also trained by the company in the past two years to equip them with the latest technical knowledge of the industry. It contributes to the growth of the firms in many ways. First, it helps in providing efficient post sales services to the buyers at their doorstep. As a result, buyers experience more convenience in receiving such services. Second, it also reduces cost of service and saves time for the consumers, which cannot be said of any new entrant. New entrants, especially Ford, Skoda Toyota, Volkswagen etc., have a limited number of authorised dealers, which discourages new consumers from purchasing their products, as they find it difficult to get their vehicles serviced. It increases the cost of service and also leads to a waste of consumers' time. New consumers and even old consumers consider all these factors before purchasing car. Third, a large market for consumer durables, including automobiles is still located in rural areas, as more than 65 per cent of India's population is still residing there. Most of them are first time buyers of passenger cars. Their choice is largely influenced by the availability of post sales services at competitive prices (Ernst et al. 2015) since roads and other infrastructure are relatively poor in rural areas, hence cars used in such areas may frequently break down or require more service as compared to those used in urban areas. Thus, it becomes difficult for consumers to go to the city every time their cars break down.

Indigenisation and Easy Availability of Spare Parts and Components at Competitive Prices: A high degree of indigenisation of the products of MUL is one of the main reasons behind the easy and cheap availability of spare parts for its products. On an average, MUL uses around 91 per cent of local components in the manufacturing of passenger vehicles (Table 5.6 in Chapter 5). It is even higher in the case of the mini and compact segments, where the share of indigenous content goes above 95 per cent (Kale 2012). Due to local manufacturing of components and other spare parts, it is easy for the firm to ensure a continuous supply of spare parts for its products, even to non-authorised service centres. Hence, consumers are able to get spare parts at their location at competitive prices, whereas it is not so easy to get components and spare parts of other car manufacturers, including Hyundai, Toyota, Honda, Ford, Fiat, General Motors, Nissan, Skoda etc., especially in rural areas. In many cases, even the authorised dealers of these firms place special orders for spare parts, which not only consume time but also increase the cost of repair. Due to this, sales of cars of these firms are largely confined to urban areas and it provides an edge to MUL over her rivals in a major part of the country. In general, consumers have a very strong perception that MUL post sales services are much more cost-effective as compared to others. To break this perception, many car manufacturers including Ford, Fiat etc. have started advertising that their post sales services are competitive as well.

Price Competitiveness: MUL not only has a wide-ranging product profile but also supplies these cars at competitive prices with maximum features. MUL's products have the lowest Total Cost of Ownership (capital cost + parts cost + maintenance) as compared to other options in the market. In addition, these products are more fuel efficient as compared to all its competitors operating in the compact segment and that makes them a good choice in a developing country like India. Price competitiveness, along with high fuel efficiency, encourages low-income consumers as they are more conscious about prices and the fuel efficiency of the cars. Price efficiency of MUL cars does not compromise on efficiency and performance of the cars. The firm's products have been time tested on Indian roads to be highly reliable, and it has helped building the positive reputation of its products. In a developing country like India, word-of-mouth publicity and bandwagon effects also have a significant effect on promoting a particular brand.

As MUL has a long existence in India, due to low total cost of ownership as well as high performance and reliability, customers have trust in the brand and word of mouth works here. Their users usually remain loyal to MUL's products and are more likely to suggest them to other first-time buyers. It is such that, owing to its first mover advantage and long existence, people feel an emotional connection with the products of MUL and it strengthens the marketing channels of the firm's products at the consumer level. Almost every Indian family had an MUL product as its first vehicle. It is difficult for any other firm to overcome this emotional connection with and trust in MUL's products that the firm has built over the years with Indian consumers.

In addition to positive publicity among consumers, MUL has also saved itself, over time, from any negative publicity. MUL has never experienced any negative marketing, for their products as has happened with other competitors at times, for instance, Tata's Nano etc. MUL has put extra efforts in maintaining its positive publicity and the firm's promotional efforts are innovative and go beyond regular media. For instance, they have a large driving school network which often helps them in building a new consumer base.

High Resale Value: The resale value of MUL's products is high owing to their easy repair and maintenance and high performance in terms of fuel efficiency, fewer breakdowns etc. Due to low maintenance cost, the firm's products enjoy a high rating and high price in terms of value-for-money in the second-hand car market. High resale value has an impact on the sale of new products, as middle-income consumers are very conscious about the resale value of the products they purchase. The buyer has a surety of getting a good return in the resale market due to less depreciation in its value. It adds to the new demand of MUL products.

Exports of Firm: As discussed in the previous chapters, the export performance of MUL was not very encouraging. The export intensity of MUL, in general, remained below 10 per cent (Tables 6.1, 6.2 and 7.1 in Chapters 6 and 7). Alternatively, more than 90 per cent of MUL's cars are sold in the local market. In its three and a half decades of existence, MUL has remained a net importer. Though the firm has not started bringing in positive foreign exchange inflows, the gap between its earnings and spending has consistently decreased over the years. The poor export performance of MUL is considered to be an outcome of the initial objective of the firm. It is well acknowledged that the basic objective of the firm at the time of entry was to serve the domestic market (Pingle 1999; Singh 2015). The firm was also committed to increasing usage of local content due to the agreement with the state at the time of its entry (Hamaguchi 1985; Venkataramani 1990). But the firm was not under a condition in the agreement to develop India as an export base. Due to this, the firm has always targeted the domestic market rather than world market. It suggests that the export performance of MUL was guided by the motives and commitment at the time of its entry.

In sum, it is the continuous efforts of MUL, along with its first mover advantage, that has contributed to maintaining an edge over other counterparts in various domains, including brand image, sales and dealership network, marketing etc.

8.2 HYUNDAI: the first runner-up of the market

Empirical exercises conducted in the previous chapters have high-lighted various unique characteristics of Hyundai Motor which require detailed discussion. First, Hyundai is the only one among the firms that entered in the 1990s or even afterwards which has been continuously and significantly indigenising its manufacturing activities. The firm has increased indigenous content in its production up to 76.94 per cent in 2013–14 as against 57.78 per cent in 2001–02 (Table 5.6 in Chapter 5). Second, it has substantially contributed to exports and even started bringing positive foreign exchange inflows for the country. It is the only firm which is a net exporter in the industry. Third, Hyundai emerged as the second largest car manufacturer in India with more than 25 per cent production share in the recent years, which is much more than 5.9 per cent, the production share of third-largest firm in the industry. All these characteristics highlight the differentiated performance of the firm as compared to other manufacturers in the industry and require detailed discussion about what motivated the firm to achieve a high degree of indigenisation and to use India as a manufacturing base for world production when none of its contemporaries did that.

Entry, Challenges and Strategy of Hyundai: Hyundai Motor entered India in 1996 and established its manufacturing facilities in Chennai. Except for Hyundai, in the 1990s, all foreign firms entered as JVs with local firms, whereas Hyundai was allowed to enter as a fully owned subsidiary of a foreign firm. The special permission to Hyundai can be seen in the context of the first ever visit of the Republic of Korea's president to India in February 1996. During the visit of the president, the discussion was focused on business, trade and investment (Tayal 2014). To promote investment, the 'Bilateral Investment Promotion Agreement' was signed between India and Korea with a target of increasing Korean investments in India to $3 billion by 2000. As a result of this,

> India's earlier-than expected approvals for Hyundai Motor and Samsung Electronics for 100 per cent FDI in their Indian projects were viewed by the Korean side as a gesture of goodwill by the Indian government, which sincerely welcomed investments from Korea.
>
> (Tayal 2014: 89)

Not only this, Hyundai received support from the government of India along with a number of incentives offered by the Tamil Nadu government, including tax holidays, subsidised land etc. (Gulyani 2001; Tewari 2001).

At the time of entry, there were a number of challenges for Hyundai to get a foothold in India. First, a major challenge was to break the monopoly of MUL, which had controlled more than 80 per cent of India's car market in the middle of the 1990s, and that too in the wake of the entry of Daewoo, Ford, General Motors with a variety of advanced cars. Second, as discussed above, MUL had already created brand loyalty among India's consumers by supplying fuel-efficient, technologically advanced cars in India since the early 1980s. Third, the passenger car industry in India was loaded with excess capacity in the late 1990s, which put pressure on the manufacturers to reduce the cost and increase the variety of cars (D'Costa 2005). Fourth, demand for cars in India was mainly concentrated in the low-end segment, as around 47 per cent of India's households fell in the low-middle and middle-income class, whereas just around 10 per cent population belonged to the upper-middle and high-income group (Table 3.6 in Chapter 3). MUL had completely monopolised the low-end car segment by introducing a variety of cars in the 1990s.

Considering all these challenges, Hyundai made its entry in a big way and tailored its strategy according to the requirements of the Indian market. As a first step, the firm established Chennai plant with a manufacturing capacity to the tune of 1,20,000 units per annum (Gulyani 2001; Paul 2009). No firm in the passenger car industry, including MUL, had ever started with such a huge production capacity and that too in a phase of competition when all the new entrants were piled up with huge un-utilised capacity. Chennai plant was the only fully integrated manufacturing plant of the company outside its parent country (South Korea). It was set up with an objective to use India as a base to supply components and CKD kits to the parent plant in South Korea as well as some of Hyundai's CKD assembling units in 14 other countries (Gulyani 2001; Park 2004; Singh 2015). This implies that the underlying objective of this firm at the time of entry in India was not just to exploit India as a market for its products but also to use India as a manufacturing location to cater to the world market.

It was both a strategy as well as a compulsion for the firm to choose India as a manufacturing base. Hyundai's bad experience in

Bromont (Canada) and final closure of the plant brought changes in its globalisation strategy (Chung 1998, 2003). The firm changed its globalisation strategy from worldwide export to regional manufacturing sites in different regions, keeping strategic functions, such as product design and R&D, centralised in the company headquarters. Among others, it was the problem with the parent firm in Korea which caused irregular and disrupted supply of components, raw material and intermediates (Freyssenet, Shimizu and Volpato 2003). At the same time, no core component units wanted to invest in the Bromont area. Instead of investing in Bromont, core components suppliers wanted Hyundai to find low-cost production locations in newly liberalised Asian economies in order to become cost-effective and to develop an alternative manufacturing base other than the parent country (Chung 1998, 2003; Carrillo, Lung and Tulder 2004). China and India were the two rapidly expanding economies with huge demand prospects for passenger vehicles. Hyundai chose India as Chinese Automotive Industry Policy 1994 allowed three large and three small passenger car projects based on foreign technology and those were already in existence there.[4]

In India, it was the underlying objective of Hyundai to localise production activities in order to be price efficient. Chennai did not have a strong ancillary base as MUL had developed near its production unit in Manesar (Tewari 2001). Most of the manufacturing facilities were located either in Pune or near Delhi. It would have taken Hyundai a huge amount of time and money to get components delivered at the Chennai plant from other parts of India. In this case, smooth production could have been done only if the firm had maintained a huge inventory, which would have adversely affected the competitiveness by adding to the cost of production.

The large initial production capacity as well as the establishment of an integrated production plant in Chennai helped the firm to attract ancillary units from various locations from India in Chennai (Gulyani 2001; Park 2004). It provided confidence to the ancillary units that Hyundai has a long-term objective to develop its production base (Tewari 2001). The firm negotiated with local ancillary units based in Delhi and Pune and asked them to establish ancillary units near its manufacturing plant in Chennai and, at the same time, the firm invited its core suppliers from Korea, with which its parent firm had established industrial clusters involving strong sub-contracting linkages in the home country (Park 2004). Hyundai's move was supported by the core component units as

16 Korean parts and components suppliers followed Hyundai to India and started ancillary production jointly with local component suppliers near the main production plant of Hyundai in Chennai (Singh 2015). As a result of this, Hyundai has over time successfully developed four industrial clusters[5] which ensure quality and timely delivery, while ancillary units also develop components and parts under the guidance of Hyundai (Park 2004). The clustering and localisation strategies of Hyundai Motor enabled the firm to reduce the inventory cost, develop better assembler-supplier relations, ensure quality and standards and achieve a high degree of indigenisation in a short span of time. Further, owing to the clustering and localisation strategy, it could implement lean production techniques with the objective of improving competitiveness by cutting costs, improving quality and enhancing their responsiveness to demand.

Product Choice, Marketing Strategy and Success of Hyundai: Given the challenges from MUL along with other new entrants and the diverse nature of demand in India, Hyundai opted for the mass versus luxury segment, as the Indian market was mainly dominated by a booming small car segment. According to Paul (2009) the management of Hyundai Motor India did not accept the decision of their headquarters to start in the luxury segment and, rather than going for their popular mid-size sedan Accent or any of their mid-size sedans made for the USA market, it made a big decision to launch a totally new Santro car for the Indian consumer in the booming compact segment. It not only was less expensive, but also was made 80 per cent indigenously and was given a distinctive 'tall boy' design to build their 'being Indian' image in the minds of consumers (Paul 2009). To increase brand awareness and to promote Santro as a 'people's car,' the firm addressed a large number of potential consumers in the regional offices through famous personalities having mass appeal (Ernst et al. 2015). Further, by roping in movie and sports stars in marketing campaigns, Hyundai successfully built its brand's positive image among potential customers. Another strategy was to raise brand awareness and exploit word-of-mouth publicity. 'The CEO personally selected the customers who would get the first few Sonatas (Hyundai's top-end luxury car brand) that rolled out of Hyundai- it was a careful mix of business leaders, socialites and political leader' (Paul 2009: 43). Their marketing strategy was a judicious mix of various factors, including building personal relationships with all their dealers, test drives with media, actively targeting women as well as children in their ads, management of relationships with financial partners to provide innovative financing deals to their customers, and projecting their products as family cars by avoiding sales to taxi and commercial car operators (Paul 2009; Ernst et al. 2015).

Product Variety and Dealership Network: Hyundai has also built a strong profile of cars in the mini and compact segment. It is closely following the market leader MUL with seven basic models in the mini and compact segment (Table 8.1), which varies in terms of price, and other features. The firm's product profile successfully serves the diversified demand of low- and middle-income consumers. If we compare MUL and products of other firms in terms of preference, then out of all other firms Hyundai's products are the second most preferred in India. It is not only true in the case of first-hand vehicles but also in the second-hand vehicle market in India. It is evident as after MUL, Hyundai has a maximum number of cars falling in the top 10 most sold cars in India (Table 8.2).

In order to cater its potential customers, Hyundai has also developed a comfortable dealer base in India (Table 8.3). In terms of dealership and service centres as well, Hyundai is following the market leader MUL. Although it is not as closely following MUL as in terms of the number of car models, it is still much further ahead than other firms in the market.

All these efforts and strategies of Hyundai management have contributed towards the success of the firm and building a sizeable market share in India and have also helped the firm to create a positive brand image among common people.

Export Performance: Unlike MUL, Hyundai Motor entered the Indian car industry with an objective to develop India as a low-cost manufacturing base (Gulyani 2001; Tewari 2001; Chung 2003; Park 2004). Given her initial objective, the firm not only started exporting cars in the early years of its entry, but the quantum of exports and export intensity of the firm has increased over the reference period and gradually it has emerged as a leading exporter of cars in the country (Singh 2015). On average, the contribution of Hyundai to total industry exports remained above 55 per cent from 2003–04 to 2013–14. In some years, export contribution of the firm increased to around 70 per cent of total industry exports. The consistently high exports and emergence of the firm as a net exporter suggests that it has worked in line with its objective of entry in the country.

8.3   Some observations

It emerges from the discussion that the initial objectives and long-term motives along with survival strategies of MUL and Hyundai differentiated their performance from their competitors in the passenger car market in India.

Despite the fact that the performance of MUL and Hyundai remained unique as compared to other firms, the implications for the host country of both the firms are different since MUL remains a net importer and Hyundai a net exporter, owing to the differences in the nature and objectives of their entry in India's car industry. Based on the case studies, it is inferred that it is not the quantum of FDI but the nature and initial objective of foreign investors which determine the extent and type of benefits for the host country.

Notes

1 The unique performance of these firms is visible in terms of market power, export performance and degree of indigenisation of production activities.
2 Besides drawing from previous analysis and existing literature, the discussion in this chapter is based on interaction with some stakeholders, such as mechanics, consumers and dealers.
3 In the corresponding years, the production figure of MUL has increased from 73762 units to 330395 units and then to 1097643 units.
4 That too under the condition that foreign equity participation of 50 per cent or more was not allowed in finished passenger cars and engine manufacturing. In addition, FDI in automobile distribution and retailing was generally prohibited.
5 Hyundai developed four industrial clusters located in Bangalore, Chennai, Delhi, and Mumbai to ensure a regular supply of automobile parts. According to Park (2004), out of its 78 vendors, 59 per cent of automobile components and parts were supplied by 46 vendors. These 46 companies were situated within a radius of 50 kilometres from her main assembling plant located in Chennai.

Chapter 9

Conclusion and policy implications

The process of liberalisation in the passenger car industry of India was initiated in the early 1980s, but major changes in policy were observed only in the early 1990s. The changes in the 1990s transformed the policy regime from one that was highly controlled to one involving substantial deregulation and decontrol. The most significant change was with respect to the restrictions on the entry of foreign firms and their operations. Entry of foreign firms was made hassle-free and the operations of foreign firms in India were made more flexible. Further, a second dose of reforms was resorted to which was applicable, specifically, to the passenger car industry in the early 2000s. Here, the explicit goal was to develop India as a manufacturing hub for small cars by attracting large inflows of foreign investment in the industry and also to promote in-house R&D. For this, foreign firms were permitted to increase equity share up to 100 per cent through the automatic route as opposed to the limit of up to 51 per cent equity prevalent in the 1990s. And the government also lifted all quantitative restrictions imposed during the second half of the 1990s on different types of imports used in the manufacture of passenger cars. As a consequence, the passenger car industry has not just attracted huge FDI but is one of those sectors which attracted the highest foreign investment after opening up of the economy. Average annual FDI received by the passenger car industry was US$ 82.63 million from 2000 to 2006 which increased to US$ 794.68 million from 2012 to 2016 (GoI 2007, 2010, 2013, 2016b). Out of the total FDI received by automobile industry from 2000 to 2016, the passenger car segment accounted for 43 per cent.

With the change in policy environment, resultant increase in foreign presence and associated strong growth, advocates of liberalisation presented India's passenger car industry as an example of the success of liberalisation. They also claim that, during the last decade and a half, the passenger car industry also performed remarkably well in terms of technology development and exports, thereby realising two goals that remained unmet during the earlier regime. Studies have argued that technology standards of passenger car firms have improved remarkably and cars manufactured in India are comparable to the ones manufactured in advanced countries.

To assess the validity of these claims, the present research addressed three issues related to the passenger car industry: (1) Changes in the structure and growth of the industry and the underlying factors explaining those changes under different economic regimes. (2) The impact of these changes in structure and foreign entry on the technological development of firms and the factors underlying the rapid emergence of technologically advanced cars in India. (3) The trade performance of foreign firms and their contribution to the balance of payments currently and the sustainability of export trends in the wake of changing strategies of foreign firms.

9.1   Major findings

The empirical analysis dealing with the structural changes and growth highlights that the principal factor behind the restructuring of this industry during the 1980s was the entry of a JV formed between the GoI and Suzuki Motors. The entry of MUL shook the stable oligopoly of HML and PAL and weakened the market position of the old and established manufactures. Within a short span of time, MUL gained leadership in the passenger car industry. By the end of the 1980s, it held more than 60 per cent of the total market. It is worth pointing out that the success of this firm was not only on account of its competitive strength but also the result of a strategy adopted by the state to support MUL's drive to become the market leader. Evidence of the government's support is the policy designed during the 1980s that provided special space to Maruti-Suzuki JV. Thus, the structural change observed by the passenger car industry during the 1980s was the result of foreign entry and, simultaneously, it was significantly shaped by the systematic intervention of the government with the only aim of ensuring the success of MUL.

Unlike the 1980s, the structural changes observed since the 1990s were mainly driven by the entry of foreign firms, as the nature of foreign presence in the industry changed completely from one of being a technology supplier to that of equity participation, though the importance of factors other than foreign presence cannot be ignored. Since the early 1990s, the government allowed foreign firms to establish manufacturing units. Accordingly, the industry witnessed the entry of leading international firms which started manufacturing cars in India. As a result of this, competition increased and the market share of the leader, MUL, declined. This competition was the result of the increasing presence of new entrants in the market, and the mounting presence of technologically advanced passenger cars. Increase in the variety of cars since the late 1990s also led to the emergence of strong segmentation within the industry.

Besides foreign presence, some other factors also significantly contributed to the restructuring and growth of the car industry in the 1990s and afterwards. As suggested by the empirical analysis, just one segment, namely, the compact segment, accounted for around 80 per cent of total cars manufactured in India since 2008–09. Detailed analysis suggests that this pattern was mainly driven by the growing importance of middle-class households which aspire to a luxury lifestyle. The growing demand of the middle class for automobiles was supported by the easy availability of credit for the automobiles which accounted for a major share of the personal loans in total credit given by the commercial banks.

On the issue of technology development, empirical analysis indicates that, in general, the spending of passenger car firms on technology acquisition and technology development has increased since the early 1980s. However, the disaggregated view of technology spending suggests that the spending of firms on technology is highly biased towards imported technology. Passenger car firms have increased the share of total spending towards technology imports and, simultaneously, have reduced the investment in in-house R&D activities.

The analysis of inter-firm variations in spending on technology revealed important features of the technology development and technology acquisition strategies of firms. Indigenous firms (HML and PAL) have directed significant resources towards technology imports during the 1980s. The higher import spending of these firms in the 1980s was mainly driven by two developments: (1) the changing policy environment, which provided opportunities to these firms to sign technical agreements with foreign firms which were not permitted during the 1960s and 1970s; and, (2) the entry of MUL in the early 1980s, which resulted in stiff competition and marginalised these indigenous firms in the market by launching a low-priced fuel-efficient car in India. To maintain their position, these firms formed technical JVs with foreign firms with the aim of upgrading their products as well as introducing new products equipped with advanced technology.

Subsequently, foreign JVs and fully owned subsidiaries too substantially increased their spending on imports of technology. And here, too, the investment in in-house R&D either remained very low or even dropped to zero. Take the case of MUL, which is the market leader and has increased spending on technology, but the spending of the firm on R&D remained less than 0.5 per cent until 2010–11 and then increased to just around 0.5 per cent. The investment of other subsidiaries of international firms, such as Hyundai, Honda, Ford, General Motors, in in-house R&D also remained meagre.

The other side of the story is that the investment in in-house R&D by the parent firms (of foreign subsidiaries operating in India) outside India varied between 2 to 7 per cent of sales. Interestingly, in the case of Honda, which has reduced investment in R&D to zero after 2004–2005, the R&D intensity of its parent firm increased from 4.7 per cent to 6.5 per cent from 2000 to 2012. Similarly, the market leader in India's car industry, MUL, invested between 0.12 to 0.60 per cent of sales value in R&D since the mid-1980s, whereas the parent firm of MUL (Suzuki Corporation) increased investment in in-house R&D from 2.7 per cent in 2002 to 4.7 per cent of sales value in 2013.

These numbers suggest that, although India has successfully attracted a large volume of foreign investment, which added to the production base of the car industry, it has failed to strengthen its technology base in terms of R&D activities undertaken in India. There may be a number of factors behind these trends. Important ones include the nature of ownership of firms and the changing characteristics of demand under globalisation. It is strategically better for the subsidiaries of international firms to gain access to the cutting-edge technology available from parent firms and modify it through small investments rather than to develop technology through in-house R&D in the host country. This strategy seems logical from the firm's point of view, given the fact that product heterogeneity across developed and developing countries is shrinking, especially in the case of consumer durables including cars.

Further, the passenger car manufacturers have resorted to huge imports of components, raw materials and intermediate goods as well. Except two firms (MUL and Hyundai), which have indigenised their manufacturing activities, other firms are recording high import content figures, and often use imported SKD/CKD units in the production of passenger cars. Selling largely assembled products not only makes it easier for firms to introduce new cars on a regular basis, but also does not require great investment in manufacturing activities.

Based on this evidence, it is apparent that those who claim that India's passenger car industry has achieved an edge in technology lack support. Measuring technology development in terms of product innovation or availability of a variety of passenger cars presents a completely misleading picture in the context of India's passenger car industry.

Another issue addressed in the present work is related to the trade performance of foreign firms and their contribution to the BoP. Analytically, it is predicted that the foreign presence would ease the BoP constraint by using India as a base to serve the world market. Empirical analysis did not lend support to this hypothesis in the context of India's car industry. Results indicate that export intensity of the industry did not record any improvement during the 1990s, whereas a positive change in the export trend was noticed after the 2000s. On the other hand, imports remained considerably high since the onset of reforms.

Firm-wise analysis showed a significant difference in the export behaviour of selected firms. Based on the export performance, we can divide firms into two groups. First, out of six selected firms, the export intensity of four firms (General Motors, Ford, Honda and HML) was very low until recently. Export intensity of General Motors and Honda remained below 0.5 per cent until 2009–10, whereas the import intensity of these firms varied between 30 to 40 per cent. The operations of these firms led to a significant drain of foreign exchange, because they were focused on exploiting the domestic market by selling highly import-intensive products. After 2010–11, Honda's exports have increased, but the gap between import and export intensity is still more than 20 per cent. Second, the other two selected firms (MUL and Hyundai) have increased their exports during the last one and a half decade. But the export performance of these two firms varied significantly. In the case of MUL, export intensity has marginally improved after 2000 but it is still lower than its import spending. Until recently, its export intensity has not gone beyond 10 per cent, which would mean that more than 90 per cent of its total output of cars is consumed in the domestic market. On the other hand, the export performance of Hyundai has consistently increased during the last decade. Average export intensity of this firm has remained around 35 per cent since 2005–06. In 2008–09, the export intensity of the firm rose to as high as 46 per cent. Due to high exports, the foreign exchange earnings of this firm exceeded its foreign exchange spending since 2008–09.

Further, we used SIAM data to analyse the importance of different firms in terms of their contribution to the exports of the industry. It shows that, out of 13 firms, eight firms have either contributed zero or close to zero (less than 0.5 per cent) to the total exports of the car industry from 2001–02 to 2011–12. The situation did not change much even from 2011–12 to 2013–14, as the contribution of six firms remained either zero or close to zero and the export contribution of four other firms varied between 1 to 6 per cent. This strongly supports our previous findings that foreign firms are mainly net importers and their presence is only worsening the BoP of the country. In recent years, the situation becomes more worrisome as Hyundai, the largest exporter in the industry, has been recording a downturn in export intensity, owing to change in its production and export strategy. Instead of focusing on the international market, this firm is trying to expand in the domestic market by strengthening its product profile in the compact and mid-size car segment. Similarly, the export intensity of other firms (Nissan, Toyota) has also been declining since 2014–15, but their presence in the local market is growing. The changing strategy of foreign firms raises serious concerns about the sustainability of export trends of the car industry in the years to come.

The case studies of MUL and Hyundai suggest that the success of these firms in the domestic market was largely shaped by the consistent efforts of these firms, including a high degree of indigenisation, variety of cars, expansion of dealership and service centres etc. But their success in terms of indigenisation and export performance was not an outcome of similar factors. In the case of MUL, it was a pressure from the government to increase usage of indigenous content as the firm entered into an agreement with GoI to increase usage of local content. Thus, indigenisation in the case of MUL was an outcome of systematic state intervention. But in the case of Hyundai, it was self-commitment and a long-term motive to develop India as a low-cost manufacturing base in Asia in order to supply components and CKD kits to the parent firm as well as to other subsidiaries the world over.

Based on the empirical results, some implications are drawn, which are as follows:

First, the experience of the car industry suggests that even after the provision of various fiscal and financial benefits to international firms under a liberal policy regime, India has failed to motivate car manufacturers to perform R&D in India as they continue to depend on imported technology. Given this tendency, it looks unlikely that India would be able to develop indigenous technology through in-house R&D as laid out in Auto Policy 2002 and various other relevant documents of the GoI. The current behaviour of manufacturing firms, especially foreign players, would not only adversely affect India's aim to achieve an edge in technology but may also favour monopolisation of technology in the hands of leading international firms outside the country. This raises serious concerns about the process of industrialisation in developing countries, including India, as technology suppliers are likely to charge higher prices, which would adversely affect the competitiveness of importing firms.

Second, it is clear that there is no direct positive relationship between FDI and exports Foreign exchange earnings of international firms in the car industry on account of exports did not improve as much as was expected. On the other hand, the foreign exchange spending of these firms on imports of capital goods, components and raw material, payments against disembodied technology imports (royalties and technical fees) and repatriation of profits as dividends registered a manifold increase in the phase of liberalisation. Further, new firms were continuously entering with the sole intention of exploiting the domestic market, and, in order to get an easy foothold in a market marked with excess capacity, they were importing technology, raw material and CKD/SKD kits to sell assembled products at competitive prices. Given this behaviour of foreign firms, it is likely that the gap between outflows and inflows of foreign exchange will widen further. Any further step towards a higher degree of liberalisation is not going to work as a remedy for the worsening BoP situation, as India's experience since the 1990s suggests.

Third, though the sales volume of manufacturers of high-end cars (Mercedes, Porsche, Rolls Royce etc.) is small, the value of their sales, the import intensity of their cars, and therefore their import bill is high. Their existence in the domestic market but absence in the export market suggests that these firms only seek to service domestic demand. This severely affects the BoP position as the outflow in the case of high-end cars is very high. Even if firms operating in the compact segment start bringing positive inflows, it is difficult to offset the negative from the high-end segment. Thus, it is important to regulate the output of this segment.

Fourth, the rate of growth of passenger car demand and production spiked after liberalisation; this was because the easy credit policies encouraged by the central bank allowed the consumers, whose income levels otherwise would not allow them to purchase a car, to enter the market. This raises serious concerns about the possibility of rising defaults and the sustainability of growth in this industry.

9.2 The way forward

Thus, it is clear that while the liberal trade and investment regime did help India to attract large inflows of FDI into the passenger car industry, this was not the kind of foreign investment which India required to boost exports, support its BoP and strengthen indigenous technological capabilities.

However, it is possible for India to attract quality FDI as: (a) India is capable of providing skilled workers at relatively low wages, at a time when wages in China have started rising. (b) India is a large market for MNCs' products, which is only likely to grow in the future, which strengthens the government's bargaining position vis-à-vis foreign firms. So, with a view to promote indigenisation and development of technology within the domestic economy, the government must come up with a differentiated policy which distinguishes between different types of FDI based on nature and quality. It should be able to provide incentives to those foreign firms which help promote exports from India (such as Hyundai) and, in addition, it should also be able to restrict the entry of those firms which are entering with the sole intention of exploiting the local market by using the liberal import regime. An absence of systematic intervention in the changing business environment at the global level would not encourage international manufacturers to use India as a base for world production. To what extent India can succeed in this direction is questionable, as the GoI has partly tied its hands by signing the Uruguay Round agreement.

Annexure

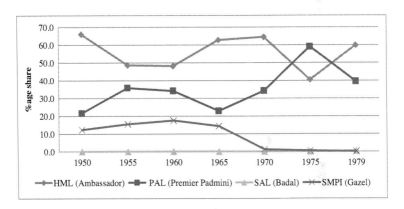

Figure A.1 Market share of car firms, 1950–79
Source: ACMA (1984, 1991).

Table A.I MNCs in car industry

Indian firm	Foreign firm	Manufacturer name	Year of entry	Collaboration details	Nature of collaboration
PAL	Fiat, Italy	PAL	1952	Production of Fiat 500 & later Fiat 1100	Technical
HML	Morris Motor Ltd., UK.	HML	1954	Ambassador based on Morris Oxford III	Technical
MUL	Suzuki Motors, Japan	MUL (renamed Maruti Suzuki India Ltd in 2007)	1982	26% share with Suzuki, & rest with GOI. Suzuki share increased 40% in 1987, 50% in 1992 & 54.2% in 2002.	Technical and Financial
HML	Vauxhall Motors	HML	1984	Contessa	Technical
HML	Isuzu	HML	1986	Engine/transmission for Contessa	Technical
PAL	Nissan Motors, Japan	PAL	1986	Engine/transmission for NE 118	Technical
HML	Ricardo Consulting Engg., UK	HML	1987	To modernise Ambassador petrol & diesel power train	Technical
PAL	Techno licence Ltd., UK	PAL	1986	To make diesel engines for Padmini	Technical
PAL	AVL, Austria	PAL	1987	To upgrade Padmini engine	Technical
Standard Motors	Austin Rover, U.K.	Standard Motors	1985	Standard 2000	Technical

				Dolphin	Technical
Sipani Automobiles			Mid-1980s		
DCM-Toyota	Daewoo Corporation, Korea	DCM- Daewoo	1994	Equity participation 51:49 with control in Daewoo's hands; to manufacture Cielo	Joint Venture (JV)
HML	General Motors, USA	General Motors India	1994	50–50 JV between HML and GM; to manufacture Opel Astra	In 1999 JV purchased by GM and it became a subsidiary of GM
HML	Mitsubishi Motors Corporation, Japan	HML	1998 and again in 2002	To produce lancer (1998) and Pajero (2002)	Technical agreement
PAL	Peugeot, France	PAL Peugeot Ltd.	1994	50:50 JV, to manufacture Peugeot model 309	Transfer of technology & manufacturing engineering know-how
PAL	Fiat, Italy	Ind. Auto Limited (renamed as Fiat India Private Ltd in 2007)	1997	Fiat (51%) and PAL (49%) to manufacture Uno	JV in 1997 and PAL stake acquired by Fiat in 2007
Mahindra and Mahindra	Ford, USA	Ford India Pvt. Ltd. (its share rose in JV)	1995	50–50 JV and in 1998 Ford share increased to 72%; it became a subsidiary of Ford	Initially JV and now subsidiary

(Continued)

Table A.1 (Continued)

Indian firm	Foreign firm	Manufacturer name	Year of entry	Collaboration details	Nature of collaboration
Shriram Group	Honda, Japan	Honda Siel Cars India Ltd. (Honda Cars India Ltd. in 2012)	1995	Shriram Group (3.16%) rest with Honda. In 2012 Honda purchased Shriram share	Initially JV and in 2012 subsidiary
TELCO	Daimler Benz, Germany	Mercedes-Benz (India) Ltd	1994	Equity share 51:49 to produce diesel version cars of E-class series	Joint Venture
Kirloskar Group	Toyota Motor Corporation, Japan	Toyota Kiloskar Motors	1997	Toyota Motor Corporation (89%) and Kirloskar Group (11%)	Joint Venture
–	Hyundai Motor, South Korea	Hyundai Motor India Limited	1997	100%	Subsidiary
–	Skoda Auto, Czech Republic, Volkswagen Group	Skoda Auto India Private Limited	2001	100%	Subsidiary
–	Audi, Germany	Audi India	2004	100%	Subsidiary
–	BMW Group	BMW India	2006	100%	Subsidiary
–	Nissan Motors, Japan	Nissan Motors India Private Limited	2005	100%	Subsidiary
–	Renault, French	Renault India Private Limited		100%	Subsidiary

Source: Compiled from the official websites of firms and *The Economic Times*.

Table A.2 Trends in capacity utilisation in passenger car industry (percentages)

Manufacturer	2002–03	2006–07	2011–12	2012–13
Mercedes-Benz India	23.49	22.81	56.83	32.36
Fiat India	0.00	2.79	8.68	3.97
Honda Cars	45.74	82.74	41.22	61.69
Ford India	15.56	41.45	59.75	54.90
BMW India	–	–	92.41	60.23
HML	30.61	17.97	8.67	9.79
Hyundai Motor	93.77	104.87	92.75	93.97
MUL	102.85	148.21	113.46	92.77
Skoda Auto	–	45.53	89.25	73.74
Toyota India	59.86	83.68	76.69	60.59
General Motors	30.21	43.39	48.46	39.54
Renault-Nissan	–	–	66.95	48.49
Volkswagen India	–	–	53.04	33.35
Tata Motors (only Passenger Vehicles)	–	–	71.42	58.82
International Cars and Motors Ltd	–	–	1.99	1.08
M&M (only Passenger Vehicles)	–	–	79.94	78.88
Average Capacity Utilisation	73.82	98.09	78.57	68.73

Source: SIAM (2006b, 2008, 2010a, 2012a, 2014a).

Note: – indicates non-availability of data.

Table A.3 Price range of passenger cars in India: segment-wise

Car segment	Price band (in Rs. Lakh)*
Mini	1.7 to 3
Compact	3 to 8
Mid-size	8 to 12
Executive	12 to 15
Premium and Luxury	Above 15

Source: Compiled by author from the official websites of firms.

Notes:
(1)*refers to price band, it is not very specific but just an indication.
(2) 1 lakh = 0.1 Million

Table A.4 R&D expenditure of selected automobile companies

Company	Year	R&D expenditure (Rs. million)	R&D expenditure as % of sales
United States			
General Motors	1980	2234	3.9
Ford Motors	1980	1675	4.5
Chrysler	1980	278	3
Japan			
Toyota Motors	1979	433.3	3.7
Nissan Motors	1979	375	3.3
Mitsubishi	1979	179.1	4.0
Honda Motors	1979	158.3	3.6
Isuzu	1979	77.5	2.9
India			
TELCO	1982–83	5.8	2.7
MICO	1982–83	2.8	1.3
Premier Auto	1982–83	1.6	1.3
Ashok Leyland	1982–83	1.6	0.4
Bajaj Auto	1982–83	0.9	0.6

Source: Gumaste (1988), Table 6.2, p. 48.

Table A.5 Import intensity of disembodied technology (percentages)***

Year	HML	MUL	Hyundai Motor	General Motors	Honda Cars	Ford India	Average of selected firms
2000–01	0.55	1.71	0.64	1.88	4.29	1.42	1.49
2001–02	0.69	2.20	0.45	4.18	3.92	1.02	1.83
2002–03	0.71	1.58	1.85	22.19	3.78	1.05	1.94
2003–04	0.59	0.92	2.99	0.00	2.64	1.31	1.57
2004–05	0.37	1.32	4.55	1.65	1.99	1.03	2.20
2005–06	0.29	1.45	4.82	1.55	3.14	1.79	2.58
2006–07	0.14	1.89	4.98	2.46	2.12	2.10	2.76
2007–08	0.59	2.30	4.53	2.69	3.49	–	3.07
2008–09	0.43	3.18	5.02	2.90	4.86	–	3.93
2009–10	0.19	3.05	6.56	2.71	3.82	–	4.26
2010–11	0.27	5.50	6.48	–	5.32	–	5.74

(Continued)

Table A.5 (Continued)

Year	HML	MUL	Hyundai Motor	General Motors	Honda Cars	Ford India	Average of selected firms
2011–12	0.29	6.22	5.71	–	5.85	–	5.97
2012–13	0.53	6.03	5.73	–	6.42	–	5.94
2013–14	–	6.13	5.92	4.39	5.35	1.84	5.52
Average import intensity							
2000–01 to 2004–05	0.57	1.50	2.64	2.75	2.89	1.16	1.88
2005–06 to 2009–10	0.33	2.53	5.37	2.55	3.48	1.98**	3.47
2010–11 to 2013–14	0.32#	5.98	5.94	4.39*	5.66	2.00*	5.77

Source: Same as Table 5.1.

Note: Same as Table 5.1.
***includes both royalty payment and expenses on other services such as technical payments.

Table A.6 Total foreign exchange spending of car firms, 1989–90 to 1999–2000 (% of sales)

Year	HML	MUL	Daewoo Motors	Average of selected firms
1989–90	16.18	21.39	–	19.62
1990–91	10.66	18.41	–	16.12
1991–92	10.80	19.11	–	17.13
1992–93	9.72	22.04	–	19.05
1993–94	7.55	27.99	–	23.14
1994–95	8.30	21.26	30.66	19.11
1995–96	8.25	19.99	85.78	23.05
1996–97	7.79	14.00	229.38	33.66
1997–98	12.07	13.11	47.44	14.30
1998–99	20.96	16.94	79.12	19.93
1999–2000	14.32	27.26	27.67	25.28
Average foreign exchange spending				
1990–91 to 1994–95	9.18	22.23	–	19.31
1995–96 to 1999–2000	13.23	18.51	98.14	23.37

Source: CMIE PROWESS 4.12.

Note: – indicates non-availability of data.

Table A.7 Total foreign exchange earnings of car firms, 1989–90 to 1999–2000 (% of sales)

Year	HML	MUL	Daewoo Motors	Average of selected firms
1989–90	2.76	3.49	–	3.24
1990–91	1.67	4.09	–	3.37
1991–92	0.86	12.60	–	9.81
1992–93	0.71	7.65	–	5.96
1993–94	3.37	7.65	–	6.63
1994–95	2.05	7.31	21.74	6.72
1995–96	2.01	7.00	8.09	6.35
1996–97	2.27	7.87	1.85	6.59
1997–98	2.13	5.25	13.13	5.15
1998–99	9.99	4.99	32.14	6.82
1999–2000	5.80	3.22	15.46	4.86
Average foreign exchange earnings				
1990–91 to 1994–95	1.85	7.87	–	6.61
1995–96 to 1999–2000	4.82	5.51	12.11	5.88

Source: Same as Table A.6.

Note: Same as Table A.6.

Table A.8 Total foreign exchange spending of car firms, 2000–01 to 2013–14 (% of sales)

Year	HML	MUL	Hyundai Motor	General Motors	Honda Cars	Ford India	Average of selected firms
2000–01	16.11	19.68	16.39	31.43	24.32	17.47	19.11
2001–02	12.93	14.46	18.29	31.93	24.74	15.79	16.53
2002–03	13.06	13.49	25.42	68.56	22.26	19.20	17.92
2003–04	10.84	12.00	29.64	42.94	33.41	18.56	20.04
2004–05	8.68	14.33	29.05	26.38	29.23	27.72	20.88
2005–06	13.32	12.33	38.27	21.68	33.57	34.44	23.62
2006–07	18.68	10.36	40.27	21.74	31.05	27.92	23.09
2007–08	26.78	13.49	32.52	41.88	34.33	–	23.97
2008–09	28.46	16.46	26.44	50.20	43.44	–	24.72
2009–10	24.78	12.59	21.78	51.87	31.40	–	19.57
2010–11	36.17	15.17	24.88	–	37.84	–	19.86
2011–12	34.05	17.48	26.45	–	36.28	–	21.90
2012–13	128.18	18.38	30.32	–	38.05	–	23.92
2013–14	0.00	16.73	30.53	34.46	26.92	40.60	24.53
Average foreign exchange spending							
2000–01 to 2004–05	12.60	14.64	25.46	33.80	28.11	20.44	19.20
2005–06 to 2009–10	22.97	13.20	29.59	40.06	34.61	30.54**	22.71
2010–11 to 2013–14	49.48#	16.99	28.31	34.46*	32.99	40.60*	22.82

Source: Same as Table 5.1.

Note: Same as Table 5.1.

Table A.9 Total foreign exchange earnings of car firms, 2000–01 to 2013–14 (% of sales)

Year	HML	MUL	Hyundai Motor	General Motors	Honda Cars	Ford India	Average of selected firms
2000–01	0.84	2.41	4.43	0.37	0.50	8.65	2.88
2001–02	0.86	2.16	3.47	0.51	0.51	18.76	3.25
2002–03	1.16	6.74	4.74	1.10	0.71	16.05	6.05
2003–04	1.16	8.46	17.17	2.41	0.50	10.76	9.81
2004–05	0.97	7.29	27.32	2.91	0.44	9.58	11.56
2005–06	0.20	3.86	30.07	5.35	0.09	6.31	11.09
2006–07	0.38	3.31	30.88	4.51	0.04	4.61	10.42
2007–08	0.05	3.49	32.41	6.48	0.03	–	11.54
2008–09	0.10	6.41	49.58	13.05	0.03	–	21.77
2009–10	0.05	14.10	47.36	5.94	0.53	–	23.74
2010–11	0.06	8.62	37.33	–	2.31	–	17.29
2011–12	0.23	9.38	35.56	–	3.99	–	18.33
2012–13	0.61	9.30	38.86	–	9.86	–	19.41
2013–14	–	8.49	40.99	1.78	9.02	37.33	20.11
Average foreign exchange earnings							
2000–01 to 2004–05	0.97	5.69	14.78	1.98	0.51	12.37	7.48
2005–06 to 2009–10	0.16	7.26	40.76	7.28	0.15	5.29**	16.94
2010–11 to 2013–14	0.20#	8.94	38.33	1.78*	7.00	37.33*	18.95

Source: Same as Table 5.1.

Note: Same as Table 5.1.

Table A.10 Net foreign exchange earnings of selected firms excluding Hyundai (% of sales)

Year	HML	MUL	Hyundai Motor	General Motors	Honda Cars	Ford India	Average of selected firms (excluding Hyundai)
2000–01	−15.27	−17.27	−11.97	−31.06	−23.82	−8.81	−17.22
2001–02	−12.07	−12.30	−14.82	−31.42	−24.23	2.96	−12.88
2002–03	−11.90	−6.75	−20.68	−67.46	−21.55	−3.15	−9.05
2003–04	−9.69	−3.53	−12.47	−40.54	−32.90	−7.79	−9.41
2004–05	−7.71	−7.04	−1.73	−23.46	−28.79	−18.14	−12.09
2005–06	−13.12	−8.47	−8.21	−16.34	−33.47	−28.14	−14.25
2006–07	−18.30	−7.05	−9.39	−17.23	−31.02	−23.32	−13.88
2007–08	−26.73	−10.00	−0.11	−35.41	−34.30	–	−17.35
2008–09	−28.37	−10.05	23.13	−37.15	−43.41	–	−17.69
2009–10	−24.72	1.51	25.58	−45.93	−30.86	–	−6.90
2010–11	−36.11	−6.55	12.45	–	−35.53	–	−9.59
2011–12	−33.83	−8.10	9.10	–	−32.29	–	−10.60
2012–13	−127.58	−9.08	8.54	–	−28.19	–	−11.28
2013–14	–	−8.24	10.46	−32.68	−17.90	−3.27	−10.23
Average net foreign exchange earnings							
2000–01 to 2004–05	−11.63	−8.95	−10.68	−31.81	−27.60	−8.07	−12.05
2005–06 to 2009–10	−22.82	−5.94	11.17	−32.78	−34.46	−25.25**	−14.02
2010–11 to 2013–14	−49.27#	−8.05	10.02	−32.68*	−25.91	−3.27*	−10.80

Source: Same as Table 5.1.

Note: Same as Table 5.1.

Bibliography

ACMA (Automotive Component Manufacturers Association). 1984. *Automotive Industry of India: Facts and Figures 1983–84*. New Delhi: Automotive Component Manufacturers Association of India.

ACMA (Automotive Component Manufacturers Association). 1991. *Automotive Industry of India: Facts and Figures 1990–91*. New Delhi: Automotive Component Manufacturers Association of India.

ACMA (Automotive Component Manufacturers Association). 2003. *Automotive Industry of India: Facts and Figures 2002–03*. New Delhi: Automotive Component Manufacturers Association of India.

Agarwal, A. 2010. 'Hyundai to Stop Production in India – Thanks to Labour Strikes!', *Track.in*, June 9. http://trak.in/tags/business/2010/06/09/hyundai-stop-car-production-india/ (accessed on 7 January 2018).

Agarwal, R. N. 1987. *Corporate Investment and Financing Behaviour: An Econometric Analysis of India Automobile Industry*. Delhi: Commonwealth Publishers.

Aggarwal, A. 2002. 'Liberalisation, Multinational Enterprises and Export Performance: Evidence from Indian Manufacturing', *The Journal of Development Studies*, 38(3): 119–137.

Ahluwalia, M. S. 1986. 'Balance of Payments Adjustment in India, 1970–71 to 1983–84', *World Development*, 14(8): 937–962.

AIAM (Association of Indian Automobile Manufacturers). 1965. *The Automobile Industry: Statistical Profile*. Bombay: Association of Indian Automobile Manufacturers.

AIAM (Association of Indian Automobile Manufacturers). 1985. *The Automobile Industry: Statistical Profile*. Bombay: Association of Indian Automobile Manufacturers.

AIAM (Association of Indian Automobile Manufacturers). 1995. *The Automobile Industry: Statistical Profile*. Bombay: Association of Indian Automobile Manufacturers.

Altenburg, T., H. Schmitz and A. Stamm. 2008. 'Breakthrough? China's and India's Transition from Production to Innovation', *World Development*, 36(2): 325–344.

Baggonkar, S. 2016. 'Maruti, Hyundai, Nissan Exports Hit a Low Gear', *Business Standard*, September 23. www.business-standard.com/article/companies/maruti-hyundai-nissan-exports-hit-a-low-gear-116092200925_1.html (accessed on 20 October 2016).

Balasubramanyam, V. N. 1971. 'Foreign Collaboration in Indian Industry', *Economic and Political Weekly*, 6(48): 159–166.

Balasubramanyam, V. N. 1973. *International Transfer of Technology to India*. New York: Praeger.

Balasubramanyam, V. N. and V. Mahambare. 2004. 'Foreign Direct Investment in India', in V. N. Balasubramanyam and Y. A. Wei (eds.), *Foreign Direct Investment: Six Country Case Studies*, pp. 47–68. London: Edward Elgar Publishing Limited.

Baranson, J. 1968. 'Automotive Industries in Developing Countries', *Report No. EC 162*. World Bank.

Basant, R. 1997. 'Technology Strategies of Large Enterprises in Indian Industry: Some Explorations', *World Development*, 25(10): 1683–1700.

Becker-Ritterspach, F. A. A. 2007. 'Maruti-Suzuki's Trajectory: From a Public-Sector Enterprise to a Japanese Owned Subsidiary', Paper presented at *15th GERPISA International Colloquium*, June 20–22.

Becker-Ritterspach, F. A. A. and J. C. E. Becker-Ritterspach. 2008. *The Sustainability of the Small Passenger Car Path in the Indian Automobile Industry*. Unpublished. www.becker-ritterspach.de/pdf/GERPISA%20 2008.pdf (accessed on 25 August 2014).

Becker-Ritterspach, F. A. A. and J. C. E. Becker-Ritterspach. 2009. 'The Development of India's Small Car Path', *Oxford Management Online Review*, 1–20. http://admin.indiaenvironmentportal.org.in/files/Small% 20Car%20Path%20India%20_MORE%20Apr09_final.pdf (accessed on 20 April 2014).

Behrman J. N. and W. A. Fischer. 1980. *Overseas R&D Activities of Transnational Companies*. Cambridge, MA: Oelgeschlager, Gunn & Hain.

Bell, M. 1984. 'Learning and Accumulation of Industrial Technological Capacity in Developing Countries', in Martin Fransman and Kenneth King (eds.), *Technological Capability in the Third World*, pp. 187–209. Hong Kong: Palgrave Macmillan.

Bell, M. and K. Pavitt. 1992. 'Accumulating Technological Capability in Developing Countries', *The World Bank Economic Review*, 6(1): 257–281.

Bell, M. and K. Pavitt. 1993. 'Technological Accumulation and Industrial Growth: Contrasts Between Developed and Developing Countries', *Industrial and Corporate Change*, 2(2): 157–210.

Bell, M. and K. Pavitt. 1997. 'Technological Accumulation and Industrial Growth: Contrasts Between Developed and Developing Countries', in Daniele Archibugi and Jonathan Michie (eds.), *Technology, Globalization and Economic Performance*, pp. 83–137. Cambridge: Cambridge University Press.

Bell, M., D. Scott-Kemmis and W. Satyarakwit. 1982. 'Limited Learning in Infant Industry: A Case Study', in Frances Stewart and J. James (eds.), *The Economics of New Technology in Developing Countries*, pp. 138–156. London: Pinter Publishers.

Beugelsdijk, S., R. Smeets and R. Zwinkels. 2008. 'The Impact of Horizontal and Vertical FDI on Host's Country Economic Growth', *International Business Review*, 17(4): 452–472.

Bhargava, R. C. and Seetha. 2010. *The Maruti Story: How a Public Sector Company put India on Wheels*. Noida: HarperCollins Publishers.

Bijapurkar, R. 2007. *Winning in the Indian Market: Understanding the Transformation of Consumer India*. Singapore: John Wiley and Sons.

Blalock, G. and P. J. Gertler. 2009. 'How Firm Capabilities Affect? *Who* Benefits from Foreign Technology', *Journal of Development Economics*, 90(2): 192–199.

Business Line. 2013. 'EEPC: India's Motor Vehicle Exports to EU to Be Hit from January', December 3. www.thehindubusinessline.com/economy/eepc-indias-motor-vehicle-exports-to-eu-to-be-hit-from-january/article23153135.ece (accessed on 10 January 2015).

Business Today. 2012. 'Strike Hits Production at Hyundai Motor India', October 31. www.businesstoday.in/sectors/auto/strike-hits-production-at-hyundai-motor-india/story/189498.html (accessed on 10 April 2014).

Carrillo, J., Y. Lung and R. V. Tulder. 2004. *Cars, Carriers of Regionalism?* New York: Palgrave Macmillan.

Chakraborty, S. 1987. *Development Planning: The Indian Experience*. New Delhi: Oxford University Press.

Chandrasekhar, C. P. 1994. 'Aspects of Growth and Structural Change in Indian Industry', in Deepak Nayyar (ed.), *Industrial Growth and Stagnation: The Debate in India*, pp. 318–345. New Delhi: Oxford University Press.

Chandrasekhar, C. P. 1997. 'The Trade-Investment Nexus and Industrialization: An Assessment Based on the Asian Experience', in Deepak Nayyar (ed.), *Trade and Industrialization*, pp. 273–292. Delhi: Oxford University Press.

Chandrasekhar, C. P. 1999. 'Firms, Markets and the State: An Analysis of Indian Oligopoly', in Amiya K. Bagchi (ed.), *Economy and Organisation: Indian Institutions Under the Neo-liberal Regime*, pp. 230–267. New Delhi: Sage Publications.

Chandrasekhar, C. P. 2002. 'Opening the Sluice Gates', *Frontline*, 19(1). www.frontline.in/static/html/fl1901/19011030.htm (accessed on 5 July 2013).

Chandrasekhar, C. P. 2010. 'From Dirgisme to Neoliberalism: Aspects of the Political Economy of the Transition in India', *Development and Society*, 39(1): 29–59.

Chandrasekhar, C. P. 2011. 'Six Decades of Industrial Development: Growth of the Manufacturing Sector in India', in D. Narayana and

Raman Mahadevan (eds.), *Shaping India: Economic Change in Historical Perspective*, pp. 206–236. New Delhi: Routledge.

Chandrasekhar, C. P. 2013. 'Knowledge and the Asian Challenge', in N. Yokokawa, J. Ghosh and R. Rowthorn (eds.), *Industrialization of China and India: Their Impacts on World Economy*, pp. 59–87. London and New York: Routledge.

Chandrasekhar, C. P. and J. Ghosh. 2002. *The Market That Failed: Neoliberal Economic Reforms in India*. Delhi: LeftWord.

Chatterjee, P. 2016. '10 Worst Labour Agitations in Indian Auto Industry', *ET Auto*, November 23. https://auto.economictimes.indiatimes.com/news/industry/10-worst-labour-agitations-in-indian-auto-industry/51099922 (accessed on 7 January 2018).

Chattopadhyay, U. 2013. 'Demystifying the Growth Story of Indian Passenger Car Industry', *International Journal of Trade, Economics and Finance*, 4(3): 111–118.

Chenoy, K. A. M. 2015. *The Rise of Big Business in India*. Delhi: Aakar Books.

Chung, M.-K. 1998. 'Globalization Strategies of Korean Motor Vehicle Industries: A Case Study of Hyundai', *Actes du GERPISA, No. 22*. http://gerpisa.org/ancien-gerpisa/actes/22/22-5.pdf (accessed on 10 June 2015).

Chung, M.-K. 2003. 'The Chance for a Peripheral Market Player: The Internationalization Strategies of the Korean Automobile Industry', in Michel Freyssenet, Koichi Shimizu and Giuseppe Volpato (eds.), *Globalization or Regionalization of the American and Asian Car Industry?* pp. 185–208. New York: Palgrave Macmillan.

Cimoli, M., G. Dosi and J. E. Stiglitz. 2009. *Industrial Policy and Development: The Political Economy of Capability Accumulation*. New York: Oxford University Press.

Cohen, W. M. and D. A. Levinthal. 1989. 'Innovation and Learning: The Two Faces of R&D', *The Economic Journal*, 99(397): 569–596.

Dahlman, C. J. 1984. 'Foreign Technology and Indigenous Technological Capability in Brazil', in Martin Fransman and Kenneth King (eds.), *Technological Capability in the Third World*, pp. 317–334. Hong Kong: Palgrave Macmillan.

D'Costa, A. P. 1995. 'The Restructuring of the Indian Automobile Industry: Indian State and Japanese Capital', *World Development*, 23(3): 485–502.

D'Costa, A. P. 2005. *The Long March to Capitalism: Embourgeoisment, Internationalization, and Industrial Transformation in India*. New York: Palgrave Macmillan.

Desai, A. V. 1972. 'Imports of Capital and Technology: A Second Look', *Margin*, 4(2): 51–62.

Desai, A. V. 1984. 'Achievements and Limitations of India's Technology Capability', in Martin Fransman and Kenneth King (eds.), *Technological*

Capability in the Third World, pp. 245–262. Hong Kong: Palgrave Macmillan.

Desai, A. V. 1985. 'Indigenous and Foreign Determinants of Technical Change in Indian Industry', *Economic and Political Weekly*, 20(45/47): 2081–2094.

Dore, R. 1984. 'Technological Self-reliance: Study Ideal or Self-serving Rhetoric', in Martin Fransman and Kenneth King (eds.), *Technological Capability in the Third World*, pp. 65–80. Hong Kong: Palgrave Macmillan.

Dosi, G., C. Freeman and R. Nelson. 1988. *Technology Change and Economic Theory*. London and New York: Pinter Publishers.

Driffield, N. 2001. 'Inward Investment and Host Country Market Structure: The Case of the U.K.', *Review of Industrial Organization*, 18(4): 363–378.

Dunning, J. H. and S. M. Lundan. 2008. *Multinational Enterprises and the Global Economy*, Second Edition. Cheltenham: Edward Elgar.

The Economic Times. 1997. 'Company History – Daewoo Motors India Ltd.'. http://economictimes.indiatimes.com/daewoo-motors-india-ltd/infocompanyhistory/companyid-13869.cms (accessed on 15 July 2014).

The Economic Times. 2011. 'India's Middle Class Population to Touch 267 Million in 5 Years', February 6. https://economictimes.indiatimes.com/news/economy/indicators/indias-middle-class-population-to-touch-267-million-in-5-yrs/articleshow/7435793.cms (accessed on 24 May 2014).

The Economic Times. 2013. 'Carmakers Maruti, Toyota, Honda and Others Plan to Invest Rs. 11000 Crore to Expand Capacity, Counter Clowdown', April 24. https://economictimes.indiatimes.com/automobiles/carmakers-maruti-toyota-honda-and-others-plan-to-invest-rs-11000-crto-expand-capacity-counter-slowdown/articleshow/19702205.cms (accessed on 24 August 2014).

The Economic Times. 2014. 'Automobile Exports from India on a Constant Decline', October 30. https://economictimes.indiatimes.com/industry/auto/news/passenger-vehicle/cars/automobile-exports-from-india-on-a-constant-decline/articleshow/44977630.cms (accessed on 25 January 2015).

Ernst et al. 2015. *Case Study: Hyundai Motor India (HMI) Ltd.: Local Marketing Strategy and Future Challenges*. www.academia.edu/7007586/Case_Study_Hyundai_Motor_India_HMI_Ltd._Local_Marketing_Strategy_and_Future_Challenges_Group_5 (accessed on 15 March 2015).

Ernst, D., T. Ganiatsos and L. Mytelke. 1998. *Technology Capability and Export Success in Asia*. London and New York: Routledge.

Evans, P. B. 1995. *Embedded Autonomy: States and Industrial Transformation*. Princeton: Princeton University Press.

Forbes, N. 2002. 'Doing Business in India: What Has Liberalization Changed?', in A. O. Krueger (ed.), *Economic Policy Reforms and the Indian Economy*, pp. 129–167. New Delhi: Oxford University Press.

Frankel, F. R. 1978. *India's Political Economy 1957–1977: The Gradual Revolution*. New Delhi: Oxford University Press.

Frankel, F. R. 2004. *India's Political Economy 1947–2004: The Gradual Revolution*. New Delhi: Oxford University Press.

Fransman, M. and K. King. 1984. *Technological Capability in the Third World*. Hong Kong: Palgrave Macmillan.

Freyssenet, M., K. Shimizu and G. Volpato. 2003. *Globalization or Regionalization of the American and Asian Car Industry?* New York: Palgrave Macmillan.

Fu, X. 2008. 'Foreign Direct Investment, Absorptive Capacity and Regional Innovation Capabilities: Evidence from China', *Oxford Development Studies*, 36(1): 89–110.

Geroski, P. A. 1990. 'Innovation, Technological Opportunity, and Market Structure', *Oxford Economic Papers*, 42(3): 586–602.

Ghosh, A. 1992. *Planning in India: The Challenge for the Nineties*. New Delhi: Sage Publications.

Ghosh, J. 1990. 'The Impact of Integration: India and the World Economy in the 1980s', in Sugata Bose (ed.), *South Asia and World Capitalism*, pp. 338–356. New Delhi: Oxford University Press.

GoI (Government of India). 1947. *Report of the Panel on Automobiles and Tractors*. New Delhi: Ministry of Industry and Supply, Government of India.

GoI (Government of India). 1948. *Industrial Policy Resolution 1948*. New Delhi: Government of India.

GoI (Government of India). 1951. *First Five Year Plan: Chapter 29 on Industrial Development and Policy*. New Delhi: Planning Commission, Government of India.

GoI (Government of India). 1953. *Report on Automobile Industry*. New Delhi: Government of India.

GoI (Government of India). 1957. *Report on the Automobile Industry*. New Delhi: Ministry of Heavy Industries, Government of India.

GoI (Government of India). 1958. *Scientific Policy Resolution 1958*, No. 131/CF/57. New Delhi. http://lakshadweep.nic.in/depts/laktech/new_page_4.htm (accessed on 12 January 2018).

GoI (Government of India). 1960. *Report of the Ad hoc Committee on Automobile Industry*. New Delhi: Ministry of Commerce & Industry, Government of India Press.

GoI (Government of India). 1961. *Third Five Year Plan: Chapter 26 on Industries*. New Delhi: Planning Commission, Government of India.

GoI (Government of India). 1968. *Report on Continuance of Protection to Automobile Industry*. New Delhi: Tariff Commission, Government of India.

GoI (Government of India). 1973. *Review of the Automobile Ancillary Industry*. New Delhi: Ministry of Commerce & Industry, Government of India.

GoI (Government of India). 1991–92. *Economic Survey 1991–92*. New Delhi: Ministry of Finance, Government of India.

GoI (Government of India). 1992–93. *Economic Survey 1992–93*. New Delhi: Ministry of Finance, Government of India.

GoI (Government of India). 1996–97. *Economic Survey 1996–97*. New Delhi: Ministry of Finance, Government of India.

GoI (Government of India). 1997. *Export-Import Policy 1997–2002*. New Delhi: Ministry of Commerce & Industry, Government of India.

GoI (Government of India). 2002. *Auto Policy, March 2002*. New Delhi: Ministry of Heavy Industries and Public Enterprises, Government of India.

GoI (Government of India). 2006. *Automotive Mission Plan 2006–2016*. New Delhi: Ministry of Heavy Industries and Public Enterprises, Government of India.

GoI (Government of India). 2007. *SIA Newsletter Annual Issue 2006*. New Delhi: Department of Industrial Policy and Promotion, Ministry of Commerce & Industry, Government of India.

GoI (Government of India). 2010. *SIA Newsletter Annual Issue 2009*. New Delhi: Department of Industrial Policy and Promotion, Ministry of Commerce & Industry, Government of India.

GoI (Government of India). 2010–11. *Annual Report 2010–11*. New Delhi: Ministry of Heavy Industries and Public Enterprises, Government of India.

GoI (Government of India). 2013. *SIA Newsletter Annual Issue 2012*. New Delhi: Department of Industrial Policy and Promotion, Ministry of Commerce & Industry, Government of India.

GoI (Government of India). 2016a. *Consolidated FDI Policy*. New Delhi: Department of Industrial Policy and Promotion, Ministry of Commerce & Industry Government of India.

GoI (Government of India). 2016b. *Foreign Direct Investment in India – Annual Issue*. New Delhi: Department of Industrial Policy and Promotion, Ministry of Commerce & Industry, Government of India.

GoI (Government of India). 2017. *Consolidated FDI Policy*. New Delhi: Department of Industrial Policy and Promotion, Ministry of Commerce & Industry Government of India.

GoI (Government of India). 2017–18. *Annual Report 2017–18*. New Delhi: Ministry of Heavy Industries and Public Enterprises, Government of India.

GoI (Government of India) and SIAM (Society of Indian Automobile Manufacturers). 2016. *Automotive Mission Plan 2016–26*. www.siamindia.com/uploads/filemanager/47AUTOMOTIVEMISSIONPLAN.pdf (accessed on 10 August 2017).

Goyal, S. K. 1979. *Monopoly Capital and Public Policy*. New Delhi: Allied Publishers Private Limited.

Green, A. E. 1992. 'South Korea's Automobile Industry: Development and Prospects', *Asian Survey*, 32(5): 411–428.

Gulyani, S. 2001. *Innovating with Infrastructure: The Automobile Industry in India*. New York: Palgrave Macmillan.

Gumaste, V. M. 1988. *Technological Self-Reliance in the Automobile and Ancillary Industries in India*. Madras: IFMR.

Gupta, S. D. 2014. 'As Hyundai Changes Strategy, India's Status as Auto Export Hub in Question', *Business and Standard*, August 20. www.businessstandard.com/article/opinion/surajeet-das-guta-hyundai-s-straws-in-the-wind-114081200376_1.html (accessed on 12 February 2015).

Haller, S. A. 2004. *The Impact of Multinational Entry on Domestic Market Structure and R&D*. Economics Department, European University Institute. www.etsg.org/ETSG2004/Papers/Haller.pdf (accessed on 15 May 2014).

Hamaguchi, T. 1985. 'Prospects for Self-Reliance and Indigenization in Automobile Industry (Case of Maruti-Suzuki Project)', *Economic and Political Weekly*, 20(35): M115–M122.

Hazari, R. K. 1966. *The Structure of the Corporate Private Sector: A Study of Concentration, Ownership and Control*. Bombay: Asia Publishing House.

HML (Hindustan Motors Limited). 1966. *The Automobile in India: A Study*. Calcutta: Department of Economic and Market Research, Hindustan Motors Limited.

Humphrey, J., A. Mukherjee, M. Zilbovicius and G. Arbix. 1998. 'Globalization, FDI and the Restructuring of Supplier Networks: The Motor Industry in Brazil and India', in M. Kagami, J. Humphrey and M. Piore (eds.), *Learning, Liberalization and Economic Adjustment*, pp. 117–189. Tokyo: Institute of Developing Economies.

IBEF (India Brand Equity Foundation). 2012. *Automobiles*. www.ibef.org (accessed on 15 May 2014).

IDRA (Industries Development and Regulation Act). 1951. *The Industries Development and Regulation Act, 1951*. www.lawsindia.com/Industrial%20Law/c_096.htm#s1 (accessed on 17 February 2014).

IIFT (Indian Institute of Foreign Trade). 1981. *Role of Transnational Corporations in India's Exports*. New Delhi: Indian Institute of Foreign Trade.

Ishigami, E. 2004. 'Competition and Corporate Strategy in Indian Automobile Industry with Special Reference to Maruti Udyog Limited and Suzuki Motor Corporation', Paper presented at *International Conference: A Comparison of Japanese Firm and Korean Firm in India Automobile Market*. Centre for Area Studies, Korea, March 5.

Ito, S. 1985. 'Technology Transfer from Japanese to Indian Firms', *Economic and Political Weekly*, 20(45/47): 2031–2042.

Jalan, B. 1991. *India's Economic Crisis: The Ways Ahead*. New Delhi: Oxford University Press.

Jenkins, R. 1979. 'The Export Performance of Multinational Corporations in Mexican Industry', *Journal of Development Studies*, 15(3): 89–107.

Jenkins, R. 2006. 'Globalization, FDI and Employment in Vietnam', *Transnational Corporations*, 15(1): 115–142.

Joseph, K. J. 1997. *Industry under Economic Liberalization: The Case of Indian Electronics*. New Delhi: Sage Publications.

Joseph, K. J. 2006. *Information Technology Innovation System and Trade Regime in Developing Countries: India and the ASEAN*. New Delhi: Palgrave Macmillan.

Joseph, K. J. and D. Abrol. 2009. 'Science, Technology and Innovation Policies in India: Achievements and Limits', in J. E. Cassiolato and V. Vitorino (eds.), *BRICS and Development Alternatives: Innovation Systems and Policies*, pp. 101–132. New York: Anthem Press.

Joseph, K. J. and C. Veeramani. 2001. 'India's External Sector after Economic Liberalization', in K. V. Kesavan (ed.), *Economic Liberalization in India: Japanese & Indian Perspectives*, pp. 137–160. New Delhi: Indian Council of Social Science Research.

Joshi, V. and I. M. D. Little. 1994. *India: Macro Economics and Political Economy 1964–1991*. New Delhi: Oxford University Press.

Kale, D. 2012. 'Sources of Innovation and Technology Capability in the Indian Automobile Industry', *Institutions and Economies*, 4(2): 121–150.

Kale, D. and S. Little. 2007. 'From Imitation to Innovation: The Evolution of Innovative R&D Capabilities in the Indian Pharmaceutical Industry', *Technology Analysis and Strategic Management*, 19(5): 589–609.

Kaplinsky, R. 1984. 'Trade in Technology-Who, What, Where and When?', in Martin Fransman and Kenneth King (eds.), *Technological Capability in the Third World*, pp. 139–160. Hong Kong: Palgrave Macmillan.

Karmokolias, Y. 1990. 'Automotive Industry Trends and Prospects for Investment in Developing Countries', *Discussion Paper No. 7*. Washington, DC: World Bank, International Finance Corporation.

Kathuria, S. 1996. *Competing Through Technology and Manufacturing: A Study of the Indian Commercial Vehicles Industry*. New Delhi: Oxford University Press.

Kathuria, S. and V. Vandana. 1990. *Competitiveness of the Indian Commercial Vehicles Industry: An Exploration*. New Delhi: Align Publications.

Kesavan, K. V. 2001. *Economic Liberalization in India: Japanese & Indian Perspectives*. New Delhi: Indian Council of Social Science Research.

Khare, A. 1997. 'Strategic Advantages of Good Relations in Indian Automobile Industry', *Technovation*, 17(10): 557–568.

Kidron, M. 1965. *Foreign Investment in India*. London: Oxford University Press.

Kim, L. and R. R. Nelson. 2000. *Technology Learning and Innovation: Experiences of Newly Industrializing Economies*. Cambridge: Cambridge University Press.

Krueger, A. O. 1975. *The Benefits and Costs of Import Substitution in India: A Microeconomic Study*. Minneapolis: University of Minnesota Press.

Krueger, A. O. 2002. *Economic Policy Reforms and the Indian Economy*. New Delhi: Oxford University Press.

Kujal, P. 1996. 'The Impact of Regulatory Controls on Industry Structure: A Study of the Car and Scooter Industry in India', *Working Paper No. 96–15*.: Department de Economia, University Carlos, Spain.

Kumar, N. 1985. 'Costs of Technology Imports: The Indian Experience', *Economic and Political Weekly*, 20(35): M103–M114.

Kumar, N. 1987. 'Technology Policy in India: An Overview of Its Evolution and an Assessment', in P. R. Brahmananda and V. R. Panchamukhi (eds.), *The Development Process of the Indian Economy*, pp. 461–492. Bombay: Himalaya Publishing House.

Kumar, N. 1990. *Multinational Enterprises in India: Industrial Distribution*. London: Routledge.

Kumar, N. 1994. *Multinational Enterprises and Industrial Organisation – The Case of India*. New Delhi: Sage Publications.

Kumar, N. 2000. *Globalization and the Quality of Foreign Direct Investment*. New York: Oxford University Press.

Kumar, N. 2005. 'Liberalisation, Foreign Direct Investment Flows and Development: Indian Experience in the 1990s', *Economic and Political Weekly*, 40(14): 1459–1469.

Kumar, N. 2007. 'Introduction', in N. Kumar and K. J. Joseph (eds.), *International Competitiveness and Knowledge Based Industries in India*, pp. 1–17. New Delhi: Oxford University Press.

Kumar, N. and K. J. Joseph. 2007. *International Competitiveness and Knowledge Based Industries in India*. New Delhi: Oxford University Press.

Kumar, N. and N. S. Siddharthan. 1994. 'Technology, Firm Size and Export Behaviour in Developing Countries: The Case of Indian Enterprises', *The Journal of Development Studies*, 31(2): 289–309.

Kumar, N. and N. S. Siddharthan. 1997. *Technology, Market Structure and Industrialization: Issues and Policies for Developing Countries*. New York: Routledge.

Kumar, P. 1985. *Growth of Industrial Corporations in India: Structure, Strategy, Determinants*. New Delhi: Deep and Deep Publications.

Lakshmikumaran & Sridharan. 2017. 'India-EU Free Trade Agreement: State of Play and Way Forward', *Lexology*, June 20. www.lexology.com/library/detail.aspx?g=afb818fa-cfce-4fdf-aecf-503d633ed5fd (accessed on 10 November 2017).

Lall, S. 1979. 'Multinational and Market Structure in an Open Developing Economy: The Case of Malaysia', *Review of World Economies*, 115(2): 325–350.

Lall, S. 1980. 'Indian Technology Exports and Technological Development', *The Annals of the American Academy of Political and Social Science*, 458: 151–162.

Lall, S. 1982. 'Technological Learning in the Third World: Some Implications of Technology Exports', in F. Stewart and J. James (eds.), *The Economics of New Technology in Developing Countries*, pp. 157–197. London: Pinter Publishers.

Lall, S. 1984. 'India's Technological Capacity: Efforts of Trade, Industrial Science and Technology Policies', in Martin Fransman and Kenneth King (eds.), *Technological Capability in the Third World*, pp. 225–244. Hong Kong: Palgrave Macmillan.

Lall, S. 1985. *Multinationals, Technology and Exports*. New York: St. Martin's Press.

Lall, S. 1986. 'Technological Development and Export Performance in LDCs: Leading Engineering and Chemical Firms in India', *Weltwirtschaftliches Archiv*, 122(1): 80–91.

Lall, S. 1987. *Learning to Industrialize: The Acquisition of Technological Capability by India*. London: Palgrave Macmillan.

Lall, S. 1992. 'Technological Capabilities and Industrialization', *World Development*, 20(2): 165–186.

Lall, S. 1996. *Learning from the Asian Tigers*. London: Palgrave Macmillan.

Lee, K. 2013. *Schumpeterian Analysis of Economic Catch-up: Knowledge, Path-Creation, and the Middle-Income Trap*. Cambridge: Cambridge University Press.

Livemint. 2009. 'Workers End Strike at Hyundai Plant; Stir on at M&M', May 7. www.livemint.com/Companies/C8hXCMn18Lmjg WgSY32OSN/Workers-end-strike-at-Hyundai-plant-stir-on-at-MampM.html (accessed on 5 June 2014).

Livemint. 2014. 'Hyundai Stops Car Exports to Europe from India', August 11. www.livemint.com/Companies/NtK5S5zclLI601xNoMnDaJ/ Hyundai-stops-car-exports-to-Europe-from-India.html (accessed on 10 July 2015).

Long, G. 2005. 'China's Policies on FDI: Review', in T. H. Moran, E. M. Graham and M. Blomstrom (eds.), *Does Foreign Direct Investment Promote Development*, pp. 315–336. Washington, DC: Center for Global Development, Institute for International Economics.

Lundin, N., F. Sjoholm, P. He and J. Qian. 2007. 'FDI, Market Structure and R&D Investments in China', *Working Paper No. 2007–04*. Japan: The International Centre for the Study of East Asian Development, IFN Research Institute of Industrial Economics.

Malik, Y. K. and D. K. Vajpeyi. 1988. *India: The Years of Indira Gandhi*. Netherlands: E.J. Brill.

Mani, S. 2011. 'The Indian Automotive Industry: Enhancing Innovation Capability with External and Internal Resources', in Patarapong Intara-kumerd (ed.), *How to Enhance Innovation Capability With Internal and External Sources*. ERIA Research Project Report No. 9.

Manor, J. 1988. 'Party and Party System', in Atul Kohli (ed.), *India's Democracy: An Analysis of Changing State-Society Relations*, pp. 62–98. Princeton: Princeton University Press.

Marathe, S. S. 1989. *Regulation and Development: India's Policy Experience of Controls over Industry*. New Delhi: Sage Publications.

Mishra, A. R. 2017. 'India, EU to Hold Free Trade Talks Next Week', *Livemint*, November 9. www.livemint.com/Politics/UDXmgxJeTNKK5Ql AUBmeoK/India-EU-to-hold-free-trade-talks-next-week.html (accessed on 15 December 2017).

Modi, A. 2016. 'Maruti Suzuki Widens Hiring from ITIs', *Business Standard*, August 22. www.business-standard.com/article/companies/maruti-suzuki-widens-hiring-from-itis-116082100624_1.html (accessed on 30 August 2016).

Mohanty, A. K., P. K. Sahu and S. C. Pati. 1994. *Technology Transfer in Indian Automobile Industry*. New Delhi: Ashish Publishing.

Moran, T. H., E. M. Graham and M. Blomstrom. 2005. *Does Foreign Direct Investment Promote Development*. Washington, DC: Center for Global Development, Institute for International Economics.

Motohashi, K. 2015. *Global Business Strategy: Multinational Corporations Venturing in Emerging Markets*. New York: Springer International Publishing.

Mrinalini, N., P. Nath and G. D. Sandhya. 2013. 'Foreign Direct Investment in R&D in India', *Current Science*, 105(6): 763–773.

Mrinalini, N. and W. Sandhya. 2008. 'Foreign R&D Centre in India: Is There Any Positive Impact?', *Current Science*, 94(4): 452–458.

Mukherjee, A. and T. Sastry. 1996. 'The Automotive Industry in Emerging Economies: A Comparison of Korea, Brazil, China and India', *Economic and Political Weekly*, 31(48): M75–M78.

Mukherjee, S. 2014. 'Hyundai Stops Car Exports to Europe from India', *Business and Standard*, August 11. www.business-standard.com/article/pti-stories/hyundai-stops-car-exports-to-europe-from-india-114081100536_1.html (accessed on 6 July 2015).

Nagaraj, R. 2013. 'India's Dream Run, 2003–08: Understanding the Boom and Its Aftermath', *Economic & Political Weekly*, xlviii(20): 39–51.

Naik, S. 2006. *Regional Determinants of FDI: A Study of Indian State under Liberalization*. Unpublished M.Phil Dissertation, Centre for Development Studies, Trivandrum, Kerala.

Najmabadi, F. and S. Lall. 1995. *Developing Industrial Technology: Lessons for Policy and Practice*. Washington, DC: World Bank.

Narayana, D. L. 1989. *The Motor Vehicle Industry in India (Growth within a Regulatory Policy Environment)*. New Delhi and Trivandrum: Oxford & IBH Publishing Co. Pvt. Ltd.

Narayana, D. L. and K. J. Joseph. 1993. 'Industry and Trade Liberalisation-Performance of Motor Vehicles and Electronics Industries, 1981–91', *Economic and Political Weekly*, 28(8/9): M13–M20.

Narayana, D. L., E. Mridul and M. Chandan. 1992. 'Growth, Technical Dynamism and Policy Change in the Indian Motor Vehicle Industry', in Arun Ghosh, K. K. Subrahmanian, M. Eapen and H. A. Drabu (eds.), *Indian Industrialization: Structure and Policy Issues*, pp. 208–236. New Delhi: Oxford University Press.

Narayanan, B. G. and P. Vashisht. 2008. 'Determinants of Competitiveness of the Indian Auto Industry', *Working Paper No. 201*. New Delhi: Indian Council for Research on International Economic Relations.

Narayanan, K. 1998. 'Technology Acquisition, De-Regulation and Competitiveness: A Study of Indian Automobile Industry', *Research Policy*, 27(2): 215–228.

Narayanan, K. 1999. *Technology, Modernization and Growth in Indian Manufacturing: A Study of the Automobile Sector*. Unpublished PhD Thesis, University of Delhi, Delhi School of Economics, Delhi.

Narayanan, K. 2001. 'Liberalization and the Differential Conduct and Performance of Firms: A Study of the Indian Automobile Sector', *Discussion Paper Series No. 414*. Japan: The Institute of Economic Research, Hitotsubashi University and United Nations University Institute of Advance Studies, Japan.

Narayanan, K. 2004. 'Technology Acquisition and Growth of Firms: Indian Automobile Sector Under Changing Policy Regimes', *Economic and Political Weekly*, 39(5): 461–470.

Narayanan, K. 2006. 'Technology Acquisition and Export Competitiveness: Evidence from Indian Automobile Industry', in Suresh D. Tendulkar, Arup Mitra, K. Narayanan and Deb Kusum Das (eds.), *India: Industrialisation in a Reforming Economy*, pp. 439–470. New Delhi: Academic Foundation.

Narula, R. 2005. 'Knowledge Creation and Why it Matters for Development: The Role of TNCs', in UNCTAD (ed.), *Globalization of R&D and Developing Countries*, pp. 43–60. New York and Geneva: United Nations.

Narula, R. and S. Lall. 2006. *Understanding FDI-Assisted Economic Development*. London and New York: Routledge.

Natarajan, R. 1988. 'Science Technology and Mrs Gandhi', in Y. K. Malik and D. K. Vajpeyi (eds.), *India: The Years of Indira Gandhi*. Netherlands: E.J. Brill.

Nayak, A. K. J. R. 2008. *Multinationals in India: FDI and Complementation Strategy in a Developing Country*. New York: Palgrave Macmillan.

Nayyar, D. 1978. 'Transnational Corporations and Manufactured Exports from Poor Countries', *Economic Journal*, 88(1): 59–84.

Nayyar, D. 1996. *Economic Liberalization in India: Analytics, Experience and Lesson*. Hyderabad: Orient Longman.

NCAER (National Council of Applied Economics Research). 2002. *India Market Demographics Report 2002*. New Delhi: National Council of Applied Economics Research (NCAER).

Nelson, R. R. and S. G. Winter. 1974. 'Neoclassical versus Evolutionary Theories of Economic Growth: Critique and Prospectus', *Economic Journal*, 84(336): 886–905.

Nelson, R. R. and S. G. Winter. 1982. *An Evolutionary Theory of Economic Change*. Cambridge: Harvard University Press.

New York Times. 1922. 'World Motor Car Census', in T. Rajnish and H. Cornelius (2014) *Aiming Big with Small Cars: Emerging of a Lead Market in India*, p. 106. Switzerland: Springer International Publishing.

Okada, A. 1998. 'Does Globalization Improve Employment and the Quality of Jobs in India: A Case from the Automobile Industry', *Research Note No. 3*. Massachusetts Institute of Technology, Department of Urban Studies and Planning, USA. https://ipc.mit.edu/sites/default/files/documents/00-012.pdf (accessed on 15 June 2014).

Okada, A. 2004. 'Skills Development and Inter-firm Learning Linkages under Globalization: Lessons from the Indian Automobile Industry', *World Development*, 32(7): 1265–1288.

Panagariya, A. 2004. 'India in the 1980s and 1990s: A Triumph of Reforms', *IMF Working Paper No 04/43*. www.imf.org/external/pubs/ft/wp/2004/wp0443.pdf (accessed on 15 June 2014).

Parhi, M. 2008. 'Technological Dynamism of Indian Automotive Firms: A Close Look at the Factors Inducing Learning and Capability Building', Paper presented at the VI Globelics Conference at Mexico, September 22–24. https://scholar.google.com/citations?user=FA_GqNoAAAAJ&hl=en&oi=sra#d=gs_md_cita-d&p=&u=%2Fcitations%3Fview_op%3Dview_citation%26hl%3Den%26user%3DFA_GqNoAAAAJ%26citation_for_view%3DFA_GqNoAAAAJ%3AzYLM7Y9cAGgC%26tzom%3D-330 (accessed on 10 January 2013).

Park, J. 2004. 'Korean Perspective on FDI in India: Hyundai Motors' Industrial Cluster', *Economic and Political Weekly*, 39(31): 3551–3555.

Parthasarthi, A. 2007. *Technology at the Core: Science and Technology with Indira Gandhi*. New Delhi: Pearson Education.

Patnaik, P. 1979. 'Industrial Development in India since Independence', *Social Scientist*, 7(11): 3–19.

Paul, J. 2009. *No Money Marketing: From Upstart to Big Brand on a Frugal Budget*. New Delhi: Tata McGraw-Hill.

Pearce, R. 1999. 'Decentralised R&D and Strategic Competitiveness: Globalised Approaches to Generation and Use of Technology in Multinational Enterprises (MNEs)', *Research Policy*, 28(2/3): 157–178.

Pearce, R. 2005. 'The Globalization of R&D: Key Features and the Role of TNCs', in UNCTAD (ed.), *Globalization of R&D and Developing Countries*, pp. 29–42. New York and Geneva: United Nations.

Peria, M. S. M. and A. Mody. 2004. 'How Foreign Participation and Market Concentration Impact Bank Spreads: Evidence from Latin America', *Working Paper 3210*. Washington, DC: World Bank Policy Research, World Bank.

Pillai, P. M. 1978. 'Multinational Corporation in Indian Industries: A Study of Its Changing Dimensions of Concentration and Diversification', *The Indian Economic Journal*, 26(3): 179–198.

Pillai, P. M. 1979. 'Technology Transfer, Adaption and Assimilation', *Economic and Political Weekly*, 14(47): M121–M126.

Pillai, P. M. and K. K. Subrahmanian. 1977. 'Rhetoric and Reality of Technology Transfer', *Social Scientist*, 5(6/7): 73–92.

Pingle, V. 1999. *Rethinking the Developmental State*. New York: St. Martin's Press.

Porter, M. E. 1990. *The Competitive Advantage of Nations*. New York: Free Press.

Pradhan, J. P. and N. Singh. 2008. 'Outward FDI and Knowledge Flows: A Study of the Indian Automotive Sector', *Working Paper No. 2008/10*. Institute for Studies in Industrial Development, New Delhi.

Rajan, R. S., E. Rongala and R. Ghosh. 2008. *Attracting Foreign Investment to India*. Unpublished. http://citeseerx.ist.psu.edu/viewdoc/download?doi=10.1.1.516.5015&rep=rep1&type=pdf (accessed on 7 September 2011).

Ranawat, R. and R. Tiwari. 2009. 'Influence of Government Policies on Industry Development: The Case of India's Automotive Industry', *Working Paper No. 57*. Germany: Hamburg University of Technology.

Ray, S. and P. K. Ray. 2011. 'Product Innovation for the People's Car in an Emerging Economy', *Technovation*, 31(5/6): 216–217.

Reddy, P. 1997. 'New Trends in Globalization of Corporate R&D and Implications for Innovation Capacity in Host Countries: A Survey from India', *World Development*, 25(11): 1821–1837.

Reddy, P. 2000. *Globalization of Corporate R&D: Implications for Innovation Systems in Host Countries*. London and New York: Routledge.

Reddy, P. 2005. 'R&D-related FDI in Developing Countries: Implications for Host Countries', in UNCTAD (ed.), *Globalization of R&D and Developing Countries*, pp. 89–108. New York and Geneva: United Nations.

Romijn, H. 1997. 'Acquisition of Technological Capability in Development: A Quantitative Case-Study of Pakistan's Capital Goods Sector', *World Development*, 25(3): 359–377.

Ronstadt, R. C. 1977. *Research and Development Abroad by US Multinationals*. New York: Praeger.

Rosenberg, N. 1982. *Inside the Black Box: Technology and Economics*. Cambridge: Cambridge University Press.

Rugman, A. M. and J. P. Doh. 2008. *Multinationals and Development*. New Haven and London: Yale University Press.

Sagar, A. D. and P. Chandra. 2004. 'Technological Change in the Indian Passenger Car Industry', *BCSIA Discussion Paper 2004–05*. Cambridge: Energy Technology Innovation Project, Kennedy School of Government, Kennedy School of Government, Harvard University. www.belfercenter.org/sites/default/files/legacy/files/2004_Sagar_Chandra.pdf (accessed on 24 July 2014).

Sahoo, P., G. Nataraj and R. K. Dash. 2014. *Foreign Direct Investment in South Asia: Policy, Impact, Determinants and Challenges.* New Delhi: Springer International Publishing.

Saripalle, M. 2012. 'Learning across Policy Regimes: A Case Study of the Indian Automobile Industry', *International Journal of Automotive Technology and Management*, 12(2): 197–217.

Scott-Kemmis, D. and M. Bell. 1988. 'Technological Dynamism and the Technological Content of Collaboration: Are Indian Firms Missing Opportunities?', In A. V. Desai (ed.), *Technology Absorption in Indian Industry*, pp. 71–86. New Delhi: Wiley Eastem.

Sharma, K. 2000. 'Export Growth in India: Has FDI Played a Role?', *Discussion Paper No. 816*. New Haven: Economic Growth Centre, Yale University.

Shirali, R. V. R. 1984. 'The Dawning of the Maruti Era', in F. A. A. Becker-Ritterspach and J. C. E. Becker-Ritterspach (2009) *The Development of India's Small Car Path*, pp. 3–4. Oxford Management Online Review, 1–20.

Shukla, R. 2010. *How India Earns, Spends and Saves: Unmasking the Real India.* New Delhi: Sage Publications.

SIAM (Society of Indian Automobile Manufacturers). 2006a. *Statistical Profile of Automobile Industry in India 2005–06.* New Delhi: Society of Indian Automobile Manufacturers.

SIAM (Society of Indian Automobile Manufacturers). 2006b. *Profile of the Automobile Industry in India 2005–06.* New Delhi: Society of Indian Automobile Manufacturers.

SIAM (Society of Indian Automobile Manufacturers). 2008. *Profile of the Automobile Industry in India 2007–08.* New Delhi: Society of Indian Automobile Manufacturers.

SIAM (Society of Indian Automobile Manufacturers). 2010a. *Statistical Profile of Automobile Industry in India 2008–09.* New Delhi: Society of Indian Automobile Manufacturers.

SIAM (Society of Indian Automobile Manufacturers). 2010b. *Profile of the Automobile Industry in India 2008–09.* New Delhi: Society of Indian Automobile Manufacturers.

SIAM (Society of Indian Automobile Manufacturers). 2012a. *Statistical Profile of Automobile Industry in India 2010–11.* New Delhi: Society of Indian Automobile Manufacturers.

SIAM (Society of Indian Automobile Manufacturers). 2012b. *Profile of the Automobile Industry in India 2010–11.* New Delhi: Society of Indian Automobile Manufacturers.

SIAM (Society of Indian Automobile Manufacturers). 2014a. *Statistical Profile of Automobile Industry in India 2012–13*. New Delhi: Society of Indian Automobile Manufacturers.

SIAM (Society of Indian Automobile Manufacturers). 2014b. *Profile of the Automobile Industry in India 2012–13*. New Delhi: Society of Indian Automobile Manufacturers.

SIAM (Society of Indian Automobile Manufacturers). 2016a. *Statistical Profile of Automobile Industry in India 2014–15*. New Delhi: Society of Indian Automobile Manufacturers.

SIAM (Society of Indian Automobile Manufacturers). 2016b. *Profile of the Automobile Industry in India 2014–15*. New Delhi: Society of Indian Automobile Manufacturers.

Singh, A. 2009. 'The Past, Present, and Future of Industrial Policy in India: Adapting to the Changing Domestic and International Environment', in M. Cimoli, G. Dosi and J. E. Stiglitz (eds.), *Industrial Policy and Development: The Political Economy of Capability Accumulation*, pp. 277–302. New York: Oxford University Press.

Singh, J. 2009. *Foreign Direct Investment and Market Structure: Evidence from India's Manufacturing Sector*. Unpublished M.Phil Dissertation, Centre for Development Studies Trivandrum, Kerala.

Singh, J. 2010. 'Economic Reforms and Foreign Direct Investment in India: Policy, Trends and Patterns', *The IUP Journal of Financial Economics*, 8(4): 59–69.

Singh, J. 2014. 'India's Automobile Industry: Growth and Export Potentials', *Journal of Applied Economics and Business Research*, 4(4): 246–262.

Singh, J. 2015. *Foreign Firms, Technological Development and Competitiveness: A Comparative Assessment of India's Passenger Car Industry under Two Policy Regimes*. Unpublished Ph.D. Thesis, Jawaharlal Nehru University, New Delhi.

Singh, J. and M. D. Cheema. 2015. 'Globalization and Industrial Development in Developing Countries: Evidence from India's Automobile Industry', *Productivity*, 56(2): 159–171.

Singh, J., S. Jha and Y. Singh. 2011. 'Impact of Liberalization on Foreign Direct Investment: An Empirical Analysis of Indian Economy in Post Reform Period', *The IUP Journal of Public Finance*, 9(3): 23–33.

Singh, J., K. J. Joseph and V. Abraham. 2011. 'Inward Investment and Market Structure in an Open Developing Economy: A Case of India's Manufacturing Sector', *Indian Journal of Economics*, XIIC(3): 286–297.

Singh, N. 2004. 'Strategic Approach to Strengthening the International Competitiveness in Knowledge Based Industries: The Case of Indian Automotive Industry', *Working Paper No. 82*. New Delhi: Research and Information Systems for the Non-Aligned and Other Developing Countries (RIS).

Singh, N. 2007. 'Automotive Industry', in N. Kumar and K. J. Joseph (eds.), *International Competitiveness and Knowledge Based Industries in India*, pp. 233–279. New Delhi: Oxford University Press.

Singh, P. and S. Kaur. 1999. 'Multinationals Enterprises and Developing Countries: An Indian Experience', in P. P. Arya and B. B. Tandon (eds.), *Multinationals versus Swadeshi Today: A Policy Framework for Economic Nationalism*, pp. 63–75. New Delhi: Deep and Deep Publications.

Sinha, J. B. P. 2004. *Multinationals in India: Managing the Interface of Cultures*. New Delhi: Sage Publications.

Stewart, F. 1984. 'Facilitating Indigenous Technical Change in Third World Countries', in Martin Fransman and Kenneth King (eds.), *Technological Capability in the Third World*, pp. 81–94. Hong Kong: Palgrave Macmillan.

Stewart, F. and J. James. 1982. *The Economics of New Technology in Developing Countries*. London: Pinter Publishers.

Subrahmanian, K. K. 1972. *Import of Capital and Technology: A Study of Foreign Collaborations in Indian Industry*. New Delhi: People's Publishing House.

Subrahmanian, K. K. 1986. 'Technology Import: Regulation Reduces Cost', *Economic and Political Weekly*, 21(32): 1412–1416.

Subrahmanian, K. K. 1987. 'Towards Technological Self-Reliance: An Assessment of Indian Strategy and Achievement in Industry', in P. R. Brahmannanda and V. R. Panchamukhi (eds.), *The Development Process of Indian Economy*. Bombay: Himalaya Publishing House, 420–446.

Subrahmanian, K. K. and P. M. Pillai. 1979. *Multinationals and Indian Export: A Study of Foreign Collaboration and Export Performance in Selected Indian Industries*. New Delhi: Allied Publishers Private Limited.

Subrahmanian, K. K., D. V. S. Sastry, S. Pattanaik and S. Hajra. 1996. *Foreign Collaboration under Liberalisation Policy: Patterns of FDI and Technology-transfer in India since 1991*. Mumbai: Department of Economic Analysis & Policy, Reserve Bank of India.

Sutton, J. 2007. *Quality, Trade and the Moving Window: The Globalization Process*. London School of Economics, Mimeo. www.ecb.europa.eu/events/pdf/conferences/global_macro/Jsutton_paper.pdf (accessed on 20 august 2013).

Tayal, S. R. 2014. *India and the Republic of Korea: Engaged Democracies*. New Delhi: Routledge.

Tewari, M. 2001. *Engaging the New Global Interlocutors: Foreign Direct Investment and the Transformation of Tamil Nadu's Automotive Supply Base*. Unpublished, Harvard University, Cambridge. www.researchgate.net/profile/Meenu_Tewari/publication/237360840_Engaging_the_New_Global_Interlocutors_Foreign_Direct_Investment_and_the_Transformation_of_Tamil_Nadu's_Automotive_Supply_Base/links/55218e230cf2f9c13052838c.pdf (accessed on 20 March 2015).

Tiwari, R. and C. Herstatt. 2014. *Aiming Big with Small Cars: Emerging of a Lead Market in India*. Switzerland: Springer International Publishing.

Tyabji, N. 2000. *Industrialization and Innovation: The Indian Experience*. New Delhi: Sage Publications.

Tyabji, N. 2015. *Forging Capitalism in Nehru's India: Neocolonialism and State, 1940–1970*. New Delhi: Oxford University Press.

UNCTAD (United Nations Conference on Trade and Development). 1997. *World Investment Report 1997: Transnational Corporations, Market Structure and Competition Policy*. New York and Geneva: United Nations Conference on Trade and Development.

UNCTAD (United Nations Conference on Trade and Development). 1999. *World Investment Report 1999: Foreign Direct Investment and the Challenge of Development*. New York and Geneva: United Nations Conference on Trade and Development.

UNCTAD (United Nations Conference on Trade and Development). 2005. *World Investment Report 2005: Transnational Corporations and the Internationalization of R&D*. New York and Geneva: United Nations Conference on Trade and Development.

UNCTAD (United Nations Conference on Trade and Development). 2006. *World Investment Report 2006: FDI from Developing and Transition Economies: Implications for Development*. New York and Geneva: United Nations Conference on Trade and Development.

UNCTAD (United Nations Conference on Trade and Development). 2013. *World Investment Report 2013: Global Value Chains, Investment and Trade for Development*. New York and Geneva: United Nations Conference on Trade and Development.

UNCTAD (United Nations Conference on Trade and Development). 2017. *World Investment Report 2017: Investment and the Digital Economy*. New York and Geneva: United Nations Conference on Trade and Development.

United Nations. 1983. *Transnational Corporations in the International Auto Industry*, ST/CTC/38. New York: United Nations Centre on Transnational Corporations.

Venkataramani, R. 1990. *Japan Enters Indian Industry: The Maruti – Suzuki Joint Venture*. New Delhi: Radiant Press.

Venugopal, R. 2001. 'TELCO's Small Car', *Asian Case Research Journal*, 5(1): 49–69.

Verma, S. 2009. 'FDI and Balance of Payments: A Comparative Study of Foreign Exchange Transactions Behaviour of FDI and Non-FDI Enterprises in Select Industrial Groups in the Manufacturing Sector of India, 1991–2008', *Centre for Economic Studies and Planning*. New Delhi: School of Social Sciences, Jawaharlal Nehru University.

Wang, M. and M. C. S. Wong. 2004. *What Drives Economic Growth?: The Case of Cross-border M&A and Greenfield FDI Activities*. http// ssrn.com/abstract=627663 (accessed on 24 May 2014).

World Bank. 1987. 'India Review of the Automobile Products Industry',
   Report No. 6667-IN. Industrial Development and Financial Division,
   South Asia Projects Department, World Bank.
World Bank. 2011. *World Development Indicators.* Washington, DC: The
   World Bank Group.
WTO (World Trade Organisation). 2002. *Dispute Settlement Report 2002:
   India-Measures Affecting the Automotive Sector.* Cambridge: Cam-
   bridge University Press.

Index

187; entry into market 60,
189–190; export contribution
167–171; export performance
of 193; import content in
high-end cars 132; imports
of disembodied technology
124; imports of embodied
technology 126; marketing
strategy 192–193; market share
63, 68, 73, 189–193; product
choice 192–193; production
capacity 76; raw material usage
130; strategy 189–192; sub-
segment wise contribution to
exports 177; success of 192–193;
technology intensity 117; total
foreign transactions 163; trade
performance 160–162, 193

import intensity 136, 140,
145–148, 157, 158–160, 178,
199, 201
import payments 9, 102, 127, 131,
141, 144, 148, 149, 160
import spending 126, 131, 158,
175, 179, 197–198, 199
Industrial Policy Statement of 1980
32, 33
Industries Development and
Regulation Act (IDRA) 23,
27–28, 93
International Bank for
Reconstruction and
Development (IBRD) 36
International Monetary Fund
(IMF) 36
investment: behaviour 57–58;
implications for strategy in
second phase of restructuring
75–77; liberal regime 8, 92, 177,
202; R&D 46–47, 109–110,
114–115, 118–119, 127–128,
132–133, 198; removal of
restrictions on 36; see also
foreign investment policy

joint ventures (JVs) 28, 33–34, 38,
50, 52, 56, 60, 78, 104, 110,
149, 151, 160

licensed capacity 19, 94
licensing policy: abolition of
licensing in early 1990s 75;
capacity re-endorsement scheme
32–33; disembodied technology
90, 123; import licensing 106,
115, 128, 156; imports of
restricted items were permitted
against specific import license
from DGFT 37, 38; Industries
Development and Regulation
Act 23, 26, 27, 93; production
subject to type of license and
production capacity of licenses
issued by government 19;
product-specific licenses 51,
58, 93; technical licensing
agreements with foreign firms
101–102; technology 85

Mahindra and Mahindra (M&M)
60, 108, 160, 168
Maruti Udyog Limited (MUL):
competitive pricing 147, 187;
downturn in market share
79, 182; export contribution
167–171; export performance
of 188; first mover advantage
and product variety 182–185;
import content in high-end cars
132; imports of disembodied
technology 124–125; imports
of high-end segment 177;
indigenisation and easy
availability of spare parts
and components 186–187;
investment behaviour 57–58;
joint ventures 34, 50, 52–55,
60, 68; leadership position.
181–188; market share 52–53,
190; political factors 53–55;
post sales services 185–186;
price competitiveness of
products 187–188; pricing
behaviour 58–59; production
capacity 76; R&D investment
120; raw material usage 130;
re-establishment by Gandhi 32;
re-sale value of products 188;

123–125; imports of embodied
technology 126–128; indirect
imports of technology 128–130;
international R&D of foreign
firms 119–123; raw material
usage 128–130; technology
intensity 116–118
technology policy: phase I
from 1947 to 1965 24–26;
phase II from 1966 to 1980
29–31; phase III of partial
liberalisation from 1982 to 1990
34–35, 96; phase IV of external
liberalisation from 1990 to
present 40–41
Technology Policy Statement
(TPS) 34
Toyota 60, 68, 171, 175, 177, 187
trade: analysis of export
contribution of firms 167–177;
conditions for foreign car
manufacturers 38; in goods

140; liberal regime 8, 75, 92,
138, 177, 202; mounting deficit
after second oil crisis 32, 36; in
non-goods 140; pending free-
trade agreement with EU 171;
performance of firms 1989–2000
145–152, 188, 193; performance
of firms during 1980s 87,
141–145; performance of firms
from 2000 to 2014 158–162,
193; performance of foreign firms
and their contribution to BoP
199; reductions in overall tariffs
to open up India for international
trade 39; removal of restrictions
36; total transactions 140

Vauxhall Motors 50

Walchand Hirachand group 16–17
World Trade Organisation (WTO)
1, 38–39